FROM BLUE TO GREY

First edition
published in 2005 by

WOODFIELD PUBLISHING
Bognor Regis, West Sussex, England
www.woodfieldpublishing.com

ISBN 1-903953-72-3

From Blue to Grey

*Recollections from the RAF careers and subsequent lives of members
of 54 Entry, Royal Air Force College, Cranwell (1949-51)*

*Prompted by thoughts of grandchildren saying
"What was it like and what did you do, Grandad?"*

COMPILED, EDITED AND TO SOME EXTENT WRITTEN BY
FRED HOSKINS, RICHARD ROBSON AND BRIAN MEADLEY
(WITH HELP FROM SOME OF THEIR FRIENDS)

Woodfield

ACKNOWLEDGMENTS

Photographs of the RAF College Cranwell are reproduced by kind permission of the Commandant, Royal Air Force College Cranwell.

The articles 'Near Things and Close Shaves' and 'Return to Earth' are based on extracts from *Waystation to the Stars* [Copyright ©1999 Colin Foale] and reproduced by kind permission of the author and Headline Publishing Limited, a division of Hodder Headline plc, 318 Euston Road, London NW1 3BH.

'Visits to the Old North West Frontier' by Colin Foale is based on extracts from *The History of 73 Squadron* and reproduced by kind permission of Mr Don Minterne.

Contents

Foreword

By Right Honourable Lord Tebbit CH

Before becoming a Member of Parliament I had made my life in aviation. Called up for National Service in 1949 I was lucky enough to be one of the few hundred selected for pilot training and gained my wings having flown Prentices and Harvards, then converting to Meteors.

On 604 Squadron R.Aux.A.F. I flew Vampires and Meteors, so I can appreciate Richard Robson's 'Remember the Meatbox' and many other recollections of the graduates of No.54 Entry of Flight Cadets of the Royal Air Force College, who were my aviation contemporaries. Having

become an Honorary Old Cranwellian in 2001 – the 50th anniversary of the graduation of No 54 Entry – I had no hesitation in writing this foreword.

Amongst its wonderfully humorous accounts of RAF life in their times are some serious or even sad. Of the 31 young men who graduated in 1951, six were killed flying in the RAF (four within two years) and another invalided out following serious injuries.

Today that would be a very high peacetime casualty rate, but not so in the 1950s. Such losses we all took in our stride just as casualties are accepted in the armed forces today, despite the "hype" of politicians and the emotional incontinence engendered by the media

Pilot Officer Norman Tebbit.

The RAF has changed in the last half century and change continues apace. So has the world and many of the stories in this book are of a world that will not return. Many of the bases at home and abroad (and the aircraft) are no more. But between them these men flew in every military role and pretty well every aircraft in service or development in those days. That width of experience was matched by the occupations they followed in civilian life, which is of itself a tribute to the preparation for life they received at Cranwell.

Originally this book was intended for families and friends, but I hope it will appeal to a wider audience. Certainly it should, for it is not just a good read but a serious contribution to the history of this Kingdom and its Royal Air Force.

Right Honourable Lord Tebbit CH

Preface

Avast there, me Hearties!

We were young in those days. We did deeds and ventured new things. We lived under discipline, and had authority ourselves, and gave orders. We accepted responsibility, and had confidence. We took risks and had a go. Sometimes we had severe frights and learnt the hard way. We had adventures and enjoyed ourselves. We did not think much about getting old.

Some of our friends did not live long enough to become old. Now, to our surprise, those of us who are left actually are getting old. We can't see and hear so well, and we get tired. Our families make decisions for us. Some of us take pills, and others need nursing care. But inside we are still young, the same as we used to be.

We have more spare time now, and can look back at our memories, sometimes even wondering if we really did all those things, or were they just imagination? Yes, we did! And no, they weren't!

So we have put together this miscellany of anecdotes, to swap amongst ourselves and also to pass on to friends and families, in a world that has already changed, and belongs to a younger generation who do not know what we did.

We are rather like those old sailors in boys' books, sitting on a bench outside the harbour inn, with our wooden legs, black eyepatches and our parrots on our shoulders. We have many tales to tell – of derring-do, of storms and fights long ago, of faraway lands and merry happenings, of people we knew and the history we saw.

Some passers-by will surely like to pause and listen.

Maybe they will buy us a pint…!

R.H.R.

Royal Air Force College Cranwell.

1.   Introduction

What the RAF College was, the way of life there, and something about the men of No 54 Entry

CRANWELL & THE FLIGHT CADET ENTRY SYSTEM
1920 – 1973

The Royal Air Force Cadet College was founded at Cranwell by Lord Trenchard as the main channel of entry for officers intended to hold permanent commissions in the new Royal Air Force. Its first course began training on the 5th February 1920 with 52 cadets.

Entrants into the Royal Air Force Cadet College had to be between the ages of 17½ and 19½ years and pass the Civil Service Examinations, but the College also offered Cadetships each year to a few Aircraft Apprentices from the Technical Training Schools at Halton and Cranwell. The courses lasted two years and the syllabus included: War Studies; English; Aeronautical Science; Aeronautical Engineering; General Service subjects; Drill and Physical Training; Aviation and Aeronautics; Flying and Airmanship; Applied Flying and Air Navigation. Participation in sports was strongly encouraged. On successful graduation, the Flight Cadets were granted permanent commissions as Pilot Officers in the General Duties Branch of the Royal Air Force.

Between 1920 and 1939 more than 1,100 Flight Cadets were trained at Cranwell and at the beginning of World War II 931 graduates were on the active list. Some, such as Douglas Bader, achieved fame for their exploits in war. Another, Frank Whittle, became famous for his work on jet propulsion. Others were to reach the highest ranks after the war and filled the most senior posts as Lord Trenchard had intended. Tragically, more than 430 Old Cranwellians lost their lives during that war – a loss rate of 46 per cent. Over 600 decorations were won, including one Victoria Cross, two George Crosses, 82 Distinguished Service Orders and 269 Distinguished Flying Crosses.

Between the wars Cranwell had been the scene of the start of some important pioneering long distance flights, landmarks in aviation history, but perhaps the most important flight ever made from Cranwell took place on the 15th May 1941, when the first jet propelled aircraft to fly in the United Kingdom took off from the South Airfield. It was the experimental Gloster-Whittle E28/39 flown by Gerry Sayer.

The College as such was closed during World War II but became the base for a number of Flying Training Schools. The training of Flight Cadets began again in 1946 and, as before the war, was limited to those who were to be pilots but the course had been extended to two years and eight months. In 1948 the scheme was widened to include an Equipment and Secretarial Wing a few miles away at RAF Digby. After a few years that wing moved over to Cranwell and by 1962 there were also Flight Cadets training as Navigators and for the Royal Air Force Regiment. In 1965 there was a merger with the Royal Air Force Technical College, Henlow, bringing engineering cadets to Cranwell so that it became the centre for the training of all entrants intended to hold permanent commissions in almost all the branches of the Royal Air Force.

The last entry of Flight Cadets, No. 101, graduated in 1973, bringing the total to 3,571 cadets having graduated since 1920. Training continued under the Graduate Entry System and was subsequently replaced by the Initial Officer Training Scheme with which the Royal Air Force College continues its traditional role of producing high calibre officers for the modern Royal Air Force.   [F.D.H.]

COLLEGE LIFE

Young men aspiring to become officers and pilots in the Royal Air Force by way of cadetships at the R A F College arrived, often in a state of nervous excitement, at Sleaford Railway station where NCOs of the RAF Regiment shepherded them to buses to take them on for the last part of the journey. They were perhaps a little surprised when the bus continued beyond the impressive college building they glimpsed on the north side of Cranwell Avenue and found themselves dumped outside Block 77, a barrack block opposite the entrance to Station Sick Quarters and used to accommodate the two junior entries.

At the start of the course lasting two years and eight months, divided into eight terms, the new cadets were allocated between "A", "B" and "C", the three squadrons forming the Cadet Wing, but there were four barrack rooms so some of each squadron were assigned to the fourth, "ABC", room. Each room housed 20 cadets. The senior of the two junior entries occupied one side of each room and the new boys the other. In alphabetical order they were allocated a bed with its wall locker and a wooden bed box, and over the next few days they were issued with uniform and other kit and packed their civilian clothes for storage until their first leave At this stage the new entrants were simply "cadets" as opposed to the Flight Cadets they hoped to become after eight months. Cadets wore the uniform of ordinary airmen, complete with the eagle shoulder flashes, and were distinguished only by white bands round their caps, a peaked cap for best and a field service or sidecap for working dress, and a coloured lanyard, red for "A" squadron, yellow for "B" and blue for "C" worn on the right shoulder.

The working uniform was known as 'battledress', with a blouse jacket with no brass buttons while the best uniform had a tunic with brass buttons and belt buckle. After two terms, on reaching the status of Flight Cadets, the eagle shoulder flashes were removed, the airman style capbadges were replaced by those issued to Warrant Officers and on their working dress Flight Cadets wore white bands on the shoulder straps with a central stripe in the squadron colour, while on the best uniform they wore white gorgette patches on the collars, again with a stripe denoting the squadron. In 1949 all Flight Cadets and cadets were issued with officer pattern uniforms made to measure by Burberrys; this brought them back to the pre-war standard of uniform. Of particular importance in junior entries was the issue of a battledress uniform in khaki denim, complete with webbing anklets, to be worn when undergoing Ground Combat Training (GCT). This entailed firing rifles, sub-machine guns and Bren Guns, and general infantry training. To cope with the cold Cranwell winters a sleeveless leather jerkin could be worn over the denims. Needless to say, steel helmets were issued and each cadet had a rifle and bayonet.

In the barrack rooms of Block 77 the cadets were initiated into the display of kit in the wall lockers and the method of lining up beds and boxes on the polished linoleum floors. Each cadet was given a room task to do each morning, such as sweeping or polishing the floors, lining up the beds and boxes, cleaning the wash basins and taps, or tidying the surrounds of the block. These tasks often occupied an evening as well, in preparation for a formal inspection of room and kit. In fact there were frequent inspections by the NCOs and by the Officer in charge of the junior entries and the barrack rooms had to be made ready to inspection standard every morning, with the kit in individual lockers set out according to a strict pattern and the blankets and sheets neatly folded into a square block wrapped in one of the blankets.

During the first few weeks there was an emphasis on drill and physical training (PT) and throughout the first two terms cadets were drilled and exercised every weekday. When the necessary standard had been reached the cadets joined the Flight Cadets for the routine drill and parades at the college and also joined them for the weekly early morning PT sessions for each squadron.

The first two terms were not entirely physical in content. Instruction began in a variety of subjects in both the Aeronautical Science and

Engineering and the Humanistics departments of the college. In the ASE Department cadets and Flight Cadets were, during the course of the eight academic terms, taught aerodynamics, thermodynamics, meteorology, weapons theory, radio and navigation. In the first two terms cadets were given instruction in mathematics including calculus and the use of the slide rule. The navigation syllabus covered the theory of compasses and other navigation instruments, the use of radio aids, the calculation of drift, speed and wind velocity, flight planning, and an introduction to astro-navigation, but in the first two terms the instruction was largely in the uses of maps, compass and watch for basic pilot navigation.

After a while the cadets had to apply these skills in Avro Anson aircraft. For these flights they were kitted out in heavy canvas Sidcot flying suits of wartime vintage, sheepskin lined boots, thick woollen sweaters, leather flying helmets and goggles, silk inner gloves and leather gauntlets. With green canvas bags of maps, log pads, pencils and Dalton computers they boarded the Ansons to fly cross country routes, keeping a log of their positions and times, working out wind velocities, using the drift sight and, in many cases, being airsick because of the uncomfortable surroundings, the heavy and hot suits and the bumpy movement of the slow aircraft. It was not the best introduction to a flying career!

Additionally, during the first two terms cadets received instruction in the Cadets' Instructional Workshops where they were taught such things as how to carry out simple repairs to airframes, how to strip down internal combustion engines and about the workings of hydraulic systems.

'Humanistics' included English, military and economic history and geography, current affairs and War Studies. The latter covered the organisation and history of the Royal Air Force and there were officers from the Royal Navy, the Army and the United States Air Force to give instruction relevant to their services. The battles and campaigns of the Second World War were studied, of course. Apart from the subjects directly relevant to professional studies, there were topics intended to broaden the mind and a memorable excursion in Junior Entries was to a coal mine in Nottinghamshire. Hours spent underground viewing at first hand the working conditions of the miners resulted in a healthy respect and sympathy for those toilers. The English course was broad and included the study of some poetry as well as the use of the language.

The Aeronautical Science and Engineering Department had most of its lecture rooms and laboratories in a building to the east of the college while the Humanistics lecture rooms were on 'A' Site, about five hundred yards to the west of the college. The navigation room was in the college building and, for the two junior entries, some lectures were given near their barrack block. The drill square for the junior entries was near their barracks but routine morning drill took place at the front of the college. The gymnasium was near the south airfield, as were the workshops and, of course, the hangars and crewrooms for flying training. Thus the main locations were at the corners of an approximate rectangle with short sides of about half a mile and long sides of almost a mile. Hence a good deal of time and physical effort was spent in moving between classes, drill and PT. Marching quickly between locations helped to improve or maintain fitness and also created an appetite. Flight Cadets ate in the beautiful dining hall in the college while cadets ate in their own mess near their barrack block. They also had a small NAAFI canteen nearby while Flight Cadets used the 'Fancy Goods Store' in the college to buy necessaries, a small selection of snack items and even a limited amount of beer.

Unlike pre-war cadets who had to pay to be at Cranwell, the post-war cadet was paid. In 54 Entry's time the initial daily rate of pay was four shillings, with three shillings Flying Instructional Pay added when flying training began. Later in the course the basic pay rose by one shilling. Those who had already served as airmen or aircrew cadets continued to receive their airman pay if it was at a higher rate.

On completing Junior Entries the cadets became Flight Cadets but, as there were not enough rooms in the college for all, they moved for one term to Daedalus House, a large house to the rear of the Station Sick Quarters. Here, as in the main college building, they enjoyed the privilege of a bedroom each, equipped also for study, and the services of a civilian batman to clean the room and perform some valeting services – which did not extend to cleaning webbing belts, boots and rifles. In the early post-war years some of the batmen and waiters had been college servants since the '20s and could tell of cadets from those early days who had achieved fame. Being in Daedalus House meant more walking or, rather, marching, as meals were taken in the college with all the more senior Flight Cadets. 'Marching' because it was simply not permissible to walk! All cadets were expected to move briskly and if two or more were moving from place to place together then they must march in step and without talking. It was not unknown for an officer on a bicycle to glide up soundlessly behind a small party heading for the college after flying and then make his presence felt. Discipline was strict and sanctions, usually 'restrictions' or extra drill, arbitrarily and swiftly imposed.

In the dining hall were three long tables, one for each squadron. The tables had a break in the middle, leaving a path from the central entrance door to the servery door. At the head of the table sat the senior entry and at the bottom the next senior entry. Immediately below the senior entry sat the most junior entry of Flight Cadets, presumably so that the seniors could keep a close watch over them. The food was reasonable in quantity and quality although there were some items frequently recurring on the menu which were not greatly appreciated, such as Brown Windsor soup and what the irreverent termed 'mutton rings', namely sliced rolled breast of lamb.

On Wednesdays, Saturdays and Sundays Flight Cadets could wear civilian clothes after duty and the evening meal was an informal supper. On the other four nights of the week they had to dress in their best 'airman pattern' uniform and sit together for a formal dinner which was attended also by some of the officers, who wore dinner jackets. Every second week one of these dinner nights was replaced by a Guest Night when officers wore mess dress and Flight Cadets wore their very best, officer pattern, uniforms with white shirts, wing collars and bow ties. At Guest Nights the college band played in the gallery above one end of the dining hall, the commandant was at the head of the top table next to the Under Officer of the King's Squadron, directly under the King's Colour of the Royal Air Force College, its staff held in the claws of a bronze eagle, and there would be some important guests from outside the college and even from outside the RAF. It could be a little unnerving for a junior Flight Cadet to find that he was to sit next to and converse with one of these senior and important people.

It could also be unnerving for the new Flight Cadets to go, in parties of four, to supper with the Commandant on a Sunday evening and thence to the cinema. However, Guest Nights could be quite jolly events for those in, as it were, the back seats, with entertaining music from the band – South Rampart Street Parade and St Louis Blues and other light music as well the more orthodox pieces. After dinner the Flight Cadets were required to assemble in the lecture hall to listen to a lecture from the principal guest, who might be a senior serving officer, a politician, senior university lecturer, engineer or an industrialist. Such lectures might be on an aspect of the RAF, on current affairs, developments in the design of aircraft and engines, or on, perhaps, exploration or a similar topic. Guest Nights were followed by a college parade the next morning – not a very good idea bearing in mind that the same very best uniform had to be worn and everyone had been late to bed. However, that was how it was, and first parade for inspection by the Under Officer and the Squadron Drill Instructor was early enough to allow for a further inspection by the Squadron Commander before finally marching onto the parade ground and, in due course, another inspection by the Commandant!

Now the college has four accommodation wings but then there were only three, one for each of 'A', 'B' and 'C' squadron. However, in addition to the flight cadets bound for the General Duties/Pilot branch there were others training for the Equipment and Secretarial branches and because of the lack of space they were located at Digby. For the college parade the E & S Flight Cadets were brought to Cranwell by bus and formed up to the east of the college, near 'C' Squadron. 'A' and 'B' Squadrons formed up to the west and on the command the squadrons marched on to the parade ground in front of the college and halted in line facing south, with the college behind them. After the preliminary dressings the King's Colour was marched on, the ensign and his escorts emerging from the main door of the college and descending through the band positioned on the steps and taking post in the centre of the parade. The parade gave the general salute and was then inspected by the commandant. During the inspection the college band played suitable music – which sometimes was very contemporary, including music from the films, such as 'The Harry Lime Theme' from 'The Third Man'. After that the squadrons marched to the west end of the parade ground and formed column of squadrons to march past by squadrons in slow time and in line. Marching in line, about 25 to 30 abreast, it is not easy to keep the lines straight and to complicate matters each squadron in turn was caused to change from close order to open order on the march, with the centre rack marking time for two paces and the rear rank for four. After the salute on the march the squadrons closed order, still on the march and, arriving at the east end, turned about and repeated the performance in the other direction in quick time. The wing then went back to its original formation in front of the college and after another dressing to get the lines straight, advanced in line in a manoeuvre called "The Advance in Review Order" and gave the General Salute. The parade commander asked permission to march off. This was not always forthcoming and on occasion the parade was made to repeat some manoeuvre before being released. Eventually the squadrons returned to their starting places and were dismissed.

Mention of the Under Officer suggests a description of how the college was run. A Squadron Leader commanded each of the three squadrons and was assisted by a Flight Lieutenant or Flying Officer known as a 'Cadet Wing Officer'. Under him was a Flight Sergeant of the RAF Regiment, who supervised drill each day, and then there were the flight cadet NCOs who acted more or less as school prefects. At the head was an Under Officer (UO) who wore a thin stripe of braid on his cuff, the stripe rising to a point. Under him were two Flight Cadet Sergeants who wore ordinary sergeants' stripes on their arms. Up to 1951 each squadron also had four Flight Cadet Corporals but these were dispensed with and all the senior entry were designated "Senior Flight Cadets". Cadets in the junior entries addressed all flight cadets as 'sir' and all flight cadets addressed the senior entry in the same way. The drill instructors addressed flight cadets as 'sir' or added 'Mr' to the front of the name, for example a flight sergeant might well say (or shout) "Mr Smith, sir! Pick your feet up!" The Cadet Wing Warrant Officer addressed flight cadets as 'sir' but was called sir in return. It is said that the Cadet Wing Warrant Officer addressed some Flight Cadets in the following terms "I call you 'Sir' and you call me 'Sir'. The difference is that when you call me 'Sir' you had better mean it!"

There were set ways of doing things and cadets had to learn very quickly. One of the first things was that only members of the senior entry were permitted to cross the front hall, or foyer, in the college. All other Flight Cadets and cadets could only cross from one wing to the other by going round the back of the lecture hall, which was immediately behind the front hall and in front of the dining hall. In this passage way were situated all the photographs of previous college entries, prize-winners and sports teams. Here also were the notice boards for the display of orders, sports fixtures and teams and notices of events such as concerts or vacation activities. The college had a thriving 'College Society' with sections for activities such as music, dramatics, aeromodelling, debating and many others. The aim was to provide voluntary activities, in addition to syllabus items, to help broaden the minds of the Flight Cadets. In the vacations there were visits to service establishments, including those of the other services, opportunities for gliding, parachuting, winter sports, sailing, climbing and shooting – to mention just a few.

There were no carpets in the corridors, as there are now, but there was a large square carpet in the front hall. Flight Cadets were permitted to wear shoes but the juniors wore studded boots all the time. Rushing round the uncarpeted corridors in those boots caused much sliding and skidding when turning the corners. The big carpet in the entrance hall figured in the penalties imposed for the third termers, the new Flight Cadets, failing to entertain their seniors after their first Guest Night. The old hands were ranged on furniture piled to the ceiling in one of the ante-rooms and the novitiates were brought in singly or in small groups to perform. One might sing, a small group might perform a sketch. One young man placed a dustbin lid on the floor, a lighted thunder flash on that, a steel helmet on the thunder flash and then stood on the steel helmet and blew himself up. He passed, but those who failed to please might find themselves riding bicycles around the Orange (the expanse of grass in front of the college) with fire hoses playing on them. Others were compelled to crawl across the entrance hall under the carpet and there were other ingenious methods of inflicting punishment and humiliation.

Flying and academics alternated day by day so when there was flying in the morning there were lectures in the afternoon, and vice versa. However, on four weekdays there was drill to start the day at 7.25 am, immediately after breakfast, and on the fifth weekday there was PT before breakfast. The latter was almost always a thoroughly miserable experience. The squadron due for early morning PT paraded in PT shorts, vests, socks and boots at 7.00 am, wearing a sweater in the winter and carrying gym shoes. The squadron ran to the gym, about half a mile, changed boots for gym shoes and then experienced 30 minutes of boring and strenuous exercise carried out in silence – but for the orders of the PT instructors. There were no games to enliven the proceedings, just straight PT exercises, with some work on the vaulting horse or box and some agonising exercise such as hanging backwards from the wall bars and slowly raising the legs to the horizontal. Towards the end the PTI would give the order to run in a circle and then "On the back of the man in front – go!" Obviously, it was as well to be quick and jump before being jumped on. Then it might be "Everyone inside the green circle. Go!" Naturally, the green circle was not big enough to accommodate everyone so much pulling and pushing ensued. Finally, "Feet on the green line – go!" and then "Double away to the changing room – go!" Very often this was followed by "Not quick enough! Back into the gym and feet on the green line – go!" Sometimes there was a long enough pause before that order for a few of the quickest to have taken off their gym shoes and be half way into their boots. Then came a run back to the college, completion of the toilet, and breakfast before either flying or lectures.

The start of flying was what everyone was looking forward to and it came with the promotion to Flight Cadet status at the beginning of the third term. There were two Flying Wings, basic and advanced, each made up of two Squadrons divided into two Flights. Cadets were allocated to instructors and shown over the aeroplanes they were to fly. The basic trainer was the Percival Prentice, with instructor and pupil sitting side by side and with a third seat behind. It was powered by a Gypsy Major 32 engine. The advanced trainer was the North American Harvard IIB with a Pratt and Whitney Wasp engine. Both types had the advantage of variable pitch propellers, and flaps, unlike the Tiger Moth biplane which the Prentice had replaced. The instructors were almost entirely of World War II vintage, many wearing the ribbon of the DFC, and with a sprinkling of DSOs as well. The Korean War was in full swing, the RAF was expanding and so many of the instructors had rejoined after several years in civilian life. Not many of the instructors ever spoke about their experiences but sometimes it was possible, on a day when the weather rendered flying impossible, to lure one of them into telling, for example, how he had flown a Lancaster in the raid to sink the Tirpitz.

Not all cadets found that flying was easy although a few were "naturals". Flying, it was found, demanded a high degree of application and concentration. At first came lessons in flying straight and level, climbing and descending and then turning, before learning to take off and land. On average it took about eight hours of dual instruction before flying solo. Possibly solo could have been achieved in less but the requirements of the RAF were demanding. Before solo, pupils were shown stalling and spinning and after solo and consolidating their practice in circuits and landings there was more stalling and spinning and also aerobatics, practice forced landings and precautionary landings. Flying on instruments was important and for this amber screens were installed inside the windscreen and the pupils wore blue goggles so the instructor could see out but to the pupil all was black as night, save for the instruments. Night flying also was taught and practised, as was flying in formation and navigation by day and by night.

Apart from the basic lessons in the effect of controls, much the same syllabus was covered during the advanced stage but with a more complicated aircraft with a retractable undercarriage and more demanding characteristics. The Harvard was capable of some vicious reactions to mishandling. During the advanced phase cadets also learned the basics of air to air firing, using camera guns, and steep glide bombing (what most people would call "dive bombing"). Again, there was night flying, formation flying and navigation.

Even with all these various studies and activities occupying the cadets, their moral welfare was not overlooked. They received talks from the chaplains of the various denominations and, of course, there was compulsory church parade every Sunday. This took the form of a full college parade but without arms, save for the colour party. On arrival at the church, then a converted hangar, the colour party waited outside and when all were seated within marched in and handed the colour to the chaplain to place on the altar. At the end of the service the colour was handed back, the parade marched back to the college and the cadets were dismissed to lunch and the only completely free afternoon of the week. Wednesday and Saturday afternoons were free of lectures but devoted to sport.

A wide variety of sports were played at Cranwell, cricket, rugby, hockey, football, swimming, water polo, squash, tennis, rowing, shooting, fencing, riding and boxing. As to the latter, instruction in boxing was given to cadets during their very first term, at the end of which they were paired off to box in the gym after a college guest night and in the presence of the commandant and other officers and the rest of the college. This ordeal was known as 'first term boxing' and lucky indeed were the very few cadets who might be excused medically. The intention appears to have been merely to see whether the cadets had a suitable level of courage. Skill was not important and the 'winner' of the evening was the cadet who had shown the most pluck, and that seemed to be judged by the quantity of blood lost.

The subject was not mentioned specifically but all cadets knew the expression 'LMF' (lacking moral fibre), something that had come out of the war when aircrew who had finally cracked were declared LMF, stripped of their aircrew badges and allocated menial and degrading tasks – *pour encourager les autres*. At Cranwell it was apparent that there were direct efforts to ensuring that cadets had 'the right stuff'. Hence, the Warrant Officer PTI had the windows of the swimming pool fixed open permanently throughout the Lincolnshire winters when the wind came directly from the steppes. Hence, cadets were caused to perform backward somersaults from the top diving board. Hence, when visiting foreign officers arrived at the swimming pool it was arranged that there was no cadet to be seen because those who were not in the pool hidden under a rubber dinghy were hidden in the rafters so that when a whistle was blown they would drop into the water, and those under the dinghy would appear, all with a loud shout. Parachuting was not compulsory but it was an activity available during vacations and for those cadets who took part the fear of being labelled LMF for not jumping was greater than the fear of the actual jump.

Another facet of the Cranwell training was the constant pressure to do well and to do better than somebody else. Every term there was an inter-squadron drill competition for the Ferris Cup, a PT competition for the Knocker Cup and inter-squadron sports competitions for the Chimay Cup. The squadron achieving the best results over all became 'The King's Squadron' for the following term and had the honour of providing the ensign and escort for the King's Colour of the Royal Air Force College and of sitting at the centre table in the dining hall, with the Colour above and behind the Under Officer.

All these competitions demanded a great deal of effort and application. Throughout the course cadets were urged to try harder, move faster, be smarter and, above all, to be 'up to standard'. This was a common expression and thus the hapless Flight Cadet whose boots were not as clean as they might be (even though highly polished to the untutored eye) would find himself on restrictions because they were not 'up to standard'. The requirement always to march and not merely walk has been mentioned as has been the distances that had to be marched between venues. The working day effectively continued until after dinner each evening and all these things combined to impose pressures over a long period of time. The marvel is that so few yielded to these pressures and asked to be withdrawn; albeit a few were withdrawn from training without having to ask.

Having said all this, it has to be recognised that there was a lighter side to life. The great choice of sports and the availability of all manner of pursuits to be followed during term and during the vacations has already been mentioned. There was also a lot of fun and camaraderie. There was tremendous spirit among the cadets, all of whom had come through a rigorous selection process, who knew that they were privileged to be trained at Cranwell and were proud to be members of what was acknowledged to be an elite group. It was a great privilege to be a "Cranwell Cadet" and to be known as such was to be a marked man in the Royal Air Force, a man of whom much was expected – but to be a Cranwell Cadet was not necessarily to meet with universal acclaim from the less privileged.

The culmination of everything was Graduation. As it approached, the Flight Cadet's mind focussed on final examinations, his Final Handling Test to qualify for his wings and on the next stage of his flying training – was he to go to fighters or bombers or coastal? Naturally, tension rose at this point but to some extent it was relieved by preparing for the "revue" put on to entertain the rest of the college after the final guest night. Graduation itself was marked by a parade under the eyes of the senior entry's families and a senior visiting officer, politician or even a member of the royal family. Wings were presented and in the evening there was the Graduation Ball with the erstwhile senior entry now clad in their brand new uniforms with wings and the very thin light blue band on the cuff denoting the rank of Pilot Officer. That was the first step on the ladder; what had passed over the previous eight terms was merely a reaching for that first rung. [F.D.H.]

OUR DAYS AT CRANWELL

This collection of stories from members of 54 Entry calls for some sort of reflections upon our time as Cranwell cadets. Wherever we came from, and whatever we did afterwards, those eight terms formed probably the most intense period of our lives, never to be forgotten

Never to be forgotten, yet difficult to describe so long afterwards. Trying to recall it all is rather like getting a tin trunk down from the attic (one of those which young officers were supposed to buy), opening it, and finding it absolutely crammed with photographs, notes, mementoes, diary pages, log books, newspaper clippings, bits of movie film and goodness knows what else. You cannot summarize it in a few pages: all you can do is ferret through the trunk and pick out things at random which bring vivid memories back.

We all arrived at Cranwell from different backgrounds, and although by the time we graduated we had come to share a great deal in common, our trunks inevitably contain our own personal recollections, selected according to our own perspective. In the paragraphs that follow, I will pick out some of the things from my trunk.

It was, of course, a very different world then, so soon after the war. We tend to forget what a restricted and drab existence the people of Britain had, compared with today. So much was shabby and second rate in quality. There was still quite strict rationing, and I don't think the nation was as well nourished as propaganda told us. There were bomb sites everywhere in the cities, and masses of people living in temporary prefabs or old army camps. Apart from the armed services, which were scattered all over the world, hardly anyone travelled much, and going abroad was tightly restricted by financial exchange controls. The country was, in fact, virtually bankrupt and dependent upon American loans, although we weren't told the full facts at the time.

When I arrived at Cranwell, I had already done eleven months as a conscript, working at a GCI radar station, and billeted in run-down, leaky huts (we used to steal the wooden steps from other huts and burn them at weekends to keep warm). The other AC2s were disgruntled and cynical shirkers, looking forward only to their demob. Officers took no interest in us or our welfare, as far as I was aware. What a contrast at Cranwell – the impression made by that splendid building just for a start, the godlike senior cadets, the smell of polish and the trim lawns, the sense of purpose, the unseen presence of the legendary people who been there before us.

Bearing in mind the financial stringencies of the times, we can see in retrospect that whatever limited resources the RAF could spare were lavished on us, Cranwell cadets, to give us the best Service education possible. This would have been in line with Trenchard's policy in the nineteen twenties, when he had little money for new aircraft but decided instead to spend what he could on developing his officer corps and his skilled apprentices. Although much was demanded of us during our course, we were privileged in many ways.

It was a time when heroes were still admired, before modern writers proved that everyone has feet of clay. We had been brought up on tales of dog-fights between Camels and Fokkers (Biggles was not a figure of fun, as he seems to be nowadays!). We knew all about aces like Ball, Mannock, Richthofen and Guynemer. During our own schooldays we had seen the Battle of Britain, and the long bomber offensive going out night after night. People not much older than us had left our school or Scout Troop, often our own families, and gone to war. In no time at all, we would hear they were POWs, or missing or dead. Films, books and radio broadcasts kept the war and the fighting men constantly in our minds.

Now, at Cranwell, we were actually surrounded by the very men we had heard about. They wore campaign ribbons, medals, Pathfinder badges. They had risked their lives in real combat. They had attacked U-boat pens, bombed Berlin, fired rockets at Tiger tanks, flown through flak, been in dog-fights, chased flying bombs, been prisoners of war, experienced all sorts of dangers and hardships. We were going to be trained by them. We may have called them nicknames behind their backs, but by God, we respected them and listened to them .

Time to open the tin trunk and see what we can find.

Ah, here's a PT vest with a faded greyish stripe across it, where it has been exposed to the air. A memento of Junior Entries, when half our shirts and vests were never worn, but permanently laid out for inspection in the top of our lockers, carefully packed round strips of cardboard to give the required sharp creases. In Junior Entries, as in all recruit training since the Roman Army, we were meant to get the civilian stuffing knocked out of us, including self-conceit, and build bonds with our mates through a common hatred of bull and our drill sergeants! One or two cadets apparently gave up during these two terms. I think all the rest of us learnt, amongst other things, what all old soldiers know – make the most of today, because tomorrow is going to be tougher!

One of the things that the staff watched us for during all our time at the College was the dreaded LMF. The initials were first heard in Bomber Command during the war, standing for lack of moral fibre, or as it might more charitably be put, too strong an instinct for self-preservation!

So Warrant Officer ('Wog') Smith and his band of merciless PTIs would have us doing backward somersaults off the high board into the swimming pool. Those like me who couldn't swim very well were allowed to do forward somersaults to begin with (this was supposed to be a concession?). There was one time, I do not remember what term we were in, when the pool had been closed and unheated all winter, and we had to dive in. By the time we got to the other end, the PTIs were having to pull us out of the water because we were numb with cold. (You can bring on heart failure by the shock of immersion in freezing water – it is known as hydrocution! Now they tell us!)

Another test of our moral fibre was the boxing tournament at the end of Junior Entries, when we had to fight each other in front of the Commandant and the assembled College, all resplendent in their mess kits and wreathed in cigar smoke. I was matched against Ted Peters, and would have beaten him too – except he was better than I was.

Now what's this – a photograph of a figure standing by the door of an Anson, completely muffled up in a heavy Sidcot flying suit, a leather helmet, gloves and fur-lined flying boots. But he is not off to drop leaflets over Germany in the winter of 1939. It is actually the height of summer in our first term. Every Thursday we had PT and swimming before lunch – swallowing chlorinated water. Lunch was liver and cabbage. Then we had to double down to the flights, where the Ansons had been standing in the sweltering sun all morning, stinking of dope and aviation fuel.

Then off we go for map reading practice, the aircraft bumping in the hot air, our teeth gritted not to be sick. Above the engine roar, the voice of the pilot, the dour Flight Lieutenant Muir –. "Cadet Number Three, what is that railway junction to port?" We peer down through the vibrating perspex. Up comes the liver, cabbage and chlorinated water! One day, someone had to be taken to Sick Quarters for three days because his stomach had come loose from its mountings. Even today, the very names Market Harborough, Oakham, Bourne, Melton Mowbray bring the misery back!

What's next? Here's the College gates seen across the Orange; the view we saw during hours and hours on the parade ground as flight cadets. I added things up and concluded that I left Cranwell with 250 flying hours, and no less than 450 hours on parade. Drill every morning before breakfast (except PT mornings), then Commandant's parades, the Ferris Inter-squadron Drill Competitions, and of course, Graduation parades and church parades. For extra measure, sometimes punishment drill would be added for some crime or another. We must have been fit. The Lee-Enfield weighed eight and a half pounds (I can't remember if this was with its bayonet or not.)

Was there not one of our drill sergeants who could hold a Lee-Enfield straight out at arm's length by its muzzle, by the way?

Church parades every Sunday must not be forgotten. The best part of these was marching back afterwards to the lively marches of the College band, with Sunday lunch and a free afternoon before us. Life was not so bad all the time, after all!

Hello, here is a horrible cheap trilby hat with bullet holes in it. We had to wear hats when in civvies. Indeed, there was a strict dress code for all occasions in those days. (Not like today, when the RAF wear T-shirts in the mess ante-room.) Hats were so we could pay compliments to any officers we met, of course. However, the definition of a hat was not strictly laid down. Fred Hoskins had one with a huge brim, so he looked a bit like a New England Puritan. I never managed to match that, but I did try to add character to mine by shooting at it on the 25 yard range.

There must be a lot in the trunk about aeroplanes. Yes, here is a picture of a Percival Prentice. They say that if an aircraft looks right, it usually is right, quoting the Spitfire and the Mosquito as examples. The poor, amiable, well-meaning old Prentice never gets such a compliment though. It had wings the span of a Wellington, undercarriage like a Ju87 Stuka, tail of a Fairey Swordfish, engine like a Tiger Moth's. Its turned up wing-tips and its anti-spin fuselage strakes told you that the designers didn't quite get it right first time.. Never mind, it did its best. Having no supercharger, its Gipsy Queen engine lost power as soon as it clambered off the ground. You had to take ages climbing to height for aerobatics, and then only managed a few because it lost height after each one. It cruised at 95 knots, but if you put the nose down and lost a couple of hundred feet, it could reach and maintain 105 on the same power. Something to do with the angle of attack, which I used to understand. Never mind, there may have been someone who got hurt in a Prentice, but I do not remember hearing of it.

Look, there's a bit of orange Perspex. Remember the horrible two-stage amber system for IF practice with those blue goggles that always steamed up despite a ventilation tube poked out into the slipstream? Didn't we have to fly something called a Pattern B, or did that come later?

There's my first instructor's signature in my log book – Harry Dryhurst. He had been shot down on his second trip as captain of a Halifax, and reckoned his ASI was showing 400 knots when he finally got out (records show your chance of getting out of a Lancaster was only 20%, and out of a Halifax no better than 25%) Then he spent years in Stalag Luft 3. One bit of his advice I followed throughout my flying career – he said he always used to say his cockpit checks loud and clear on the intercom, because it reassured his frightened crew before taking off on a raid. To such experience, we paid attention.

Let's find something on the Harvard. Here is a recording of one starting! The radial engine and long glass cockpit made the Harvard look like one of those dive bombers in American films. The mounting whine of the inertia starter, followed by the coughing pick-up of the Pratt and Whitney completed the resemblance – a real aeroplane at last!

Those old films always had an aircraft crashing fatally on a terminal velocity dive, and then the hero would have to take up another machine and repeat the death-defying test (God only knows what it was supposed to prove, but the Americans insisted on it in the thirties), and of course, the heroine would plead for him not to go. Her entreaties would be drowned by a cinema full of cadets telling her to shut up and let him get on with it.

Another QFI's name to remember, this time on Harvards. Keith Panter had been decorated for baling out of a Mosquito holding his navigator, whose parachute had been shot to ribbons. They came down on the one chute. What did he make of us kids, still wet behind the ears?

A special memory is of bringing a Harvard back to Cranwell late on a summer's afternoon, with the cockpit canopy open, cool fresh air blowing in the smell of new-mown grass, the engine rumbling along, while below the College and the green north and south airfields are bathed in sunshine and tiny white figures dot the cricket field. Soon there will be tea to look forward to – life is not so bad after all. And the King paying for it all!

What is this picture of us wearing silly hats and harnesses? Memories of half a dozen of us standing in the back of a lorry under the canvas tilt, looking at a gap in the tailboard. Except it wasn't the back of a lorry, but a platform hanging underneath a barrage balloon, swaying and surging as the cold dawn wind moaned through the rigging. We were going to jump out of that gap in the tailboard, into eight hundred feet of empty space. The streetlights of Abingdon still twinkled in the early morning. Never was there such an overwhelming desire to be somewhere else!

But out we went, and after a forty foot drop with our hearts in our mouths, our parachutes did indeed blossom (no reserve chute in those days, by the way.). Another lesson learnt – the fear of chickening out in front of everybody else does wonders to overcome LMF! Jumping from a Dakota afterwards wasn't so bad – less cold-blooded. Even then, when the cockpit door opened and the navigator came through and asked someone for his comic "because you won't want it in a minute", a few faces blanched.

Sport played a large part in our lives, but as well as the normal games, we were given the opportunity to try all sorts of other things – gliding, horse riding, skiing, rowing, fencing and much else. I managed a place on the shooting team, but only just, and enviously watched people like Dave Keats shooting possibles. At Sandhurst once, we were drenched by heavy rain. When it had cleared and we began shooting again, none of us scored any hits at all. In fact, no shots were observed at the butts. A sergeant major gently pointed out that we had let our ammunition get wet, so the bullets were being pursued down the barrel by superheated steam as well as cordite. They were going right over the top of the targets and, presumably, into Camberley.

Here's a cigar butt. Guest nights! We still had to wear stiff winged collars then, and learnt that only waiters tuck their bow ties under the wings. When the time for toasts came, Creek Cowper would challenge us to pour a meniscus in our port glasses. There were always foreign visitors, whose national anthems would be played – our resident USAF officer meant that the Star Spangled Banner would inevitably follow God Save the King. It was difficult enough not to beat time to that tune, but with some of the weirder ones it was torment looking at Ken Bones across the table and trying to keep a straight face. ("Mr. Vice, the Umboko of Fallulaland!" "Gentlemen, the Umboko of Mumble-mumble!" *Tumpty tumpty boom crash tiddly tum, etc*, etc.)

The cigars we were proffered were, of course, far too big for us callow youths. (And I am sure the mess stewards knew it, and chuckled to themselves!) They burned on and on, and on, until some of us, at any rate, became quite ill. It cured me of smoking for ever. After dinner, we would be treated to talks by some very famous speakers, such as Professor Jones or Sir Frederick Handley Page, to name but two. And sometimes, the thought might cross your mind whether at that very same time, in some Air Force Academy across the Iron Curtain, other young officer cadets in their best uniforms were maybe toasting the Revolution, and listening to a talk by Tupolev or Zhukov ……..

There's a funny smell in the corner of the tin trunk. It's from those German aircraft in the weapons hangar. Among the many opportunities Cranwell gave us was the odd one of sitting in a FW 190 or a Messerschmitt 262. (Try getting permission to do that at the RAF Museum these days, and see what sort of dusty response you get!) There was also a Japanese Baka piloted bomb. The smallest of our Entry (unkind to mention who!) couldn't resist climbing in, and was promptly locked in by his friends. The place was under the care of a warrant officer armourer (was his name Collins?), a man who could flick the muzzle of a 303 with his thumb, and tell you how well it would shoot. (He was supposedly showing visitors round one day, and holding forth about the FW 190, when a voice said "Ach, I know ziss machine. I heff 700 hours on type").

Some old faded notebooks turn up next. Thermodynamics – did we really once know all that stuff about carpet diagrams, and gamma over gamma minus one? Aerodynamics too – Bernouilli's Theorem with all its bits in brackets stretching across a full page, and slugs per cubic feet and all the rest. What about Met, and the T-Phigram. Well, of course, we could easily brush it up again if we needed to, couldn't we?

What about the struggle to stay awake in lectures after so much physical activity! As though stalling, we would suddenly find ourselves tipping over on one wing, and have to recover smartly. Or else we would find the blackboard covered with writing or maths, without our having the faintest idea how it got there. Let us not name who it was sitting at the back of war studies, making lecherous noises every time the port of Brest was mentioned!

We could go rummaging in the trunk for ever. We have only looked at the things on top so far. What about the visit of the West Point cadets, with their extraordinarily harsh discipline that would frighten a Prussian, and their honour code that obliged them to tell tales on each other? Then there were the French cadets who came in a Ju52, one of whom began a randy song in the bar in Boston? We didn't quite get the words but the actions spoke for themselves, until his horrified companions got him to shut up! There must somewhere in the trunk be souvenirs of all those visits the College fixed up for us in our turn, to fly with the USAF, or navigate to Malta in a Wellington, for example.

But let's look at just one more photograph, a favourite. It was taken when the whole Entry was all on a visit to De Havilland's at Hatfield. We had been round the production line all afternoon, and been treated to a low-level aerobatic display by John Derry, flying a Venom straight off the production line. It was not even painted, and on a high speed low pass, an engine panel fell off. So what! Press on regardless, chaps! Flying was like that in of those days.

We had also seen a Sprite rocket motor fired. It poked out of a sort of garage, with a roped-off grass area outside. The noise was absolutely hellish. When everyone recovered their senses after it shut down, it had dug a great long trench right in front of us. (No sissy ear defenders in those days, of course. Sorry, what did you just say…?))

Now we are photographed in the hospitality suite of the factory, surrounded by demonstration engines on stands. We have had nothing to eat since lunchtime, and our empty stomachs are being plied with sherry at the firm's expense. It is one of the best, most cheerful group photographs in my album, with all of us beaming at the camera through a happy alcoholic haze.

On that note, time to close the trunk, and stand back and look at it. There, solidly packed inside is all the content of two pretty tough years and eight months. During all that period of our young lives, we were disciplined, chased, challenged, observed, stretched, reported on, given all sorts of experiences, taught to fly and to drill, given an ethos and a pride – we must have been very different when finally we graduated from when we started. So how was it when we packed that trunk and set out into the "real Air Force"?

Had we been "brainwashed"? Were we not a bit priggish? Some in the Air Force outside certainly thought so. My wife was a WRAF officer, and she heard enough snide comments about Cranwell officers to confirm that there was quite a bit of jealousy and resentment of us. Definitely there were those who watched for the slightest mistake or fall from grace, and gleefully seized upon it.

We, in our turn, had sometimes to come to terms with serving alongside old sweats who had been in the war, and now had liquid lunches and spent most of their time in the crewroom playing cards, or with bored and sullen National Servicemen who had no incentive, and had to be coerced into working. Standards in the "real RAF" were not always those we had imbibed at Cranwell. Sometimes too, I think, our commanding officers looked to us for more than we, in our relative inexperience, could deliver. (I remember realising that I could quite well have run a bomber offensive from High Wycombe, but didn't know much about being squadron adjutant!)

One view from an Old Cranwellian friend, whose father was a cadet in the twenties, is that we were given a superb education for an Air Force that had actually ceased to exist many years before – the Air Force perhaps which died in Fairey Battles in France in 1940.

We had not been long out of Cranwell before others were coming into the Service and getting permanent commissions like us, but based on university degrees and short officer training courses. They resembled us to look at, but must surely have been very different animals from us inside.

I am able to make a direct comparison here. When I left full-time service, I thought to myself that if university graduates could get permanent commissions, a Cranwell officer could equally well get himself a degree. So I went to university as a mature student, and eventually graduated MA Hons.

Student life was the complete opposite of Cranwell; certainly in my experience. There was absolutely no discipline, other than self-discipline and the requirement to produce written work on time. You could get up when you liked, wear what you liked, not wash and shave if you didn't want to. If you thought you could afford to miss a lecture, you could do so and nobody checked. A lot of the day was spent sitting round talking and drinking coffee. Everyone argued and questioned everything (although the tutors had ways of putting you down verbally), and spouted a lot of pretentious rubbish with their hands in their pockets. You could spend all evening getting legless, and go to bed when you liked, and where you liked, and with whom you liked (I speak here of the general scene, not myself personally, of course!)

The sole criteria for gaining your degree were your exam answers, and a thesis of sufficient quality. No drill, no early morning PT, no standing to attention or marching in squads to and from lectures, nobody driving you along morning, noon and night. And above all, no testing for the dreaded LMF – no backward somersaults, no parachute jumps, no compulsory boxing, – it was up to you what sports or adventure activities you took up, if any whatsoever. And, of course, you were surrounded by women, whereas I cannot remember a single one involved in our life at Cranwell, unless you count Sunday afternoon assignations with totty from one of the local Teacher Training Colleges. What a totally different upbringing from our Cadet Wing days.

It is no good speculating which route to a permanent commission has given the Service the best officers in the long run. Suffice to say that the Cadet Wing as we knew it is no more. For whatever reasons, those in the Corridors of Power chose other options for building their officer cadres

So be it. They shall not see our like again.

We could end with the old toast....

"Here's tae us, wha's like us!

Damn few, and they're a' deid!"

However, I prefer to look at my tin trunk and remember the finest compliment I could have wished for. I was checking out on Sunday morning after an Old Cranwellian reunion about twelve years ago. Several mess staff were drinking cups of tea in the hall porter's cubby hole. I thanked them for looking after us over the weekend.

One of them said: "That's all right, Sir. We like seeing you all back again, after so many years. *You were GENTLEMEN*." [R.H.R.]

THE ENTRY

All 40 of the young men who entered the RAF College as No 54 Entry in April 1949 did so with the aim of becoming commissioned into the General Duties Branch as pilots. In those days cadets intended for the Equipment and Secretarial branches were trained at Digby and there was no training at Cranwell for navigators or any other aircrew category or branch. As to background, roughly half of the entry came from grammar schools and half from public schools – including five from the same school, Bedford. Two of the three from Ceylon also came from the same school, St Thomas' College. Some of the new entrants were already in RAF uniform as they included several aircrew cadets, a former aircraft apprentice and some called up for National Service. One was in the uniform of a sergeant in the Royal Army Education Corps.

Along the way the entry gained two additional members from the previous entry, No 53, lost one to the next junior entry and two who transferred to the Equipment Branch and continued at Digby. Only 31 actually graduated as Pilot Officers in the GD Branch. This means that of the original 40, eleven fell by the wayside during the course, either for insufficient aptitude for flying, insufficient progress in academic subjects or medical reasons and one for a disciplinary reason.

After graduating on the 12th December 1951, the entry dispersed to various Advanced Flying Schools to fly Meteors, Vampires, Mosquitos or Varsities preparatory to yet more training at Operational Conversion Units either still on Meteors or Vampires in the case of those destined to fly jet fighters, or to Sunderland flying boats or Lancasters for those heading for Coastal Command and for conversion to Hornets in Singapore for three posted to the Far East Air Force. At the end of that stage of training all were posted to squadrons save for a few who were "creamed off" to train as flying instructors. In the course of time members of 54 Entry found themselves at many stations at home and abroad, including Germany, Korea, Japan, Malaya, Egypt, Iraq, Aden, Malta, Cyprus and Gibraltar.

As time went on more became flying instructors, two became test pilots and some moved to flying transport aircraft and more advanced types including Canberras, Vulcans, Javelins, Swifts, Hunters, Hastings, Vallettas, Comets, Britannias. A list of types flown and roles in which members of the entry were employed is to be seen as an appendix.

Sadly, seven members of the entry were killed in flying accidents, including three during the first year after graduation, and one flying as a passenger in a civil aircraft. Another retired on medical grounds as the result of serious injuries received in a flying accident.

As time passed there were some promotions to Squadron Leader and some attended courses at the Staff College. Further promotions came and two members of the entry rose to the rank of Air Commodore. A variety of ground appointments came, regardless of rank. One member left the service after six years and ten of the entry decided to leave the service at the first official exit point, at the age of 38, with an entitlement to a relatively small pension. Others applied to leave between the ages of 38 and 55, the age for a full pension, and only a very few remained for that length of time. After retirement members followed a diverse selection of careers including as air line pilots, as flying instructors and examiners, an air accident investigator, school bursar, bank official, civil servants, teacher, commodity broker, hotelier, solicitor, antique dealer and stock broker. These callings took some to Africa, the Middle East, Canada and the USA and although most remained in the United Kingdom on final retirement some are now living in Australia, New Zealand, Canada and Spain. Five have died of natural causes.

Almost three years living in close proximity and sharing the same experiences, some of physical hardship, some boring, some very enjoyable and some very funny, created a strong bond between young men in their late teens and early twenties, a bond which in the vast majority of cases has lasted into old age.

There can be few other experiences in life to match that enjoyed by the men of this entry.   [F.D.H.]

2.   College Days

How we got there and some of what we did…

SO YOU WANT TO BE A PILOT?

I grew up as a hangar boy in British Guiana where an American friend of my father ran a small charter company. He had been a pilot in the US Army in WW1 and, on leaving, had bought a crated new Curtis Jenny trainer for $25 and then sold the crate at a profit. After years of barnstorming and, reputedly, a short stint as a pilot for Al Capone, he had settled down to bush flying in Guiana. He operated two five seater bi-plane flying boats (similar to the Walrus) and later a Grumman Goose. In 1946 Ian Worby's (49 Entry B Sqn) father (ex-RNAS) joined as a pilot. Not surprisingly. when my family returned to England in 1947 I decided to join the RAF. My father was not in favour but eventually came round to the idea. I got the brochures on aircrew vacancies from the Air Ministry and decided to try for Cranwell.

   First I had to take the Civil Service Commission exam for entry to the three service cadet colleges, as I did not come under any of the categories who were exempt. My father arranged for me to attend Messrs Davies, Laing and Dick (Tutors), commonly called a "crammer", who were housed in a rambling mansion in Holland Park. There were all sorts and both sexes there – candidates for the Higher School Certificate, aspirants for Sandhurst and Dartmouth, and ex-servicemen trying for a University place. The staff also were a mixed group. I recall my geography tutor, a clergyman, telling me a lengthy story about his previous life as a medieval monk. Our little group used to travel by tube to Marble Arch for a two-course three shilling lunch (with orchestra) at the Lyons Corner House.

   All sitting the exam had to take English, a General Paper, Maths, plus a choice of two other subjects – I opted for Physics and Geography. My first attempt, in June 1948, was a disaster. The exam was held in a windowless room painted pale green and with fluorescent lights. After some eye problems in the English and Geography papers, during the maths paper my eyes went out of focus and I could not read the questions. After persevering to no effect I decided to retire ill before the end of the time allowed but without mentioning the cause. I decided not to go to our GP in case he was contacted by the RAF should I be considered on a subsequent occasion. I reported instead to Moorfields

Eye Hospital where I was shown to a seat on one of a row of benches with many people waiting ahead of me. A nurse took my details and within a few minutes I was summoned to a room in which were three doctors. It seemed my case had attracted their attention, being unusual. After exhaustive tests they said they could find nothing wrong with my eyes and decided it must have been fatigue coupled with the effect of the fluorescent lights and the colour of the walls. I said nothing about the RAF – again, just in case.

Soon I received the results of the examination – there I was at the bottom of a very long list. However I resolved to try again and returned to the crammers. In October I again found myself in the same room, but this time I was equipped with a pair of my father's reading glasses (I had noted at the first exam that a number of candidates wore spectacles; so I was not going to stand out). After almost half an hour of the first exam the same phenomenon recurred but the spectacles did the trick and when the results came I found myself on page one.

Next came the aircrew medical examination at the RAF Central Medical Establishment in Goodge Street, London. Various tests ensued – blood pressure, a stethoscope examination, standing on one leg without falling over, taps on the knees with a rubber mallet whose shaft was then used to tickle the feet, blowing up a column of mercury, sitting on the opposite side of the room to the doctor who whispered words for me to repeat whilst his WAAF assistant twiddled in my other ear with a beautifully manicured finger, and the infamous cough test. Finally came the eye examination; my heart beat faster as I feigned nonchalance but all was well. I had passed.

After this came a couple of days at RAF North Weald, Essex, for flying aptitude tests. I had done a few hours dual in an Auster a couple of months before in preparation. The test I best recall was keeping a spot central on a cathode ray tube using a joy stick – the Army Air Corps Museum at Middle Wallop still has one of these devices. There were tests for manual dexterity, paper tests with an aeronautical and mechanical basis (if Cog A is turned clockwise how will Cog G move?) and interviews.

Finally I found myself invited for a 3 day stay at the RAF Selection Board at Ramridge House in Hampshire. Ramridge was an extended Robert Adam house originally built in 1779, which had been requisitioned by the RAF in 1939. There is still a mural of a Spitfire on a ground floor wall but I cannot recall it.

I found there were 36 hopefuls in all. We were divided into teams of 6 and allocated to huts. My team eagerly discussed what might lie ahead of us – unlike today, the Services' selection methods were unknown to outsiders. Our lot were all friendly lads and we decided to co-operate to our mutual benefit – agreeing not to upstage the leader in the team events. One ex -Worcester training ship candidate said we were to call on him for any knots required in the practical work. Someone else said the staff would watch our table manners like hawks! I recall one of the group discussions – "If you were Captain Scott would you have let Oates commit suicide?"

I thought, "Scott is a national hero – better not to gainsay him."

Then there were the practical tests for which we were dressed in brown overalls with a large number on the back. They involved exercises like crossing a crocodile infested river marked on the ground with what seemed to be quite inadequate equipment – barrels, heavy planks and too-short lengths of rope. Officers with clipboards watched and made notes. I also remember being aware of a group of civilians watching from the sidelines. Especially I recall being selected for assessment by the team psychologist. It took place in a grand sitting room. We two sat in armchairs in front of a fire blazing in a splendid marble fireplace (Robert Adam?). He explained one in each team of six got this special treatment – "Purely a random choice you understand, Cooper." I was not so sure. Then he asked me to tell him all about my life to date. Not all, by any means, I thought to myself and had it all over in one minute flat. "Splendid," he said, and asked what books I read. "Biggles" I replied and hastily added some others. While this was going on I spotted him surreptitiously taking a small object from a pocket and tossing it into the fire. When the bang occurred I thus sat quite still, showing no surprise. "Splendid," he said, and explained that his assessment would not be available to the Board; it would be confidential to the Air Ministry and in later years would be compared with my performance in the RAF to see whether psychological tests were of any use in selecting officers. In mid March 1949 a letter came from the Air Ministry. My eyes rapidly scanned it: "I am commanded by the Air Council – successfully passed – awarded a cadetship." Happy days!

Fast forward now to being in Junior Entries, lined up in a corridor on the first floor of the College building awaiting an initial interview with the Director of Studies. Along came a civilian in a smart suit who entered the Director's office. When my turn came I found him sitting behind a desk perusing some papers.

"Ah", he said, "an educated man, I see." Then he asked if I had seen him before. Cautiously, I simply said "Yes".

"What an observant lad you are to remember that I was one of a group of headmasters visiting Ramridge House when you were undergoing selection. Well done!" I kept quiet.   [D.A.C.]

ON BECOMING A "GENERAL"

I sometimes wondered if the correct procedure had been followed in my case and that everyone else was therefore in error, or they were all correct and that I was in the wrong.

I had already applied for a Cranwell cadetship when I received my National Service call-up papers. The local recruiting office should be able to solve the problem, I considered, and so there I went. The Recruiting Sergeant explained in no uncertain terms that he had heard all the excuses before, many times, including this one.

"But", I insisted, "I can't join the Army and the Air Force, and since I want to join the RAF, I must politely decline the Army's invitation."

"Listen to me, lad" he replied, a contemptuous sneer spreading across his face, "If you don't show up at the appointed time and place, you will be arrested and sent to prison. That would scupper your chances of a cadetship, eh?"

I knew even less then about the law than I do now, but what he said seemed convincing. I decided to obey the summons. And it is true what they say about the Army; the pay is poor and the boots are heavy.

It was easy to contrive a few days leave in order to attend the RAF Selection Board. The difficulty arose when, having been successful, I wanted to leave for good. I was referred up and up the chain of command until I reached the Colonel – a fearsome, red-faced officer who fidgeted with his cane as if he were about to strike me with it. Among his many medals were several which showed that he had served not only in the Second World War, but in the First one too.

"You want to join what?" he barked.

The adjutant leaned over and spoke softly to his Colonel.

"What?" barked the Colonel, "What's that?"

The adjutant spoke a little louder. I could not hear all he said, but he seemed to be explaining that I was referring to a novel service, which, it appeared, had taken over some of the duties of the cavalry.

"Humph!" the Colonel exclaimed, "Humph! You will serve your King and country properly for two years in accordance with the law of the land. After that, you can go and join whatever new-fangled service that you like. Dismissed!"

"Right turn. Quick march. Left, right, left right" bawled the Sergeant Major.

I was determined to take up my cadetship, and if I could not leave with permission, I would leave without it. I knew enough law to realize that if I abandoned my kit and travelled in plain clothes, I could be charged with desertion. So it was that I arrived at Cranwell in army uniform with all my kit.

Within the day I had been nicknamed 'General'; the name stuck and sometimes I am still so addressed. Now, with my careworn face and greying hair, I could, perhaps, pass as a real retired general!

I was assigned to B Squadron under the renowned Bob Weighill. He welcomed us and invited anyone with a problem to go and see him. I had a problem.....A few weeks later my discharge certificate from the Army arrived by post. At last I was no longer in jeopardy with the Military Police.

But I still sometimes wonder, why did it happen only to me?   [B.M.]

A MEETING WITH A SENIOR NAVAL PERSON

During my first term at Cranwell as a member of the junior entries, the three cadets from Ceylon (that included me) were invited to a reception at the Ceylon High Commission, which was a very impressive place in those days. We were the first Ceylonese to be accepted by Cranwell and I suspect the authorities were keen to show us off. Naturally we were expected to arrive in number one uniform.

The reception was in full swing when we arrived and I noticed that there were other military people amongst the mainly diplomatic guests. The food was excellent – it always was at Ceylon functions – and drink was flowing freely. I soon began to enjoy the feeling of being treated like a celebrity and the effect of too much champagne began to make me overconfident. I was entirely at ease with all the important people to whom I was introduced and was not at all hesitant in airing my views freely.

In time I was gently ushered towards a small group of naval officers. I had not yet learned the rank structure in the Royal Navy but had just enough sense to notice that one of the gentleman had sleeves covered in gold bands and a chest full of medals. Wisely, I decided that I should call him 'Sir'. I still cringe at the exchange that followed.

The heavily-banded gentleman greeted me with, "And how's the Air Force, young man?"

I had just started being taught the 'History of the Royal Air Force' so, without hesitation, I told him what a superb service it was. All the naval officers listened politely and asked the kind of questions that showed they had been listening. I replied expansively and with great confidence. This was my subject.

Suddenly it dawned on me that I had been dominating the conversation and decided to put things right by switching the conversation to the navy. A very short while later I was pulled away by our hosts to meet another group of guests. Before leaving I had to get in the last word.

"The navy is finished, sir." I heard myself saying.

"Oh! I'm sure we will still serve some purpose in the future."

Then as a matter of courtesy I asked, "May I know your name, sir?"

"Fraser, my boy, Fraser."

We said our farewells and I thought no more about it.

At Cranwell, the following day, my fellow cadets were interested in finding out how the reception had gone. I told them how I had enjoyed myself and about the naval gentleman I had met. "Who was he?" they asked. "He said his name was Fraser."

"What was he wearing?"

I described his uniform as best I could.

There was a short, shocked silence. One of the lads, who was far more up-to-date in military matters, said in awe "That's Lord Fraser, the First Sea Lord ".

I was stunned but consoled myself in the sure knowledge that I was never likely to meet Lord Fraser again and that he would never recognise an impudent young cadet.

A few terms later Lord Fraser was the reviewing officer at a Graduation Parade. I occupied an anonymous position in the third rank of my squadron during the reviewing officer's inspection and wished myself invisible as Lord Fraser moved through the front rank and started on the middle one. I breathed an inaudible sigh of relief as he passed me by. But the old gentleman was playing games with me. He turned abruptly and walking up to me asked in a voice audible to all, "And how's the Navy now, my boy?"

He said it kindly, but I can only imagine that I had either turned white or pink by that stage. Lord Fraser had decided to keep the joke private because none of the other accompanying officers, nor my fellow cadets understood his question. Even the Commandant asked me about it later. I did not tell them at the time though the story did eventually come out.

Some years later I overheard another cadet from Ceylon tell this story as if it had happened to him. I found that amusing because the Ceylon High Commission did not have a similar reception thereafter, because Lord Fraser was no longer First Sea Lord and because he was never the reviewing officer at Cranwell again.[1]   [C.G.D.J.]

---

[1] Postscript: When The First Sea Lord, Admiral of the Fleet Lord Fraser of North Cape, came to Cranwell as Reviewing Officer of the Graduation of No 52 Entry he told several little anecdotes as cautionary words to the cadets.

As a young officer attending the Gunnery Course at Whale Island, he was a little late getting on parade one morning. He said to the Chief Petty Officer Instructor, "Sorry Chief, I'm late." The Chief replied *That's all right, son, but – Them that's keen gets fell in early!* Lord Fraser said that he had remembered that all his life and most of those who heard him tell this tale will have remembered it too. I think it was Lord Fraser who said

MY FIRST INSTRUCTOR

It is said that every student pilot considers that his first instructor is the greatest man in the world. In my case it was true; my instructor, Harry Dryhurst, really was.

He was, of course, a very good pilot and a very good instructor (two very different things!). He had infinite patience and gave terrific support and encouragement both on and off duty. When I had a minor medical problem and was put in sick quarters for a few days, he visited me twice a day, and urged me to get better and resume training.

Only the best was good enough both for his students and himself – he was totally dedicated to the RAF and expected everyone else to be so too.

In the war he had been shot down on his second trip as captain of a Halifax– a bomber mission to Berlin. He once confided that he would never forgive the Germans. But not because of the privations and hardships and misery he had had to endure as a POW, but because by shooting him down the Germans had deprived him of the opportunity of achieving his aim of becoming the best pilot in Bomber Command.

Sadly, Harry was killed many years later in a HS125 due to a combination of malfunctions which was beyond even his skill to control. But in a way he is still with us; sometimes, when I am at the controls of an aircraft, especially if there is some sort of a problem, I still think of him.   [B.M.]

FINGER TROUBLE – OR A FUEL COCK-UP

In the early 1950s the basic trainer at Cranwell was the Percival Prentice, a fairly large and underpowered monoplane with three seats. The pupil and instructor sat side by side and behind them was a third seat. The Prentice had a fuel tank in each wing which fed the engine by way of a fuel cock on the floor between the front seats and this fuel cock had three positions, namely Left, Off and Right.

Learning to carry out forced landings after engine failure was an important part of the training syllabus and engine failure was simulated by closing the throttle; there was no question of switching the engine off. The instructor having closed the throttle, it was the task of the pupil to select a suitable spot for landing, to carry out a circuit and approach as if to land and, during that procedure, carry out various checks to find out what might have caused the engine to fail and, if possible, to restart it. These checks included engine temperatures and pressures, magneto

---

that, on the same course, as part of their education, the young officers were taken to see the Naval Detention Barracks. Here they were told by a CPO on the staff; "I want all you young gentlemen to remember one thing; every man here is a volunteer!" F.D.H.

switches and the availability of fuel. All these things having been done, and assuming that the approach to a field turned out to be satisfactory, the instructor would tell the pupil to put on power and climb away from about 50 feet above the ground. These exercises were carried out in the area reserved for low-flying to the east of Sleaford and, with perhaps 50 or so aircraft flying from Cranwell every day, this was often a busy place to be and, for those who lived and worked there, a noisy place to be.

The star of this tale was Flight Cadet David de la Harpe, one of three young men who had come from Ceylon to join the Royal Air Force. Unfortunately he did not survive long after gaining his wings.

One day de la Harpe was in the low flying area with his instructor practising forced landings. All was going well and David carried out the checks including that relating to the fuel, which was to change from the tank in use to the other tank. Unfortunately, instead of turning the fuel cock through 180 degrees he turned it through only 90 to the "Off" position. The engine, for that very good reason, stopped. The instructor took control and continued what had been a skilful approach to land safely in the selected field. David looked down, saw what he had done, turned the fuel on again and said nothing.

As he and his instructor sat there pondering their plight, a figure with, as David described it, a thatched head, climbed through the hedge from the next field where he had been working with his hoe and said, or growled, "Was yow buzzin' us just now? 'Cos if yow was, I said to my mate as I 'oped as 'ow, yow'd crash – and yow 'ave!" With that he went back to his mate and his hoeing, showing no sympathy at all for the distressed airmen.

It is not clear now whether the instructor tried to restart the engine, succeeded and then took off or whether ground crew went to inspect, found nothing wrong and then they restarted. What is clear is that the failure of the engine remained a mystery – except to the few told the tale by David. [F.D.H.[2]]

A GROUND LOOP – I LEARNT ABOUT FLYING FROM THAT

The Harvard was an aircraft to be treated with respect, after the amiable lumbering Prentice. There were five reasons for swing on take-off, and it made use of all of them (let me think – spiral slipstream on the fin, torque reaction, advancing blade effect, gyroscopic effect on raising the tail – what was the fifth?)

It also ground-looped on landing if given the slightest chance.

---

[2] With grateful acknowledgements to, and memories of, David, a good friend.

One day, before I went solo on the Harvard, my instructor was giving me dual circuits and bumps at Barkston Heath. After a roller landing with full flap down, I opened the throttle and we left the ground. Suddenly my instructor seemed to take control, because we banked ninety degrees to the left and went into a maximum rate turn. He had been a wartime fighter pilot, and I thought for an instant that he was showing me what real hairy low-level flying was like.

Things happened fast after that. There was a stream of blasphemies from the back, the engine suddenly cut, and lumps of turf were flying past the canopy. Next thing, we were on the ground, facing the way we had come, rolling gently backwards. The port wing had developed a turned-up wing-tip, just like the Prentice.

He hadn't taken control at all. I think he had been asleep. Others may have ground-looped on landing, but I think I was the only one in our Entry to do so on take-off.

A case, as Churchill is supposed once to have said, of stalling between two fools? [R.H.R.]

NIGHT LIGHTS – OR AERONAUTICAL SERENDIPITY

Our Harvard night flying phase had been delayed by persistent bad weather, and so when we were finally able to get started we were all keen to go.

The Harvard, like other aircraft with retractable gear, had undercarriage lights on the panel, green for locked down, red for unlocked, and out for locked up. These lights were important and so had to be bright enough to be conspicuous on a sunny day. This meant that at night they would have been impossibly bright had there not been a device to dim them. This consisted of a filter that was rotated over the bulbs by a knob in the centre of the instrument.

In our aircraft this device was not working and so the lights were very bright indeed. Those were the good old days before the invention of "go" and "no go" lists – the captain or instructor made the decision.

" Hum," said my instructor, "It's not really suitable for night flying, especially for student solo. (Super! So he plans to send me solo tonight!) "But the programme is running late and there are no spare aircraft tonight, so I think you can manage it, don't you?"

Anyone who has been a cadet will know that when an officer of the staff asks a cadet if he agrees with him, not a great deal of contemplation is required to arrive at a suitable conclusion.

"Of course, Sir." I promptly replied.

"Good, just make sure that you don't look directly at the lights or you will mess up your night vision."

I must have got something right that night, for just over an hour later we taxied in, my instructor got out and told me to do circuits and bumps for another hour. I completed that exercise, and finally turned off the runway after a very long day. Perhaps I was a little tired, (that's my excuse anyway!) but when I went to raise the flaps, I wrongly raised the gear lever instead. Immediately a very bright green light went out and a very bright red light came on. In what the BBC now calls a "knee jerk reaction", I instantly put the lever down again, and instantly the red light went out and the green light came back on again. The aircraft was behaving normally, so I cautiously continued to taxi back to the apron.

I went to "Chiefie" and told him exactly what had happened, explaining that if there was any damage at all, I would have to put in a report. He replied that he had come across this situation before and knew exactly what to check for. A little later he came and said that he had done a thorough inspection and that there was absolutely nothing wrong with the aircraft.

We had already studied security and had been introduced to the concept of "need to know", and I took the view that no one, except me and "Chiefie" had a need to know about it.

"But surely", I hear you ask, "Surely you told your flying instructor?"

Of course I did – on graduation day when my wings were sown securely to my tunic.   [B.M.]

THE LAMB THAT WENT ASTRAY

The erring Flight Cadet in this story is not named as, sadly, he is no longer with us, but he was of a very relaxed and generous nature and we feel sure that he would have approved, and smiled at our recounting his adventure.

Towards the end of basic training on the Prentice, we were all sent up to do solo navigation cross-country flights. Imagine, then, our hero nearing the end of the triangular route, bumbling along at 95 knots in his faithful machine, when he found himself over eight-eighths cloud. Having had many warnings about not descending through cloud unless absolutely certain of position, he decided to use Cranwell's Standard Beam Approach System to find his way home safely.

Put simply, the SBA transmitted the morse letters "N" (dash-dot) to the north of its beam, and letters "A" (dot-dash) to the south. When the aircraft reached a line running east to west through Cranwell, the two letters merged to give a continuous note in the pilot's earphones. He could then turn to fly along the beam to the airfield (assuming he was not so lost that he didn't know whether he was east or west of base to start with).

Having switched on the set and checked it was Cranwell's frequency, our lone aviator heard 'A's. Amongst the many admirable qualities God had given him, the ability to distinguish morse letters was not included. He turned south to intercept the beam.

Not surprisingly, it seemed to be a very long way to the beam. As he motored on and on without reaching it, the 'A's in his earphones got quieter and quieter, until they faded away altogether.

He had been airborne far longer than planned and fuel was getting low. Fortunately, the cloud below him began to break up, and he saw fields through a gap. Descending, he executed a successful forced landing in one of them. It was lunch time, and the local school was nearby. Hordes of children rushed over, soon joined by a reporter from the local paper. Our hero's photograph was taken, standing by the Prentice, looking like Biggles, while grown-ups shooed children off the machine.

Where was he, he asked the natives. The answer was south east of London, somewhere near Croydon. He had unwittingly gone right through the London Air Traffic Control Zone. He had landed about 115 miles as the crow flies from Cranwell.

Back at the College, we flight cadets did not, of course, learn what was going on until later. It seems that once telephone communication had been achieved, a QFI had to go by staff car down to Croydon, presumably taking some groundcrew with him, to inspect the aircraft, start it up, then fly it back. Our hero eventually reappeared amongst us, none the worse for his adventure, but we never heard exactly what his flight commander said to him.   [R.H.R.]

STEEP GLIDE BOMBING

One of the perks of our extended training at Cranwell was that we were taught to dive-bomb in Harvards, with 25 pounder smoke bombs. My first dual instruction in this was with my regular instructor – a gentle flying man, ex-Transport Command. That detail went off without a problem, as far as I remember.

However, my second dual bombing was with a Flying Officer "E", known affectionately to all of us cadets as "Eff E" because of his frequent use of that Anglo-Saxon expletive! We flew over to the bombing range at Bassingham Fen and "Eff E" let me have first go. My modest 30 degree dive produced a reasonable score but then, from the rear cockpit, came the cry: "No! No! No! That's not nearly effin steep enough! You won't hit the effin ground! You're much too effin scared! I'll show you how it should be effin done!!"

We climbed up and he launched us into what seemed to me like a near vertical dive, released the bomb and pulled out – and did he PULL!! I blacked out, completely unconscious! When I came round we were in the climb and for a moment I didn't know if I was punched, bored or countersunk! We flew home rather quietly. I reckon he "cooked it" and frightened himself!

I continued with my modest technique and surprised "Eff E" by getting the best scores for bombing in "H" Flight.

Later, on 45 Squadron, based in Singapore and flying Hornets, I did many dive bombing sorties over the Malayan jungle and usually produced good results; I wasn't an advocate of the 60 degree dive.

Mind you. Old "Eff E" was right about one thing. I never did hit the ground. I was much too effin scared! [E.A.P.]

IN A SPIN

At one time there was, and possibly still is, an RAF flight safety publication or journal called "Air Clues" and in it was a column entitled "I Learnt About Flying From That!" in which pilots would confess various errors from which they claimed to have learnt and which were intended to help others from avoiding the same. I often wondered how many confessions had still to be told and lately I have been thinking of a few of my own.

In 1950 I started my pilot training at Cranwell on an aircraft called the Percival Prentice T1, which had replaced the Tiger Moth. The Prentice had a fixed undercarriage, and was fairly spacious, with side by side seats for instructor and pupil under a large canopy with a sliding hatch or window on each side. There was a third seat in the back for, it was alleged, a second pupil to sit and learn from what was going on in front. The adverse effect on the pupil struggling in the front of having an audience in the back had presumably not been considered. However, the only time the back seat was used, so far as I am aware, was when an instructor took two pupils to a satellite airfield for a spell of circuits and landings. Perhaps the Prentice might reasonably be described as being like a taxi with wings, a good aircraft for going away for the weekend – not that we Flight Cadets were permitted such liberties.

Not long after my first solo I was sent up to do a session of solo spinning and when spinning or doing aerobatics solo the rule was to recover by 5,000 feet, so this meant starting the manoeuvres at about 7,000 feet. With the low power of the Prentice it took quite a long time to climb to that great height. Naturally, the weather had to be good for inexperienced pupils like me to carry out the exercise and so I enjoyed climbing out over Lincolnshire looking for a space to do my spins. I had actually enjoyed the spinning I had done dual but as it was my first time solo I was a bit apprehensive. Remembering the drills and checks, on reaching 7,000 feet I had a good look round to see that all was clear (there could be a lot of activity around Cranwell at that time), tightened and locked my harness, checked there were no loose articles in the cockpit, that the flaps were up, that there was enough fuel and that the engine temperatures and pressures were within limits.

At last, the spin! Straight and level, reducing power, nose above the horizon, speed falling off, throttle closed, stick further back and as the judder of the stall started, stick right back into the stomach and full left rudder. A flick and, success, a veritable spin to the left as per the book! As I said, I quite enjoyed spinning so I let it continue for a while and then I thought about recovering, the procedure for which is to apply full opposite rudder, pause and then ease the stick forward and when the spin stops, ease out of the dive and put on power to climb up again. So, I started the recovery action. At least, I thought that was what I was doing but, read on...

I applied full opposite rudder and waited. The spin to the left continued unabated and I sat there with the stick still hard back in my stomach. Becoming aware that the altimeter needle was turning rather rapidly I decided not to wait any longer but to put the stick forward. A few more turns and to my delight the spin actually stopped! I eased back on the stick, opened the throttle and as I levelled out and began to climb away saw that the altimeter needle was just coming up to the 2,000 foot mark – from the lower side. For some reason this made me feel a little peculiar, as evidenced by a some shaking all over and sweating of the palms and forehead, so I opened my side hatch to get a little cool air. At that moment I made a thank-offering to the gods of the air by sharing my breakfast with them, scattering it in the slipstream. The cynical might say that this was merely "yawning in technicolor" but I prefer the more reverent interpretation. I did not venture another spin that morning.

Did you spot the mistake? Yes, of course! I said the recovery action was "opposite rudder, pause, stick forward", but I put on opposite rudder and then, instead of just pausing briefly, waited for the rotation to stop before putting the stick forward. Thinking about it afterwards I realised that in my dual spinning we had recovered almost as soon as we entered the spin and I had come to believe that rudder alone would stop the spin and only then was it necessary to put the stick forward. My putting the stick forward was done in desperation and in the belief that I was not doing the right thing! So, I can safely say that I learnt from that little fright and I can also say that when I became an instructor none of my pupils were left in any doubt as to the correct way of recovering from a spin even though they were not permitted to spin solo in the Vampire, with all the complications of "B over A ratio" and the effects of applying in-spin aileron.

It was not long after the spinning incident that I was sent off to do circuits and landings to include some flapless landings. Unusually, the grass runway in use was the short one running south to north at the village end of the south airfield. As I said, it was short and there was little or no wind. I recall that it was rather a hazy morning. After a few uneventful circuits I turned on finals for a flapless landing. By definition this would entail a longish flat approach and it was made longer and flatter by the absence of wind. I did not do it very well, came over the hedge a bit too fast and just floated on and on instead of putting on power and going round again. So when I finally touched down there was very little runway left, and having run out of grass I had perforce to use the field full of cabbages at the end of the runway.

I found that it is not easy to taxy a Prentice in a field of cabbages so I had to shut down the engine and sit there waiting for help. I called the tower, which was then situated near the old swimming pool and gymnasium, and told them what must have been obvious if they had been looking. Quite probably they had not been looking, as it seemed that they had not been listening either. I came to that conclusion because although our callsigns indicated our flights they asked me my flight so that they could telephone the flight commander to arrange to get me out. Not understanding what I had been asked, I repeated that I was in the cabbage field whereupon a laconic voice, presumably that of an instructor, intruded with the drawling remark "They want to know your flight, you fool, not your plight".

The Prentice? There was no damage, just a bucket or so of earth and some greenery in the undercarriage fairings. What happened to me? I can't remember. [F.D.H.]

HOW NOT TO JUMP FROM A BALLOON

As a member of the Cranwell party taking a course at No 1 Parachute Training School, in 1950, I found myself standing in a large "basket", in fact something like the platform of a lorry with a canvas tilt on it, beneath a barrage balloon during its ascent, along with five others and a sergeant parachute training instructor. This was to be our first jump and we all made corny jokes and tried hard to appear nonchalant as though this sort of event was a common occurrence in our everyday life.

I was trying hard to remember all the many dos and don'ts we had been taught by the tough, almost sadistic NCO instructors. One of these points which they had stressed was the need, in preparation for jumps from the side of an aircraft, to jump out horizontally as far as possible, to avoid contact with the tailplane of the aircraft.

We lined up, ready to step to the exit. The person immediately in front of me was a good friend – or, at least he was until he reads this. When it was his turn to jump he suddenly rolled up like a Swiss roll and just fell out of the basket. I still can't believe how he didn't do himself an injury because he was so very close to the edge. This perturbed me somewhat and I wondered if I had missed something which we had been told. Several of the instructors were dispersed about the airfield below us, armed with powerful megaphones which were quite audible from a distance because there was little other noise, and their task was to express their views on our performance whilst we were on the descent. As the aforementioned chap was just below me, the PJIs were venting their feelings in no uncertain manner.

As soon as I landed I gathered up my parachute very quickly and ran across to the other chap as I was concerned about his welfare. However, he was quite all right.

I asked " What the hell had happened?" and, very calmly, he replied "When at the door I looked out and just simply fainted!".

However, I'm sure he covered himself in glory on our subsequent jumps.[3]   [D.J.B.K]

BELT UP

Scene: A lecture room in the Aeronautical Science and Engineering block of the Royal Air Force College, Cranwell. The year is 1951 and a navigator, Squadron Leader D F Miller, DFC, is addressing 54 Entry on the subject of guns and ammunition. He stresses the importance of clean ammunition and links to ensure the smooth feed of belts into the breech in order to minimise the risk of jamming. He tells the eager Flight Cadets how, in the 1914 –18 war, many of the best fighter pilots made up their own belts of ammunition after personally cleaning each round and link. He mentions Major Edward Mannock VC DSO MC as being one of this dedicated band:

Sqn Ldr Miller: Major Mannock or "Mick", as he was known, being of Irish extraction, was a very interesting character. He only had one eye.

---

[3] **Postscript**: This was not the only minor mishap on that course. Malcolm Cowper spent most of his first descent from a Dakota trying to get his feet untangled from the rigging lines through which he had somehow managed to somersault. Although he was the first of his stick out of the Dakota he was the last to reach the ground! Malcolm was our smallest cadet and cox of the College rowing eight. Sadly, he was also the first to lose his life, in 1952.

He came of a humble backgound and could be said to have been a self-made man."

A Voice from the Back: "Then why didn't he give himself two eyes?"

N.B. In fact Mannock had two eyes, but severe astigmatism in his left eye meant that he was virtually blind in that eye. He experienced difficulties in landing aeroplanes but was otherwise skilful and managed to conceal his disability.   F.D.H.

THE COMMANDANT

When we were cadets our Commandant was the renowned Air Commodore George Beamish. He was a bachelor and lived in solitary splendour in "The Lodge" also known as "The Commandant's Residence", a large house situated in its own grounds on the other side of the road from the College.

Once during his cadetship every cadet was invited to dinner at the Lodge followed by a visit to the station cinema as the Commandant's guest, sharing his private box.

We went in groups of four on Sunday evenings, in our third term.

One of the features of the officers who supervised our training was their obsession with sport. They seemed more interested in that than in flying and aeroplanes. Most cadets liked the odd game and some were quite good at their chosen ones. But we were all obsessed with flying and aeroplanes, and sport was of secondary (or lower) importance. George Beamish was no exception: it was said that he had played for Ireland in more than one sport, and for the RAF in several.

He was clearly a big tough man, and the story told about his parachute training in the thirties was certainly plausible. In those days the trainee parachutist stood on a platform built at the base of a wing strut on a Vickers Virginia biplane and clung on to the strut. When the jump area was reached, he would pull the ripcord, the parachute would deploy, and he would leave go of the strut and make his descent. It was said that when George's turn came, he pulled the cord as briefed but did not let go of the strut. It was not revealed whether this was a momentary lapse of co-ordination or a fleeting reluctance to leave the perch, but the consequence was that he took the strut with him. A now misshapen Virginia was safely landed.

Dinner was a formal, not to say stuffy, affair, and everyone was on their best behaviour lest an improper word or deed brought about the rapid end of the cadetship. The food was simple and plain as befits the table of a man more interested in sport than the pleasures of the flesh. A small beer was offered, and those who considered that their careers would not be affected (or had not thought of that angle) and accepted found that it was either home made or had been opened the previous week or had been bought at a fire sale. Whatever the reason, it was quite undrinkable. Nevertheless we drank it. How could a cadet tell his Commandant that his beer was awful? Perhaps it was a test of our stamina and stoicism, rather like first-term boxing.

We used to hope that the table talk would be of derring-do in the war or in the pre-war Empire beyond the Seas. Instead we were regaled with sporting tales in which we did our best to feign an interest.

A fixture of the College calendar in those days was the "College Run" – a seven mile cross country race in which everyone was expected to take part. This event had occurred in the week of Dave de la Harpe's invitation to supper.

"Tell me, de la Harpe," asked George, "Where did you come in the College Run?"

Dave, not renowned for his athletic prowess, replied miserably "215th, Sir."

"What!" exclaimed George, who was getting a little hard of hearing, "Fifteenth! That was not very good, was it?"

Dave decided that the better part of valour was not to correct the Commandant.

On another occasion, George asked "Tell me, Dawes, what games do you play?"

"Tennis, Squash and Fives, Sir", replied Tony, who was in fact rather good at those games.

"No, no, no, Dawes, what *team* games?"

"Well Sir, I prefer my games to team games."

"Oh really, Dawes! Do you think you are being fair to yourself?"

When I was being entertained, the Commandant opened a handsome cigarette box and offered me a cigarette. I was a smoker in those days and reached out to take one. I was nearly there when the box was snapped shut very firmly, George remarking: "How silly of me – healthy young cadets do not smoke, of course." A furtive check revealed that my finger tips were still attached to my fingers.

After dinner George would announce that it was time to go and we would all walk the short distance to the station cinema. We would go into the box, the Commandant telling us where to sit and making sure that we were all comfortable. The NCO in charge would discreetly observe all this ritual and when the Commandant and his guests appeared settled he would make a signal, whether we were on time or not, and the house lights would start to dim.

At this point George always remarked, "Just in time, gentlemen. Just in time!"

This procedure was well known to all, having been related many times. When Jock Christie enjoyed the Commandant's hospitality, as the house lights dimmed and before George had time to say anything, he remarked: "Just in time, Sir, just in time." George said nothing but gave a look that said everything.

That same evening the film being shown was an Abbott and Costello comedy in which the duo were trainee pilots. In the course of their misadventures they abandoned their aircraft but only one parachute opened and the other actor was saved by sitting on top of his colleague's open canopy. Discussing the film afterwards, George said "But that was impossible. It could not possibly happen, gentlemen".

George had a most powerful personality and his integrity shone forth clearly. He was firm but scrupulously fair. He had no wife, but he was wedded – to the Royal Air Force.

He and his staff turned an ill-disciplined, scruffy, ignorant rabble into Cranwellians and then into Air Force officers. They changed us for ever and it is a measure of their calibre that we still talk about him and them fifty and more years later. [B.M.]

A REVUE REVIEWED

A feature of coming to the end of the course and impending Graduation was the "54 Entry Review", a stage performance put on after the entry's final guest night with the primary aim of entertaining, but with the subsidiary aim of conveying a few messages to the staff! The title of the Revue relates to two of the firms of tailors supplying RAF uniforms.

Here follows the Review of the Revue as written by Brian Huxley (57 Entry) for the R.A.F. College Journal of March 1952.

Senior Entry Revue Revived: 'Ali Burberry and the 40 Gieves'

On 10th December, after the Final Guest Night, the College was privileged to witness the renaissance of the Senior Entry Revue. Produced by Philip Jevons (and integrated by Robson), *Ali Burberry and the Forty Gieves* proved an unqualified success.

After a rousing opening chorus, the show got away to a good start with some excellent harmonica playing by Paddy King. The more intellectual members of the audience were then catered for by "Barrimillova" in the beautiful "Ballet of the Beam". Our three 'Uncle Oboes' showed themselves in their true colours, confirming a strongly held belief that their exemplary behaviour was merely a cloak for juvenile delinquency of the worst kind.

We were granted two glimpses of the future. First (by courtesy of Horlicks) we joined Dan Dawes and the pilots of outer spaceships at their pre-flight briefing, and then retired to a London club-room to witness a most convincing display of decrepitude.

The first half of the show culminated in ten minutes of 'Chronic Opera'; this explained only too well why, during the last few weeks of the Autumn Term, our peace had been shattered by squads of denim-clad senior flight cadets looking radiantly happy in tin hats and webbing straps.

The second half of *Ali Burberry* started with a polished exhibition of sleight of hand by that renowned fiddler, Sandy Innes-Smith. This was followed by a sketch giving the inside story of the Combined Operations team at 'A' site. In Rastus and Sambo, 'B' Squadron (represented by Barry Mills and 'General' Meadley) put up a couple of excellent blacks. Then came perhaps the best performance of the evening – the tragic ballad of "Frankie and Johnnie", sung by Bones, Wood and King (this time with his guitar), and enacted with much sincerity by Francis and Christie. While the corpses were being removed after this sad ditty, Flight Sergeant 'Orskins kept the audience helpless with laughter with his monologue on a 'belt whitening fluid container housing'. Another lively song brought '*Ali Burberry and the Forty Gieves*' to a close. The revue was compered by Philip Jevons, against heavy odds, and the music was well supplied by the College Band.

There is a saying that "Blessed are they that that expect nothing, for they shall not be disappointed". Most of us did not know what to expect, but it is certain that nobody was disappointed. The hilarious sight of that dark satanic Mills pirouetting with his pupils around an S.B.A. and an agonized Frankie being dragged to the chair after shooting her lover compensated for all the indignities we suffered last term at the hands of '54' and will long remain in our minds.

While this success has made the Revue a 'must' for terms to come, we fear that future entries will be hard put to it to equal the talent displayed by '54'. But we shall see!   [B.H.]

3. The Early Years after Graduation

Mainly about our first flying tours in squadrons or as instructors, but with a few incidents on the ground for good measure.

WELCOME TO STRAD!

After graduating at Cranwell in December 1951 and doing a conversion course on the Gloster Meteor at No 202 Advanced Flying School at Middleton St George, Co Durham, I was sent to No 226 Operational Conversion Unit at Stradishall, Suffolk. Here, new pilots joining Fighter Command were taught tactical formation flying, the rudiments of air combat, and gunnery.

On the first day the course assembled – keen and bushy-tailed – to be welcomed by the Officer Commanding the Flying Wing. He was a well-known Battle of Britain pilot and, we were to realise later, of a rather eccentric nature. Anyhow, on this sunny April morning, here he was on a platform in front of this new course eager to hear what he had to say. After introducing himself and the senior members of his staff he started to have a closer look at what fate had just brought him. "Stand up all the National Service officers!" he ordered. Then, after a long look at them, he told them that he knew they were only in the air force for what they could get out of it. Furthermore, they were a shower and should all watch their step while they were at Stradishall.

Next came "Stand up all the Cranwell officers!" Again, a long look at each of us. Then he declared he knew all about us (Oh dear! He had been reading our previous reports!) We apparently all thought we had "made it" just because we had been trained at Cranwell. Anyway, we would not be of much use and he would, of course, be keeping a careful eye on us.

Then the Wing Commander turned his attention to the third element of the course. "Stand up the Short Service Officers!" They were "Fine fellows, the salt of the earth, the backbone of the RAF". No mention of keeping an eye on them!

Finally our service knowledge was briefly probed. "Who is the Commander in Chief of Fighter Command?" we were asked. The name of Sir Basil Embry was no doubt known to all of us, but not a mouth opened. We were all determined not to respond. After a dressing down on this aspect of our ignorance the welcome came to an end.   [D.A.C.]

VAMPIRES OVER GERMANY

After the confines of Cranwell and following the AFS course at Valley, I was posted in early 1952, together with Les Francis and Cecil Jonklaas, to No.112 Fighter/Ground Attack squadron at RAF Jever in 2nd Tactical Air Force (2nd TAF) in Germany. We were, in fact, "guinea pigs" in a new trial system of sending some pilots straight to their squadrons without going first to OCU. Indeed, we were guinea pigs in more ways than one in that we were flying Vampires which had no pressurisation, no heating and no ejector seat. That said, the next 2 ½ years proved to be a breath of fresh air and a period of varied and exhilarating flying.

The dual role of F/GA entailed flying HL (High Level) interceptions and ground attack sorties. Interceptions were often flown against Vampires from other squadrons in 2nd TAF, as well as against large formations of "friendly" bomber forces. There were certainly lots of aircraft in the skies over north Germany in those days – with squadrons at Oldenburg, Celle, Fassberg, Ahlhorn, Wunstorf, Gutersloh, Geilenkirchen, Wahn and Wildenrath – later to be joined by Bruggen and Laarbruch. Ground attack sorties were often against Army units in the close air support role and we flew regular trips to our nearby ranges to carry out strafing and rocketing.

Mobility was another feature of squadrons in those days and 112 squadron had its fair share. For example, within three weeks of our arrival at Jever the squadron was detached to the Royal Netherlands Air Force base at Twenthe for ten days. This was followed by other detachments, almost fortnightly, to Buckeburg, Sylt and Butzweilerhof (all in 2nd TAF), to the French Air Force base at Friedrichshaven in the French zone of Germany and to Filton and Odiham in the UK. What diverse and exhilarating flying it was, too, and flying four or five sorties a day was not unusual. Two of the detachments in particular come to mind – namely to Butzweilerhof and Sylt. The purpose of the four week detachment to Butzweilerhof, a few miles from Cologne, was to carry out continuous landing trials on PSP (Pierced Steel Planking) to test its suitability for use in the "field" as a quickly laid temporary runway. Circuits and bumps and short landings may seem pretty mundane, but there was some compensation with Cologne on our doorstep, and the famous Cologne Carnival was in full swing at the time.

The whole squadron went to the island of Sylt twice a year to carry out live air to air firing. We would carry out parallel and opposite quarter attacks on a target flag towed by a Tempest of the Target Towing Squadron. With more and more detachments there under your belt, your proficiency in hitting the flag increased – at least you got in closer and improved the range, line and deflection parameters. One or two hairy moments come to mind. One pilot managed to get his line absolutely spot on except that his aim was far ahead of the flag and his long burst broke the cable towing the flag and shot it off. The other pilots on that particular flag awaiting their turn were livid since they had to abort their sorties. On another occasion a pilot got too close to the flag on his attack, struck it and came back to base with the flag embedded in his tailplane! Another story has it that a pilot got so carried away with pressing home his attack that he "pulled right through" the flag still firing and the tug pilot still has the bullet scar on his thigh to prove it!

Large formation practices ("wing dings") were also quite exciting, with three squadrons of aircraft having to return to base through 8/8 cloud. Letting down in 4-ship formations at set timed intervals was always a bit hairy, with there being only a manual homer at Jever that necessitated long transmissions. Often breaking cloud at 500 feet – and no GCA either at Jever at that time – entailed a scramble to join the circuit and land. On one occasion one of the pilots ahead of me had engine failure in the circuit, didn't quite make the runway and ploughed in on the approach. He survived, luckily.

Large formation flypasts for special occasions could also be quite exciting and two instances come to mind. The first was in honour of the Duke of Edinburgh visiting 2nd TAF in March 1953. He took the salute at a parade at RAF Wunstorf and the flypast comprised 32 Vampires. Any turns in large formations have to be done smoothly and gently and not too tightly so as not to cause undue disturbance to the formation. We – that is 32 Vampires in boxes of four – were approaching the airfield when the leader called out "Turn about port. Go!" Either his timing was too early or the Duke's programme was running 30 seconds late. Whatever the reason, we were struggling to maintain close formation in a gaggle of 32 aircraft in a steeply banked turn through 360 degrees. We just made it, with everyone settling down on the run-in over the airfield. We had "lost" the 30 seconds.

The second occasion was a flypast in honour of the Queen's coronation in June 1953. This time we were to provide a formation of 36 Vampires with a wing of Meteor night-fighters to join us at an airborne rendezvous. We were lined up on the runway for take-off at 10 second intervals in pairs. Under nil or light wind conditions the combined jetwash from a large number of aircraft could cause a problem – and it did on that day. As I was rolling in my pair, and was half way down the runway, I saw one of the aircraft ahead catch some jetwash as he was getting airborne. He lost lift, wobbled, flipped on his side and cartwheeled to the left. The pilot was extremely lucky and lived to fly another day.

Final memories of 2nd TAF are of the squadron flying in to RAF Bruggen to open it up in 1953 and the subsequent conversion course on to the F86 Sabre. I use the word "course" loosely as, after two days of ground school followed by 10 minutes taxying practice getting used to the sensitive nose-wheel steering, we were dispatched on our first solo – no dual Sabres! A similar system to that at Valley two years earlier with dual on the Meteor and solo on the Vampire, but this time on a much faster swept-wing aircraft. Heating, demisting and an ejection seat were luxuries. On a final, let's say supersonic, note we would each fly a "mach" run entailing a wing over and steep dive from 43,000 feet until the Mach meter showed Mach 1. There were no worries in those days about doing it over the sea or in a special area under GCI control. We could break all the greenhouse windows we wanted!

Carefree, exciting flying days that are, regrettably long gone. Ah....those were the days! [A.D.R.D]

CARTWHEELS IN A VAMPIRE

I was in the aircraft involved in the crash at Wahn mentioned by Tony Dawes in "Vampires Over Germany". The Vampire was never the most stable platform with full drop tanks and the "Hi-Lo" technique for large formation take offs had not yet been evolved. The full implication of jetwash and turbulence were also not fully understood.

Naturally, I was not able to see the full splendour of my crash because I was too busy wrestling with a control column and a throttle, but an air trafficker described it to me in spectacular detail later in the day. Apparently the two drop tanks came off first as I cartwheeled. The nose of the Vampire was too short to strike the ground so the tail took the next impact, then each wing and the tailplane again until I was left in a bare cockpit connected to nothing. Unknowingly, I was making use of the crumple zone engineering built into modern cars. But I didn't know that at the time.

In frustration I watched the rest of the formation assemble overhead and fly off into the distance. I felt I had to do something right so I closed down the engine and meticulously shut off the fuel; the engine was actually isolated and on its own, 200 metres behind me. Then I caged the DI (gyro direction indicator). Not knowing whether I had suffered any injuries, I decided to stay put in the cockpit as I could see the Rescue and Fire trucks racing towards me. They had just come to a halt when I noticed a VW Beetle approach from the side. Out popped the Engineering Officer and, without a word, he plucked up the detachable clock from the cockpit and rushed away. Obviously, this was the most valuable part of the aircraft.

The final indignity was when the boss rang me from Filton and told me that as I could not be trusted with one of his aircraft I would have to rejoin the squadron there by using the Military Train. I did fly back, though.

I would also like to add to Tony's recollection of the infamous 360 degree turn incident. I was Number 3 in the left hand box and when "he who shall not be named" made a hard left turn I became aware of just how close to the trees I was, and also that my airspeed was a bit lower than it should have been. Can one fly formation with one eye on your box leader and one on your height and airspeed? Definitely yes, if the adrenaline is pumping fast enough.

He who shall not be named had his comeuppance on a similar large formation flypast over Brussels. Having briefed us on the radio frequency changes required and the correct frequencies to contact Brussels, our leader used the wrong one. The ensuing R/T went something like this:

"Brussels Control, this is Blue Leader. "Do you read"

No answer.

Louder and more insistent "Brussels, Blue Leader, do you read?!

Still silence.

Half a dozen calls in a similar vein followed.

Then an exasperated "Can anyone hear Brussels?"

The result was spontaneous and as slick as they come:

"Blue 2 negative"

"Blue 3 negative"

"Blue 4 negative"

"Red 1 negative"

"Red 2 negative"

and so on down to the 32nd aircraft.

These experiences served me well when, in my turn, I had to lead large formation flypasts. I tried to make my briefings accurate and relevant and I was always conscious of the poor sod on each extremity or at the tail end of a large formation and made sure his flight would not be endangered by me.   [C.G.D.J.]

A MAN'S AIR FORCE

I had not been on the Squadron long enough to have the seniority to qualify me for a place in the formation. I did, however, have just enough to be made "Reserve 1"

It was 1953 and the formation was part of the ceremony to celebrate the Coronation of Queen Elizabeth II. Flypasts were to be flown by the RAF in UK over Buckingham Palace, by MEAF in Egypt, FEAF in Singapore, and the largest by far, the 2nd TAF in Germany (where I was stationed) over Cologne. There were ten or twelve Wings in 2nd TAF in those days, each of at least three Squadrons. Every Squadron was to take part and each was to put up twelve aircraft. It was going to be the biggest formation most of us had ever seen or were likely to see again.

For rehearsals, the reserves were to start engines with the rest of the formation in case someone failed to start. If there were no problems, they were to shut down and dismiss. On The Day, they were to take off and lurk in the vicinity so that they could be called in if needed. The giant formation was formed up by the lead Wing flying a large polygon and at each turning point another Wing, already established on the new track, would slot in from the rear. This mostly worked well, but on one rehearsal a Wing Leader was a few seconds too early and took his Wing right through the one that was supposed to be ahead. The unflappable Bob Weighill, who could see it coming, ordered "Tuck in tight and keep your eyes on your leader". Those pilots unfortunate enough to have good peripheral vision saw nine boxes of four go through another nine boxes of four without a single collision. Subsequent bar talk brought the realization that it was entirely possible that all 72 aircraft could have been in a huge mid-air collision.

On another rehearsal, when the formation approached the saluting base at the High Commission in Cologne, a light aircraft flew across its path towing a banner that urged anyone reading it to buy more of 'Der Persil'. There is no record of what the towing pilot said or thought when 400 odd aircraft flew in front, behind, over or under him.

The day before the Coronation, my Squadron, which was based at Gutersloh, was detached to Wahn for reasons of fuel and range. Fortunately for me, one of the assigned pilots could not start and so I was ordered to take his place.

On The Day, when the wings were taking off in stream, a Vampire (or was it a Venom?) crashed on take off. It was later considered that the pilot was not familiar with the characteristics of his aircraft with two full drop tanks, and had flicked. The leader of the pair behind him advised his Wing Leader (who, of course, was already airborne): "Green 3 has gone in on takeoff and has burst into flames off the end of the runway. Runway clear."

It was not necessary to say that the chances of survival for the unfortunate pilot were zero.

The Wing Leader paused for at least three quarters of a second then ordered: "The rest of the wing continue the take off as briefed. Green 4 become Green 3, Reserve 1 become Green 4, Reserve 2 become Reserve 1. Acknowledge with your new call signs".

There followed, very crisply, "Green 3"

"Green 4"

"Reserve 1"

It was then that I knew that I was no longer a cadet, but had joined the man's Service.   [B.M.]

THE FLYPAST THAT NEVER WAS

On the fiftieth anniversary of the Queen's coronation I looked back to an interesting event in my time as a fighter pilot – the flypast that never was!

For Coronation Day (2nd June 1953) the RAF planned a very special flypast over Buckingham Palace and the task was given to the C-in-C of Fighter Command. He instructed the AOC No 11 Group, which covered southern England, to organise the event. Air Vice-Marshal the Earl of Bandon (an Irishman from Cork) was a greatly respected and much-liked character. He approached the task with his usual enthusiasm.

The plan he came up with was to fly 12 Meteor 8 squadrons from Fighter Command and one F86 Sabre squadron from the 2nd Tactical Air Force in Germany in one large formation. Each squadron would put up 12 aircraft, making a total of 156. Usually, large flypasts – such as the annual Battle of Britain ones over Buckingham Palace – were flown with Wings each of two squadrons in line astern following at 30 second intervals, a relatively straight forward affair.

However, this event was to be rather special and so more difficult to achieve. It was to be an Arrow shaped formation. Three Wings each of two Meteor squadrons in a "Vic" formed the head of the arrow. Then came the arrow's shaft in the form of four vics of three F86 Sabres in line astern. Finally, the tail feathers comprised another three Meteor Wings in vic.

The head was made up of three Wings based in East Anglia. The plan called for them to assemble there and fly to Southend where the Sabres would take up station, and head and shaft would then fly to the Canterbury area. Meantime the three Wings from southern airfields would form up in their area and join up with the others to make up the arrow. The whole formation would then make for the Thames estuary and thence to London.

Naturally, no rehearsals could take place over London so RAF Biggin Hill in Kent was chosen as the venue for the practice flypasts. Here the AOC would peruse the practices and confer with the Wing Leaders after each. The Wing Leaders were all distinguished fighter pilots of great experience, some dating back to the Battle of Britain, and all held the DSO and DFC.

Nevertheless it was not going to be plain sailing. Leading even a single wing in close formation called for very smooth flying, especially in bumpy conditions. The Squadron and Flight Commanders also had to fly smoothly so that the pilots at the extremities of the formation did not have too hard a time. In the heat of summer – at 1,500 feet and 300 knots – it was hot work.

Once the Wings were assembled into the Arrow formation all the difficulties were magnified. The leader could only make the gentlest of turns lest those further out became unable to hold their positions. Moreover, any disturbance due to sudden movements of the controls or to turbulence was magnified as the effects rippled outwards through the formation.

The first couple of exercises involved the head and tail elements practising separately in their own areas. I was a Flying Officer in No 247 Squadron which, together with No 54 Squadron, formed the Odiham Wing. We were based at RAF Tangmere as Odiham was being prepared for the Queen's Review of the RAF. Our Wing Leader was Dennis Crowley-Milling, a particularly smooth pilot who never indulged in throttle bashing. He led 54 Squadron, with 247 in close line astern. My position was No 4 to the CO, formating close behind and slightly lower than his machine. The two squadrons started up together and taxied out to line up on the runway and then took off two at a time in formation at five second intervals – resulting in the later aircraft experiencing quite a lot of turbulence.

Before long we were at 1,500 feet and I could see the other two wings manoeuvring to join us. Soon afterwards the Wing on the right found they couldn't hold their position during a starboard turn and I watched all 24 aircraft slide over us. A few months earlier I had seen my Flight Commander lose his life in a collision in similar circumstances when I was flying as his wing man. Thus I was especially wary and dropped down a few feet, planning an escape manoeuvre in case of necessity. However, all was well and the wandering Wing soon rejoined the formation.

Next came the full formation practices. Joining up now became a somewhat tamer affair. The formation flew past Paddy Bandon at Biggin Hill on several days in the later half of May, with tactical changes being made each time following representations by the Wing Leaders. Finally he expressed his satisfaction and reportedly told them that the net result of all the changes was that the final plan was now exactly the same as the original one!

Sadly, Coronation Day saw the arrival of a warm front with low cloud and rain, so the great formation was scrapped and a simpler flypast flown instead. However, the Arrow will always be remembered by those who had the good fortune to take part in it. Never again did the RAF mount a single formation of anywhere near its size. [D.A.C.]

THE CORONATION PARADE – LONDON, 2ND JUNE 1953

In May 1953 my Station Commander called me to his office and I thought over all my sins, recent and distant, as one does on these occasions. However the adjutant smiled at me as he wheeled me in, which was encouraging.

"Paddy, my dear chap, you're off to the Coronation as a flight commander on the route-lining force."

I was delighted, "That's jolly nice, Sir."

"You're taking the place of a chap who has fallen out for various reasons and they want a smart replacement. Off you go and enjoy yourself."

I joined the Flying Training Command part of the Coronation force at Royal Air Force Cranwell, my old Alma Mater; but this time there were no smart college rooms. Scruffy wooden huts on the old Cranwell airfield were our lot.

I was allocated a flight of very diverse chaps and together with the rest of that part of the Coronation force we spent the days drilling and route marching round the Lincolnshire countryside and practising spreading out on the march to line a simulated Coronation route with some semblance of skill and precision.

During these rehearsals quite a few car drivers were amazed to see a country road lined with hundreds of airmen at the "present" with fixed bayonets and young officers like myself at the salute. One or two rose to the occasion and raised their hats but most crouched lower over the steering wheel and accelerated furtively away.

We were formed into wings of three squadrons of three flights per squadron, still only a fraction of the whole contingent, and in the three weeks of training a tremendous morale built up. The troops were then issued with their new RAF No 1 uniform, a much finer and better tailored outfit than the old horse blanket they used to have. And that really did it!! There was a certain swagger in their every movement and they were very smart indeed.

We were loaded onto a train at Main Stores where the old railway came from Sleaford to offload the mass of paraphernalia required to run a very large Air Force base, and we were delighted to see our Coronation Commander and his Adjutant driving the train under the watchful eye of the regular driver. Of course, it was a proper steam locomotive so they had to shovel a bit of coal at least once in the ten mile journey to

Sleaford. There we were hooked onto another RAF Special and we sped off to Olympia, London, and thence by truck to Hyde Park.

"From here you go to the seventh tree on the left and five tents in". Those were my instructions to my billet; one of thousands of identical tents in Kensington Gardens alone and it became hilarious at night after dinner in the mess tent to find your way home. Most tents sprouted name plates, "Dunroamin", "Airmen's Rest", "Home Sweet Home" and others of a less salubrious and more vulgar theme. And it rained and drizzled and my uniform for the great day grew fungi hitherto undiscovered by natural science. And we began to smell fairly badly.

But the Army, God bless them, hauled in a large mobile bathroom from the Victorian era. The walls unfolded outwards to reveal large cast iron baths surrounded by modesty screens and the central part apparently formed the boiler house. When smoke appeared from the chimney there was a great cheer and we approached cautiously, each carrying a towel and a bar of soap in pious hope. Then we sat down on the grass and waited in a very wide circle. We began to think that Queen Victoria's soldiers were well looked after if this was an example.

Hope faded in an instant when there was a colossal BANG and a cloud of steam shot skywards, the curtains disintegrated and the whole issue was covered in cinders and steam. We crept back silently to our tents and resumed our normal ablutions with a cold wet rag and a bar of Wright's Coal Tar Soap.

The latrines worked better. Termed "Thunderboxes", they boasted about twenty holes in a row surrounded by hessian screens and one could find some relief in some style. These were dotted about all over Hyde Park and were the subject of much favourable comment since among other things light banter and conversations were possible and I found myself early one morning discussing things in general with no less a person than "Boom" Trenchard, the Father of the Royal Air Force.

For practice, very early every morning for a week we would march out complete with bands and march up Oxford Street in two files and separate at a given signal and stop on our allotted spaces while the rest of the huge contingent carried on to their places on the roadside along the Coronation route. It was simple manoeuvre and worked very well considering the thousands involved. Then we all marched back for breakfast. The Army and Air Force field kitchens fed us right on time every time with food fit for kings; they did wonders in very primitive conditions.

The afternoon before the great day found me looking in despair at my No 1 uniform so I carried it off to a cleaners in Bayswater.

"Got to see the Queen tomorrow."

"In that, Darlin'?"

"In that."

"Gawd! Let's see what we can do!"

An hour later I had what looked like new uniform and the lady charged me a shilling.

"Special rates, of course, Dearie" she said.

Early morning on Coronation Day saw us at breakfast in the mess tents with the newspaper headlines reading "The Crowning Glory – Everest Conquered!" News had arrived by man with cleft stick that Hillary and Sherpa Tensing had made it to the top. It was an auspicious start to one of the most memorable and delightful days of my life.

Everything newsworthy in the modern world has been covered by books and films but none so well as this occasion. Just opposite my spot in Oxford Street was a large open stand with tiered seats full of obviously American tourists. Their clockwork movie camera whirred and whirred at every single occurrence that might be of future interest and at last they were richly rewarded with a real occurrence which caused the expenditure of miles of film.

The Route Marshal was a magnificent specimen of Guards Major on a beautiful horse and he arrived on his cursory inspection, doubtless to see there were no fenians about, and the horse obligingly defecated on the street beside me. The crowds shrieked and cheered, the cameras whirred and, right on cue, a municipal street cleaner appeared with brand new galvanised barrow, new brooms, new shovel, new waistcoat and regulation gorblimey cap, and he made a magnificent occasion of sweeping it up. There was a band stationed along the road every few hundred yards and the nearby bandmaster rose to the challenge and the whole operation was completed to hysterical applause and the strains of "Land of Hope and Glory".

It drizzled and rained and dripped and nobody gave a damn. The waiting crowds sang and cheered at the smallest provocation and I was permitted during these long hours to dismiss every second man on one side of the road in turn to go for whatever comfort he could find.

During one of these reliefs the Army appeared in the shape of two very smart soldiers pulling a huge laundry basket on wheels, full of packed lunches which they doled out as they moved along. I had a word and asked them to leave two packs with every man on that side of my patch and there seemed to be no problem with that. The relief men came back and the inevitable had happened; one man didn't get any lunch and the Army by this time had vanished down Regent Street distributing their goodies. By this time too I had examined the meal and decided the sandwiches were inedible, being curly and stuffed with sweating cheese.

"Sir! Sir! I ain't got no lunch!"

"Have mine." I said.

"No, no. Sir"

"Yes, yes, my dear chap. Here you are."

The cameras whirred and whirred, the crowd cheered and from behind:

"Ooh! What a nice officer. Give the man his lunch!"

"'Scuse me Sir" a large Bobby was standing beside me with a huge box of Black Magic chocolates "but the girls in Woolworths sent these for you. Got to keep up your strength, they said." I waved and they blew kisses.

Then the procession. Soldiers sailors and airmen of every part of the British Commonwealth and Empire; crowned heads, turbaned heads, elected heads and unelected heads all in their little carriages. Bands played, crowds cheered and cameras whirred. There were roars for Winston Churchill. There were shrieks of laughter and cheers for the entire Royal Air Force Air Council mounted on horseback and looking damned uncomfortable. There were shrieks of delight for the vast smiling bulk of Queen Salote of Tonga who insisted on lowering the tonneau cover of her carriage to the evident displeasure and discomfiture of the Sultan of Zanzibar, who shared her conveyance.

"Oo's that 'orrible little man, then?"

"That's 'er lunch, dearie!" Shriek shriek, whirr, whirr.

Roars of delight greeted the Fijian Army contingent who marched past in bare feet on the rain sodden surface now well mixed with an ever increasing amount of horse dung. Sympathetic laughter and cheers for the Royal Marines whose white blanco was running from their pith helmets down their soggy uniforms. Then a continuous roar like thunder for the Queen herself!

How the hell could I call "Present Arms" over that? I just saluted and noticed that all my chaps had the wit to watch me and we were all in perfect time.

That night. London was something else. I finished up in the Fighter Command Club in Soho drinking beer with Jimmy Edwards and a bunch of Battle of Britain fighter aces. Nobody minded that I was just a sprog Flying Officer and we all finished up at Buckingham Palace. The wireless had said there were vast crowds but we saw nobody.

"The Queen! The Queen! We want the Queen!" we said, hanging on the railings.

"Move along there, lads," said a Bobby. "It's three o'clock in the morning and she's had a busy day."

We disbanded at Cranwell with great sadness. We'd had a grand time and made many new friends and I set off to my own base, once again to be summoned by the Station Commander.

"This is for you", he said, and handed me a stiff envelope which I opened to find a lovely solid silver Coronation Medal with a chit from Buckingham Palace: "By command of Her Majesty for Flying Officer R P J King... etc etc". I hadn't known this was in the offing. They were very few and far between and wearing it on ceremonial occasions always gives me something of the thrill which the whole occasion engendered.

GOD SAVE THE QUEEN! [R.P.J.K.]

THE GREENHORN AND THE FORM 252

A cautionary tale for young officers.

You have just joined your first squadron after leaving Cranwell. Today you are doing Orderly Officer for the first time. The Orderly Sergeant is Archie Piercy, a long-serving sergeant pilot on the same squadron.

At 0800 hrs you are ready at the flag pole for the raising of the ensign. There is no sign of Archie or the ensign. For about ten minutes you hang around, trying to be inconspicuous and wondering desperately what to do.

Finally Archie appears, red-faced and puffing, with the ensign under his arm. He took it home last evening and put it under his bed. This morning, he slept in, didn't he? Now he hurriedly fumbles with the halliards and finally up it goes, while you salute, hoping no one is looking out of SHQ with a watch.

Then what do you do? It is obvious. You put Sergeant Piercy on a charge, don't you?

About lunch time, you are summoned to the squadron commander's office. A small piece of useful advice is added to the Service Knowledge you learnt at Cranwell. The F252, charge form, seems to have disappeared without trace. Archie too gets an interview. What is said to him you do not learn, but the other two NCO pilots go round grinning all afternoon. It might be some sort of record that the only person you ever put on a charge during your whole service career was a sergeant fighter pilot... [R.H.R.]

AN ORIENTAL FIRST TOUR AT
THE END OF COLONIAL TIMES

After getting my wings, and that almost invisibly thin ring on my sleeve, I moved all the way from Cranwell to Swinderby, some 12 miles, to join No 204 Advanced Flying School with colleagues Ted Peters and Cecil

('Chico') Cooper. We then went with the same AFS when it was transferred to Bassingbourn. Having completed the course on the Mosquito T3 and FB6, all three of us were posted to Singapore, in the Far East Air Force (FEAF). We travelled separately so I cannot speak for the others but my journey out was hot and tedious, in a Hastings, and involved night stops at Idris (formerly Castel Benito) in Libya, Habbaniya in Iraq, Mauripur (Karachi) in Pakistan and Negombo in Ceylon. After what seemed like an age we arrived at Changi and experienced for the first time the heat and humidity of Singapore and what at that time was its distinctive smell – something of hot damp vegetation and perhaps a little spice. From Changi, I and several others, were taken to Seletar where I met Ted and Chico again and joined the Far East Training Squadron to convert onto the Hornet, another de Havilland design.

The year was 1952, only seven years after the end of the second world war, and it might be said that this was to some extent illustrated by the aircraft of FEAF. There was one squadron of Vampire jet fighters at Tengah, in Singapore and another at Hong Kong but the rest of the command's aircraft were powered by piston engines. There were Sunderland flying boats, Valletta transports, Mosquitos and Spitfires in the Photographic Reconnaissance squadron, Hornets for fighter/ground attack, Brigands in the ground attack role with Buckmasters for training and there were Beaufighters for towing targets. In addition there were Lincolns on detachment from Bomber Command and from the Royal Australian Air Force. Another indicator of how far off those days were is the fact that when I arrived at my first squadron, excluding the squadron commander, only half of the pilots were commissioned.

In hindsight, it appears that we had perhaps not quite reached the end of the Raj or, more accurately, the colonial era, not that we thought of it in those terms at the time. However, if we had thought about it, there were several things that might have conveyed that to us when we arrived from home, for example the questions of dress and how things were done in the mess. First, we soon found out how we were required to dress in Singapore. For civilian dress during the day, officers were required to wear white shirts, white shorts and white stockings – no Hawaian shirts and coloured shorts for us. In the evenings long trousers, long sleeves and a tie were mandatory. Obviously, we wore khaki drill uniforms and on arrival discovered that we had erred in buying kit at home. My shorts from Messrs Gieves, of London, were too long, too narrow, of a heavier material than was available in Singapore and fastened by a strange combination of buckles. My shirts were long-sleeved and almost green. Furthermore they all cost more than the more fashionable and much better items made to measure overnight at little cost by the tailors of

Seletar and Changi villages or the tailors with shops in the mess. So we bought extra kit within days of arriving. While we were at it we also bought evening wear of black trousers, a white sharkskin jacket and a black cummerbund.

The mess in Seletar was a very long pre-war structure with two accommodation wings either side of a central block with mess offices and dining room. There was no ante-room as such but a large covered area to the rear of the centre section, looking out over the airfield and towards the straits separating Singapore from the mainland of Malaya. There was no bar and thus no drinking on one's feet. Instead, one sat in an armchair and "boys" stood round at the end of the verandah and came when beckoned or if, in good colonial fashion one called "Boy!" In practice a raised hand or simply a look sufficed. The bar boys were all Chinese and extremely intelligent; they knew the name of every officer in a very large mess and when drinks were ordered would always come back with the correct bar book; cash payments were not allowed. The term "boy" is, of course, not politically correct these days but then it was normal and accepted by all, including the "boys", even when they were grandfathers. European men could be called "tuan", but this was not often heard, if at all, in Singapore, and in Malaya it was more likely to be heard from Malay servants or shopkeepers. European married ladies were addressed as "Mem" and unmarried ones as "Missy", as in India.

In 1952 the rationing of clothes and some food items was still in force in the United Kingdom and so it was with wonder that we saw unlimited chocolate and sweets and sundry other food items available in Singapore. I sent home tins of ham and cream and similar luxuries, all of which had come from Holland. As Holland had suffered more than the UK during the war it was surprising to see all this food exported and, in retrospect, it seems strange that we could buy Dutch food in Singapore to send home instead of it being sent straight across the North Sea.

The conversion course at FETS was fairly brief but covered the usual aspects of learning to fly a new type, some formation flying, navigation and, at the end, armament practice at Butterworth. The Hornet had a long range and long endurance and the navigation exercises included one from Singapore across the South China Sea to the western tip of Borneo and then via the Anambas Islands to the north of Malaya and back to Seletar. With aileron trim as well as the usual elevator and rudder trim, and with a seat that could be tilted back, the Hornet was comfortable for these long flights. The navigation was easy but the weather sometimes exciting, with cloud formations developing to very high altitudes.

At the end of the course we were asked to state a preference for either 33 Squadron at Butterworth, 45 Squadron at Tengah or 80 Squadron at Kai Tak, in Hong Kong. Having no interest in the bright lights of Singapore and Hong Kong, and thinking that Butterworth would be more interesting, I chose 33 Squadron and was fortunate enough to get my choice. Ted and Chico remained on Singapore island, joining 45 Squadron at Tengah.

Butterworth is in the north of Malaya, on the west coast right opposite the island of Penang. In stark contrast to the stations on Singapore, R A F Butterworth was a small station in those days and was commanded by a Wing Commander, having only just upgraded from a Squadron Leader post. Effectively, the station comprised just 33 Squadron, an Armament Practice Camp and the support for those units. This was my first squadron and in due course it turned out to be my last as I had the added good fortune to command No 33 at Odiham from 1971 to 1973 when first equipped with Puma helicopters.

At the date of which I write, 1952, No 33 Squadron was equipped with the Hornet F3, and it also had a few Mk F4s which could carry a vertical camera for photographic reconnaissance, but the primary role of the squadron was fighter/ground attack. The Hornet was, to put it simply, a smaller and single seat derivative of the Mosquito, with a wingspan of 45 feet instead of 54 feet and entry to the cockpit was through a sliding canopy instead of, as in the Mosquito, squeezing up through a small hatch in the bottom corner of the cabin. In my eyes the Hornet was one of the best looking aircraft ever built, its sleek lines enhanced by the de Havilland trademark, the elliptical tail fin and rudder and, in the case of the Hornet, made even sleeker by a dorsal fairing into the fin. The Hornet had been intended for long-range bomber escort in the war with Japan but the war ended before it could be used in that role. In Malaya it was employed on strikes against the Communist Terrorists (CTs), and for that purpose was armed with two 500 pound bombs, four 60 pound rockets and four 20mm cannon. It was fast (420 knots) and as the propellors were "handed", that is to say they rotated in opposite directions, it had no tendency to swing on take-off, unlike the Mosquito where it was necessary to lead with the port throttle and then bring up the starboard, repeating this process several times, because if you opened both throttles together you would find yourself going at an angle across the grass instead of along the runway.

Butterworth in 1952 had the reputation of being somewhat "wild". This reputation had something to do with its remoteness – far from the delights and constraints of Singapore – and something to do with drinking Tiger Beer, I seem to recall. Indeed, the instructors on FETS advised us that we would have to be prepared to play liar dice and drink Tiger beer when we went to Butterworth for the armament training phase of our course. Without those attributes it seemed that we would lack what is now known as "street cred". In fact, the favoured tipple was Anchor Beer and those who drank Tiger were thought to be a bit on the rough side, even by Butterworth standards. Anchor was so popular that there was a hush of disbelief and horror when the Padre referred one day to St Paul, when caught out in a storm at sea, as "casting out four anchors". Anchor was even consumed at table on dining-in nights without the knowledge of the top table; all that was necessary was for those preferring it to wine to ask the bar boy to bring "Chateau Anchor", whereupon a bottle would be produced wrapped in a napkin and poured very carefully to minimise the head. The drink so often mentioned in connection with colonial Malaya was the whisky and soda, known as a "stengah", meaning "half and half" (from the Malay "sa tengah", a half) but it was rarely called for in the mess, a gin and tonic or a brandy or whisky sour being more popular for those preferring spirits.

But I digress. Butterworth's reputation was also related to the fact that everyone had been living in attap huts until just before I arrived and to the fact that all the aircrew and officers carried pistols at all times (this was during the Malayan Emergency). At lunch-time all weapons were deposited (ie left lying about) on a table in the entrance to the mess. So it might be said that there was a certain element of the Wild West – particularly as it was known that in the old mess a few of the more unconventional souls would think little of firing at, eg, a snake if such were to be seen in the mess. In the new mess, when a very small snake was seen curled around the top of one of the pillars of the covered way between the main mess and the north wing, a certain officer ran to his room, fetched his revolver and, leaning against the adjacent pillar, took careful aim at the snake from a range of five feet. Luckily, some of us were able to persuade him of the likely results of a bullet striking the brickwork at so short a distance and he desisted. Once, when Station Duty Officer, I almost succumbed to this culture myself. My shouts having failed to arouse two Malay auxiliary policemen I found sleeping while supposedly guarding the transmitter station in the early hours of the morning, I drew my pistol intending to fire a persuasive shot. Luckily, and perhaps influenced by the fact that a shot might have drawn a response from two rifles, I decided that a louder shout would suffice.

Our new mess was very comfortable, with each officer having a fairly large room with a high ceiling and the usual slots around the tops of the walls to allow air to circulate, assisted by the electric fan fitted to the ceiling. The floor was tiled and there was just one small rug. The windows had no glass and were closed with louvred shutters. The double doors were partly glazed and were usually hooked open, some privacy being maintained by louvred swing half doors as in saloons in Western films. Each room had a wash-basin and running water but the showers were in a separate block. Furniture and fittings comprised a chest of drawers, a table and chair and a bed with an iron frame for the suspension of a mosquito net. The bedstead was of wood with woven webbing to hold the mattress. It was like the well-known Indian 'charpoy' except for the webbing in place of string. The built-in wardrobes were fitted with a lockable compartment, in which we kept our pistols when off duty, and in the bottom, protected by a wire cage, was a light bulb providing enough warmth to keep the contents of the wardrobe dry. Damp was a problem and giving a frequent airing to the clothes kept in the chest of drawers was a continuing task for the room boys. The latter were mainly Tamils, with a few Chinese. They looked after two or three rooms each and were agreeably efficient. Mine was a Tamil named Vencatasalam, a tubby and very cheerful lad who brought the early morning tea with a big smile, cleaned my room and saw to my laundry in a very satisfactory way. Our relationship with the mess staff was very good.

The staff in the kitchen, dining room and bar were also predominantly Chinese and Tamil. Several Tamils had similar names ending in "...samy" and so the one in the bar became "Bar Sammy" and the one in the kitchen was "Kitchen Sammy". The chef was Mr Lee and he kept us well fed. His curries were excellent as were his Nasi Goreng (fried rice) and his Mah Mee (thick egg noodles garnished with pork and prawns). His European cooking was also good but this was my first introduction to real oriental food. Mr Ong, the mess clerk was also a Chinese and when I was given the task of auditing the mess accounts he taught me how to use an abacus. On the same subject, after a temporary incapacity caused by a motorcycle accident I stood in for the Station Adjutant for a few weeks and thereby came to know the merits of Mr Oh Kim Sun, usually referred to as "Kim", the chief clerk and, effectively, the king pin and continuity man in the administration of the station. Kim was in his 30s and had been well educated in one of the excellent schools in Georgetown. He was a walking filing system, with a memory for everything that had happened at Butterworth for years and he was indeed a "rock". He was kind enough to invite me to his house in Penang and to show me some of the sights as seen through Chinese eyes.

As an aside, while on the subject of the Chinese, we noticed that when we took films to a shop in Butterworth town for processing the shopkeeper never asked for a name. Present during a discussion on this in the mess one day was a rather large meteorological officer who lived off the station in a house in Pantai Road, in Butterworth. He happened to have a beard. He also happened to have with him the packet from his last film for developing. It just had some Chinese characters on it so we asked the mess clerk to translate. He burst out laughing and explained that it simply said "Fat man with beard, Pantai Road".

I have mentioned drink several times but I do not wish to give the impression that it created a problem. Far from it, we had plenty to do both on and off duty so there was no time for alcoholic brooding. Nevertheless, there were one or two who lived life to the full and I recollect the rule that cash could not be paid for drinks but instead one had to sign one's bar book and have the total included in the mess bill each month. Bar expenditure was limited to about M$60 or M$70 each month (roughly seven or eight pounds in the money of the time, when the monthly pay of a Pilot Officer was in the order of £40 including local overseas allowance). One young officer found this somewhat irksome and so prevailed upon the dentist, a young and teetotal National Service officer, to allow him to use his bar book if he reached his own limit. Came the day when the dentist was called before the President of the Mess Committee to explain how it came about that he had exceeded the limit!

A few of us rode BSA Bantam 125cc motorcyles and a certain F Howard Stirling (we never knew what the "F" stood for), an Air Traffic Control officer, would occasionally take a friendly shot at these with a Verey pistol as one crossed the runway on the way to or from the squadron, once hitting a rear wheel. Howard also liked to produce a pair of sabres at the end of a dining-in night so as to fence in the Billiard Room without helmets or protective clothing. In my mind's eye I can still see a target figure scratched on the wall – and a few ripped shirts.

It was Howard who crammed the spring from a Sten magazine into his pistol holster to give him a "quick on the draw" capability. When, during the AOC's inspection, he demonstrated this to the great man on the balcony of the ATC tower the weapon left the holster at great speed when the flap was flipped open, just as intended, but, unfortunately, Howard failed to catch it and as he had not fitted a lanyard the pistol flew down to the ground outside. Then there was the boat or hydroplane he built out of two Sunderland wing tip floats with a structure of 3 inch rocket motor tubes supporting a salvaged engine and propeller from a crashed Auster. It was not a success. A quirk of Howard's was to give ATC instructions in rhyme, eg "Aircraft waiting with engines turning, take off by permission of F Howard Stirling.".

Howard was not alone in his ways in air traffic and I recall Ken Duke's ready wit as regards rhyming R/T. It was Ken who deflated one of our number who had just come from the Day Fighter Leaders' Course and, having flown the mighty Meteor, felt himself undervalued by being posted to a Hornet squadron. He brought with him all the latest jargon. His name was Crowe and one of our pilots was named Duck so, when Jim Crowe led six aircraft one day and after take off called, in DFLS fashion it would appear, "How many chicks have I airborne?", Ken replied "Four chicks, one duck and a crow!"

On another occasion, a pilot approaching Butterworth and wishing to know the direction to land asked, in rather sloppy fashion, it has to be said, "What's the runway?". Ken's reply was "It's a sort of concrete thing laid out on the grass for 'planes to land on". I mention these things to illustrate the fact that we were far from any other station and out of range of some kinds of supervision.

There were other eccentrics and eccentricities. In the crewroom were several lemonade bottles containing small snakes and other creatures pickled in, I assume, alcohol. One pilot kept a small monkey which was a nuisance in the crewroom and went almost berserk if shown one of these bottled snakes at close range. The owner took the monkey to fly with him, chained to the ammunition boxes behind the pilot's seat. He disgraced himself, the monkey, that is, by getting somewhat over familiar with the AOC during the inspection referred to earlier. I believe the monkey died with its master when he failed to pull out from a dive attack in mountainous jungle.

All in all, Butterworth was an interesting and exciting place to be, with Penang for off duty pursuits and most of us belonging to the Penang Sports Club (PSC) for the rugby, and the Penang Swimming Club for the swimming and some social life. These clubs were not to be confused with "the" Penang Club, which was something like London's Athenaeum and frequented by the great and important members of the establishment such as the Resident Commissioner, District Officers, senior administrators, members of the judiciary, pillars of the commercial world and so on. With rugby on Wednesday and Saturday afternoons and perhaps two games of water polo on Sunday mornings I can see now why I was just a little slimmer in those days. Rugby in the enervating heat and humidity was hard going, but the consolation when playing at the PSC was that the bar boys would bring trays of pints of cold shandy into the changing room.

Perhaps I should say that the PSC and the Penang Swimming Club were clubs for Europeans. These years followed not all that long after the partition of India and Pakistan and, as I have suggested, might be said to be some of the last days of the old-style colonial life, with a certain amount of actual, but unofficial, segregation. The Eurasians had their own sports club known as the Penang Recreation Club and the Chinese had their own club as well. We played each other at various games but stuck to our own clubs. A British acquaintance had married a Dutch woman of part Javanese descent and so he was not supposed to take her to the Penang Swimming club – but he did, from time to time, and was never to my knowledge taken to task by the committee. All in all, despite these segregational practices the various races seemed to co-exist without rancour or friction and, so far as I could tell, were only too happy to have their own clubs and adhere to their own cultures.

There was some social life and we did get to know some of the local British residents, a few of whom had spent most of their lives in Malaya and had spent the war years in prison camps or in the services elsewhere in the Far East. Our local District Officer won the DSO for his activities with those in the jungles and mountains resisting the Japanese throughout the occupation. The Europeans, mainly British but some Dutch who had previously lived in Sumatra and Java, worked in the banks and commercial firms, in the mines and, of course, in the plantations. The planters were very vulnerable to terrorist attacks and their casualty rate was high. Accordingly, they tended to live on the basis of "Eat drink and be merry... etc" and were renowned for carousing when they hit town. They all carried weapons in a variety of forms and travelled in large cars such as Buicks fitted with armour plate to taste. Up country they had clubs where they would meet at weekends and they even had some teams to play rugby, but only for fun and the drinking!

Some social activity arose from the sports and swimming clubs and there were also some hotels where there were the usual expatriate celebratory functions such as the St Andrew's Ball and the St George's Ball. I do not recall that the adherents of St Patrick and St David went in for such things in Penang. On Sundays one might go to the Swimming Club or stay in the mess for the curry. Alternatively one might go for curry tiffin at the Lone Pine Hotel on the beautiful palm-lined beach on the north coast at Batu Ferringhi or to the Peak Hotel on the delightfully cool top of the island and reached by the funicular railway. Once I was invited by some Dutch people to a *rijstafel*, a regular feature of life in the old Dutch East Indies and which consisted of course after course of rice and various curries accompanied by oceans of beer and lasting for hours. I regret to say that I did not enjoy it as much as I expected because I was hungry after playing water polo, food did not even start to appear until 3.00pm, and filling up with beer was no substitute.

In keeping with it being the last days of the colonies, in the mess at Butterworth we unconsciously emulated the young British men in the Penang of the 19th century who, according to some photographs dating from that time which I have since seen, would gather in the evening for a drink and would wear sarongs, shirts and sandals as a cool alternative to the European clothes with high necked jackets they wore during the day. So also at Butterworth the officers living in the mess would often gather on the verandah at the back of the mess in the evening, wearing sarongs and flip-flops, to drink a beer and watch the sun go down behind Penang Hill. Perhaps I should have said that the mess was about 60 yards from the edge of the sea and level with the northern tip of the island, so there was a very romantic view to be had of Penang, particularly in the evening as the lights came on to dot the slopes of the hills and to be followed by what was usually a spectacular sunset.

Adding a little spice to the lives of those at Butterworth, in 1954 a civil DC4 was diverted to Butterworth because of heavy rains and flooding in Singapore. In the aircraft was Ava Gardner, on her way to open the Asian premiere of her latest film 'The Barefoot Contessa'. Although the passengers were taken to hotels in Penang for the night, Miss Gardner remained with the RAF. She spent the evening in the Officers' Mess and the night in OC 33 Squadron's married quarter. The young pilot who carried her bag from the aircraft was rewarded with a kiss on the cheek and went around next day swearing that he would never wash that side of his face again!

As to work, we had plenty of opportunity for dive-bombing, rocketing and firing on our own ranges near some islands to the north of Penang and, this being at the height of the Emergency, we also had plenty of the real thing on strikes against the Communist Terrorists (CTs).

Thinking back to the weapons ranges, I recall that shortly after I arrived a new bombing target was anchored on the range after being towed about 350 miles from Singapore. It was a large and magnificent steel raft, triangular in shape, painted yellow and intended to withstand only our 20 lb practice bombs. Our normal weapon for strikes against the CTs was the 500-pounder but there were some 250 lb bombs in store and it was decided to dispose of them. The squadron had 12 Hornets serviceable and so a grand exercise was planned. Hornets were sent off in pairs along different routes to rendezvous points where they joined into fours and finally merged into the whole squadron a few miles from Butterworth. From there we headed for the range with the intention of bombing a reef off the end of one of the islands and not all that far from the new official target. In the manner of the US Navy dive bombers as seen in films of the Pacific in World War II, we approached in echelon and peeled off to make our dive attacks, each Hornet dropping both bombs together.

In such a formation the 12th aircraft is quite a long way from the leader and the dives get more and more shallow with that distance unless practice and experience bring greater expertise. I believe the plan was to carry out 30 degree dives (as opposed to 60 degrees) and so by the time it came to the turn of this very new and inexperienced pilot, at No 12, my dive was very shallow indeed and all chance of accuracy was lost. I saw the sea around the reef seemingly boiling from the explosions and then splashes falling more and more short until a ring of churned-up water could be seen expanding on the sea at one corner of the new target raft. Did I do this? The bombs could have come from number 11 or even from someone else but I rather think they were mine. However, very little was said about it and I assume the target was not badly damaged or there would have been a Board of Enquiry.

Just before Christmas 1952 there was a discussion in the crew room as to the desirability of delivering some toilet rolls by air to RAF Tengah, Singapore, where our sister Hornet squadron, No 45, was based, together with 60 Squadron (Vampires) and visiting Lincoln squadrons. The usual method of delivering toilet rolls by air, and I do not mean in the normal course of supply, was to lower the flaps, put in the rolls, and then close the flaps again. Over the target the flaps were lowered and out would fall the rolls of paper. Obviously, speed had to be reduced to below the maximum for lowering the flaps so as not to damage the aircraft. This method, we thought, was somewhat basic and, indeed, pedestrian. How much better it would be to devise a way of delivering at speed, preferably in a dive attack! Bombs would be out of the question, of course, whether dummy or live, but we also had rockets which were fired in a dive attack so, after some consideration, we came up with a way of using the rockets without actually firing a live projectile .

The rockets comprised iron tubes with a bore of three inches into which the cordite propellant was inserted. The 60 lb warhead was attached to the front end of the tube and in the rear was a venturi restriction to speed up the flow of gases when the cordite was ignited. On pressing the firing button on the control column ignition was achieved electrically through cables culminating in a "pigtail" connection to the rocket itself. For our peaceful employment of the rocket we took the empty tubes and mounted them, reversed, on the rocket rails under the wings. Thus the venturi was at the front end, leaving what had become the rear end open for the toilet rolls to be loaded and ejected. To prevent the airflow in flight from pushing the rolls out we taped fabric over the front ends of the tubes and also taped paper over the rear ends to keep the rolls in place. On the cloth at the front we taped detonators which we connected to the rocket circuits. Our calculation was that on pressing the firing button the detonators would blow away the fabric, the airflow would enter the tubes with sufficient force to break the paper at the tail ends and the rolls would be ejected. So it proved to be.

Two Hornets were "armed" with four tubes loaded with toilet rolls and on Christmas morning they flew to Tengah and back, a distance of 320 nautical miles each way. By the time they reached Tengah the traditional Christmas programme was in full swing and it was apparent from the crowd outside the Sergeants' Mess that the officers had arrived there to gather refreshment before going on to the Airmen's Mess to serve the turkey and pudding. The crowd looked up with surprise as two Hornets dived on them with some élan and streams of toilet paper floated down. Witty inscriptions had been added to some of the paper, including "Hang this on your Christmas tree, Champion de Crespigny" – that being the name of the Tengah Station Commander. I cannot imagine anything like that happening today.

As well as having the benefit of armament ranges close at hand, the squadron also had the advantage of having a few of its aircraft fitted with hooks to tow targets, so air-to-air firing was quite often on the training programme, taking place on tow-lines over the sea towards what is now the popular holiday resort of Pulau Langkawi. As to air to ground armament practice, the squadron sometimes supplied a pilot to act as Range Safety Officer and he would travel to and from the ranges in a launch of the RAF Marine Craft Section based at Glugor, on Penang. At the end of one day's work on the ranges the launch was returning along the coast when, on rounding a headland, the crew spotted a cruiser of the Royal Navy at anchor, from whence it was going to shell targets on the mainland. David Caris (52 Entry), the RSO for the day, immediately asked the coxswain what they ought to do. The Flight Sergeant replied, "Well, sir, I suggest we all put our shirts on for a start!" That having been done, they considered how to pay compliments and as the launch passed along the side of the cruiser David saluted, the crew stood to attention and the cox'n dipped the RAF ensign. At that, great activity was seen on the cruiser, with sailors running about to the sound of a bugle and bosun's call. From this it was deduced that the cruiser had either not seen the launch coming or had not recognised it for what it was.

By the time I arrived at Butterworth brick buildings had been erected but the squadron offices were still in tents and the crewroom was an attap shelter with no sides – much more romantic than the brick edifice that took its place, and a sight cooler. It was in one of those tents that I had my arrival interview with the Squadron Commander, Squadron

Leader CCF Cooper. After the usual exchanges he said "Tell me, Hoskins, have you ever had an accident?" "Oh, no sir!" I replied, forgetting about overshooting a Prentice into a cabbage patch, to which he responded "Good. Keep it up." – or words to that effect. Thinking back, he might well also have said "Then make sure you don't start now".

Our aircraft were parked in line along the disused north-south runway, which was not very wide, and it was necessary to taxi into the line from the front and then execute a tight 180 degree turn to end up facing forward. This entailed using a lot of brake on the inside wheel and a lot of power on the outside engine. Not long after my interview I returned from a flight to find that I was being marshalled into a rather narrow gap in the line. I started my 180 degree left turn and could see that it was going to be tight but had the reassurance of an airman at the starboard wingtip giving me the thumbs up. By this means I managed to slide my starboard wingtip over the port wingtip of the next aircraft. Looking back, I wonder if the national serviceman thought he would get his revenge for being called up, was bored and thought it would be funny or whether he put his thumb up in mistake for down. Nevertheless it was my fault, but I do not recall receiving any punishment for this offence. In fact. I am not sure whether the situation became known beyond the flight commander because good old Chiefie Sinfield just took off the wingtip fairings, knocked out the dents and screwed them back on again.

Not even Chiefie could mend other aircraft that were less fortunate. Shortly after I arrived one of the sergeant pilots had to abandon his Hornet just off the end of the runway. Some of us standing outside the crewroom saw the Hornet disappear below our line of sight over the palm trees along the beach and so we did not see a parachute and concluded the worst. However, the pilot did get out and open his 'chute and lived, although he struck the tailplane and sustained some serious injuries. There were several fatalities, including the owner of the monkey, who left pulling out of a dive attack too late, and a young pilot who carried out a single engine landing much too fast, overshot the runway, turned over and was killed. Then we lost our Ground Liaison Officer who parachuted into jungle with the SAS, became entangled in the top of a tall tree and fell to his death. Apart from that, there were several wheels-up landings and when an engine failed on one Hornet in a formation take-off it swung into the leader and chopped the fuselage in two. The electrical circuits for rockets were notoriously dangerous if the proper precautions were not observed and failure to follow the correct procedure led to a rocket being fired while the armourers were arming up an aircraft. The efflux hit an armourer, a pleasant lad named

Malpass, and the young National Service Medical Officer had to amputate the arm. The rocket flew across the airfield into a small village and hit a shophouse; luckily nobody in the village was hurt.

In addition to the Hornets the squadron also had two Mosquito T3s for dual checks and for instrument flying training. They were not very serviceable and so one did not get the chance to fly them very often and when the day came it all seemed a bit difficult after the sweet little Hornet. Shortly after joining 33 I was detailed for some solo instrument flying (IF) in a Mosquito which entailed flying out to sea north of Penang to find a cloud to fly about in. However, that was not the problem. The only useable runway at that time ran east-west. There was a taxi track running to the east end of the runway and it was here that trouble started. I thought to myself that it would save a lot of time if I were to do my checks before take-off while taxying instead of at the halt just before moving onto the runway. I got to the bit where you check that the flaps are up and reached for the flap lever..... you've guessed!

The undercarriage, flaps and bomb doors were controlled by three levers grouped together in the centre of the bottom of the Mosquito's instrument panel. To avoid confusion each lever had a different shaped knob and the undercarriage lever also had a safety catch on it which had to be depressed in order to unlock the lever and lift it. This was intended to prevent the lever being moved by mistake – vain hope! Taxying along, I reached out my right hand and grasped the undercarriage lever instead of the flap lever, released the catch and raised the lever. Immediately, there was an amazingly loud noise in my earphones coming from the undercarriage warning horn. This device came on when the aircraft was below a certain speed if the undercarriage had not been lowered and locked down and was intended to prevent pilots from inadvertently landing with the wheels up. Obviously, taxiing speed was well below the operative speed! Fortunately, the shock of the noise caused me to jam the lever down again but when I looked at the undercarriage indicator lights I saw that one was red and it would not return to green. My thought processes were dominated by this noise in my ears and my reaction was to think that everyone at Butterworth could hear it and must know what an idiot I was. That ought to have caused me to do the sensible thing, namely, to stop the engines, tell the tower and wait for someone to come out and put in the undercarriage locking pins. Remember, the Mosquito had a tail wheel so the backwards tilt of the fuselage and the undercarriage legs created a geometric lock and there was really no likelihood of the undercarriage collapsing if I shut down.

However, this did not occur to me and my one thought was to get into the air as soon as I could! Therefore I continued to taxi, cautiously, using the brakes as little as possible and pushing down on the undercarriage lever every few seconds. I simply cannot now remember whether I ran up the engines and checked the magnetos before going onto the runway but I suppose I must have done. The red light was for the port wheel, and the turn was to starboard so at least the brakes were not acting against the unlocked leg. However, it might be argued that the extra power on the port engine for the turn would have the same effect.

Nevertheless, I lined up for take off and began to open the throttles. As I have explained, the Mosquito had a marked tendency to swing and to prevent this it was necessary to lead with the port throttle and then bring up the starboard, repeating the process several times before reaching flying speed. In itself this could be a little challenging if one was relatively new and did not have much continuity on the Mosquito, but I was also intent on changing hands from throttles to stick so as to free my right hand to push on the undercarriage lever as often as possible. Also, the wretched horn was still blasting away at me! Suffice it to say that there was a decidedly dodgy feeling about the take-off run. In the event, the port leg held until I attained flying speed – just. I felt the leg go and the wing drop just at that moment and put on opposite aileron to lift the wing at the same time as I eased back the stick to get off the ground.

After climbing away and settling down I found a cloud and did some IF as if nothing had happened – well, almost. Then I returned to base and was glad to find that the undercarriage came down satisfactorily and locked with both warning lights green. It had not occurred to me that the undercarriage system might perhaps have been damaged by the lurching take-off but luckily there was no harm done. The landing was not too good and after I had signed the Form 700 my flight commander told me so. I acknowledged this with due humility and forebore to say what I was thinking – "You should have seen the take-off!"

The role of the squadron was Fighter/Ground Attack and there was plenty of the latter. So far as the "fighter" aspect was concerned, air-to-air firing was practised regularly, as was battle formation, but there was little opportunity for practice interceptions. At the south east tip of Penang Island there was a radar manned by the Malayan Auxiliary Air Force but it was almost at sea level and masked by Penang Hill to the north so its useful scanning area was strictly limited. At night, when the auxiliaries were available, it was possible to carry out interceptions over a small area of sea to the south of the island but even though there would not be more than two aircraft in the area it was usually necessary to give one's precise position to the radar station or they would not be able to start the procedure! Once we had the excitement of trying to intercept some B29s of the USAF overflying Malaya one afternoon. However, we saw them pass overhead before we were even scrambled and so by the time we got to height the "interception" became a long tail chase and we simply did not have enough speed to catch up.

Throughout the service young junior officers were expected to perform a variety of secondary duties and Butterworth was no exception. Checking inventories was perhaps the most common but another which came up from time to time was opening sealed tenders by civilian contractors for the supply of services. Witnessing pay parade was another and at Butterworth this was a real chore if it was the civil pay, because all the civilian staff were paid in notes and coins right down to the last cent. There were coins for 50, 20, 10, 5 cents and even for one cent. Usually one saw notes only down to one dollar but there were notes for as little as 5 cents and very grubby and flimsy they tended to be. So to pay, say, a labourer M$76.87 could result in an unwieldy collection of small notes and coins. Auditing mess accounts was an arduous and time-consuming task allotted to me soon after I joined 33 Squadron but at least I came out of it with the ability to use an abacus – as I have mentioned. Not only were the intricacies of double-entry book-keeping thrown in my path (I would not say they were revealed to me) but in those first few months I found myself carrying out a Unit Enquiry at the Marine Craft Unit at Glugor, on Penang Island, into the loss of an anchor. There I was fed all manner of nautical expressions such as "the cable was up and down". One would expect the anchor cable to be up and down but what was meant was that the cable was vertical, indicating that the launch was immediately above the anchor. Another extraneous job that came up from time to time was invigilating at the airmen's education examinations. I remember one question in the general knowledge paper: "Why is it often said that the advent of air travel has made the world a smaller place?" The answer given by one bright spark was "Because the higher you go in a 'plane, the smaller things look on the ground."

I suppose all officers have had to take part in courts martial in one capacity or another and we had our share at Butterworth. So as an officer under instruction I listened to a case involving an airman who had been driving a car in one of the main streets of Georgetown and ran down a Chinese civilian. There was an interpreter for the Chinese witnesses. In answer to a question, such a witness spoke for what seemed like five minutes and when asked what the witness had said the interpreter replied "He said "yes"". The defendant gave evidence and said "As I was driving along the street I saw a Chinese man start to cross. So I sounded the horn and then ran him over".

Sadly, other tasks included bearing coffins at funerals and one in particular sticks in my mind. The cemetery was in Georgetown, on

Penang, so the funeral party was conveyed over the strait in an RAF launch. We embarked on the Butterworth side with the coffin on the stern deck and we six bearers standing three on each side. Unfortunately, on arriving at Kedah Pier on the Penang side there was something of a swell and the launch was not stationary alongside but was moving out and back with the swell. Picking the right moment, the first pair of bearers stepped onto the pier with the front end of the coffin on their shoulders, the middle pair followed safely but as I and my colleague at the head end put our outside feet on solid ground the launch swayed out and our legs got further and further apart until I felt sure we would be in the sea complete with coffin. There was not much in the coffin and it would have floated, but that would not have been a good thing. Fortunately, and probably due to the efforts of the crew on the mooring lines, the outward movement stopped when we were at the extreme extent of our leg span and all was saved.

This account of my time in 33 Squadron in Malaya from 1952 to 1955 would not be complete without paying tribute to our groundcrew. A large proportion were men called up for National Service and thus relatively inexperienced, but they were headed by two Flight Sergeants of great experience and ability. There was a great spirit and pride in the squadron and men who could have been resentful at having their lives interrupted and being posted overseas worked hard, cheerfully and willingly in conditions of tropical heat and high humidity. In recent years I have met some of them at squadron functions and found that a group of them had been holding annual reunion weekends for many years. They still maintain a very strong loyalty to the Service and to their squadron and it is clear that to these men their time in the Royal Air Force and, in particular, in 33 Squadron, were the greatest days of their lives.

Although I realise that those who went from Cranwell to Meteors and Vampires in Fighter Command or in Germany would say that they had the best of the postings, I would take issue with them and say that for diversity of interest and excitement in exotic surroundings my first squadron tour, flying Hornets in Malaya, was unbeatable.   [F.D.H]

A STRANGE EXPERIENCE

It was May 1953. I was a Flying Officer in "A" Flight of No 247 Squadron at RAF Tangmere, Sussex, where the RAF Odiham Wing of Meteors had been sent to clear the way for the Coronation Review of the RAF, which was to take place there.

One bright sunny morning I was detailed to fly as leader of the second pair of aircraft in a flight of four. We lined up on the runway and the flight leader and his wingman started their take-off run. The procedure was that I should start five seconds later, that the lead pair should pull up as soon as they were airborne and that the second pair should stay low – so avoiding the turbulent effects of jetwash.

This procedure worked well if followed precisely – unfortunately it was not on this occasion. First, my hand slipped on the brake lever after only three seconds and I decided to start my take-off; one safety margin was now eroded. Second, the leader of the first pair did not pull up. Thus, on leaving the ground my wingman and I met severe turbulence just as I was selecting my wheels up.

My aircraft rolled rapidly to starboard. Then, suddenly, I found myself mentally out of the aircraft, apparently floating about 1,000 feet above the airfield. This memory remains vivid and unchanged to this day 50 years later. I could see an airfield, but not in detail – only green grass, a runway and the underside of a silver Meteor; I particularly noticed the large ventral fuel tank.

At the same time I found myself thinking very slowly – again the exact words are engrained on my memory – "That silly bugger's going to kill himself. He's got full aileron and full rudder on and the aircraft is still rolling, and now the nose is beginning to drop. The only thing he can do now is to shut down the port engine." All this seemed very slow and scientifically deliberate.

Suddenly I found myself back in the cockpit, the aircraft climbing away under control with the wings level but with the port engine's throttle closed – and heart pounding. After the relief of seeing my wingman still there we carried on with our sortie.

On the ground I found that my wingman had also encountered the jetwash but had rolled to port. I had to explain to the CO what had happened. I thought it prudent not to mention my out of body experience lest he send for the men in white coats.

In fact I told no one until the early 1960s when I was at the RAF Institute of Aviation Medicine on a Flight Safety Officers' Course. During a session on spatial disorientation the tutor said that they were aware of aircrew experiencing out of body sensations and asked us to recall any. I told my story, which did not seem to surprise him. He told us of reports by pilots on long flights in cloud sitting on the wing watching themselves in the cockpit.

One point that interests me is that although I had other out of control incidents later, I never had such an experience again. Perhaps the patron saint of aviators decided that I had learnt enough to do without his help in the future!   [D.A.C.]

REMEMBER THE MEATBOX?

When we graduated from Cranwell, the Meteor and the Vampire were Britain's front line fighters. It is a sobering thought that we are now further from the time we began our operational flying careers than we were then from the Wright biplane. Those brand new jets we flew in the fifties are now in museums. Even so, in their day they were truly awesome beasts to those of us who had just gained our wings on Harvards.

A bunch of us from 54 – Ronny Lund, Malcolm Cowper, Ken Bones, Dave Keats, Barry Mills, Don Cooper and I – arrived one dark and wet January night at Middleton St. George, having first been to Driffield to be fired up a ramp in an ejection seat (to which I attribute recurrent backache ever since.) Night flying was in progress and, in addition to the howl of jet engines, there was a strong smell of paraffin everywhere.

Daylight revealed a number of wrecks around the countryside, and the frontal silhouette of a Meteor in new bricks on the Officers' Mess wall, where some hapless youth had gone to meet his ancestors. You also passed a sort of elephants' graveyard of broken aircraft alongside the taxiway. (Even visiting aircraft seemed to be jinxed. A Wellington's undercarriage collapsed halfway down the runway, and I think it ended up in the scrapyard too.)

The Meteors themselves seemed enormous, in contrast to our Prentices and Harvards. We rapidly found that everything we were used to was multiplied four or even fivefold.... weight, power, speed, rate of climb, ceiling, G-forces, fuel consumption, not to mention the number of accidents. There was one guy on the course whose first two dual trips both ended in wheels-up landings for some reason or another. I think we had a major accident every week, and a fatal accident at least once a month. The Korean War had brought about a big expansion in aircrew training, and the place teemed with National Service and reservist student pilots, many of whom were terrified of the Meteor.

The press made a big sensation out of all these "jet" crashes, as though there was something special about them (compare the F104 Starfighter later on). In fact, we can now look back and see two obvious causes. One was simply that the management, only seven years after the war, just took danger for granted, and everyone "pressed on regardless". Accidents were expected.

The other was that the new jet engines had given such a huge leap in performance that everyone was on a steep learning curve, from aircraft designers and senior officers down to junior pilots. Aircraft systems, flight instruments, safety equipment and navigation aids had barely advanced since the days of the Spitfire.

(By the way, why have so many aircraft been named after things, which whiz across the sky in flames and hit the ground with a bang –not just the Meteor, but the Comet, Shooting Star, Thunderbolt and even the Ryan Fireball!)

We first met the two-seat trainer, the T7. Despite its longer nose, this was lighter and climbed better than the fighter versions because it had no guns. The tandem cockpit had a long heavily framed canopy, which opened sideways. Before take-off, its locks had to be carefully checked, because if the canopy opened in flight, control was difficult. If it was jettisoned when open, it could pivot round and behead the pilots. (My station commander at Leuchars died that way). There were no ejection seats, nor was the aircraft pressurized. Apart from these minor drawbacks, the T7 was exciting to fly, especially for those accustomed to trundling round at 90 knots in a Harvard. When taxying out, its two Derwents sounded almost like giant electric motors after the vibration and chuntering of the old Pratt and Whitney. They gave the Meteor a thrust:weight ratio of about 1:2, comparable with many current aircraft.

(On the subject of names again; Rolls-Royce jet engines were all called after rivers – Nene, Welland, Trent, Avon, Tyne, and so on, although there was never an "Ouse" for some reason.)

The Derwent had a centrifugal compressor, and I always found it incongruous to look down the streamlined intake only to see it apparently blocked completely by a huge mass of black-enamelled machinery covered with filters, pipes, pumps and levers. Closer inspection would reveal that the tons of high-speed air needed by the engine had to force its way past all this clutter and squeeze into the compressor through insignificant wire mesh grills. Indeed, since the compressor was double-sided, some of the air had to do a 180-degree turn and get in round the back.

It was quite reliable, and mechanically simpler than contemporary axial-flow engines, lacking such things as variable inlet guide-vanes, bleed valves or acceleration control units. It did not worry too much about swallowing birds (or even hats on occasion). However, the jet pipe would resonate if the throttle was opened too quickly, and sometimes the compressor would surge momentarily at high RPM and high altitude, which the pilot heard rather like a rubber mallet thumping the cockpit. If ignored, this would quickly snap off some turbine blades. (Of which, of course, there were 54!)

I can only remember having two genuine engine failures, plus a refusal to relight after a deliberate flame-out. The Derwent could be relit quite reliably in flight, at least up to medium altitude, whereas if the single DH Goblin engine in a Vampire 5 flamed out, Pilot's Notes seemed to suggest that it could only be relit by sheer luck The Derwent could even keep on running minus a turbine blade or two, provided you put your glove over the jet pipe temperature gauge!

Asymmetric flight in the Meteor was not much fun at circuit speeds. Its rudder had no power assistance or electric trim. A single-engined overshoot was a rather white-knuckle affair. Indeed, unless the pilot lowered his seat, locked his leg and had his straps extremely tight, the footload was enough to lift him out of his seat instead of holding full rudder on. If the dead engine happened to be the one that had the hydraulic pump (there was no duplicate in the early Meteors), and the hydraulic reservoir had been exhausted earlier, the only way to raise the undercarriage was to use the handpump, so you needed three arms as well.

The main problem, as with all these early low compression engines, was their thirst. You didn't time a sortie so much by the clock as by the fuel gauges (if you had any – some of the early T7s only had them in the front cockpit, so the instructor in the back had to bite his nails and hope his pupil was reading them correctly.) The average sortie was only 40 minutes. A full ventral tank added 20 minutes or so, but aerobatics or circuits and bumps were not allowed until it ran dry.

Despite the risk, the original training syllabus actually required us novices to do a number of real flameout landings solo. Even more idiotically, pupils short of fuel were instructed to flame out an engine deliberately. The idea was that it was marginally more economical to run one engine on high power than to have two at cruising power. In some Meteors of that time, there was only one generator and one hydraulic pump, and one or the other was lost according to the engine being shut down. The extra endurance bought by this dubious procedure was probably only about five minutes, and of course, if the dead engine failed to relight before landing you were in trouble.

Many of us will remember going up to 35,000 ft in the unpressurized T7 to do a Mach run. This is an experience unknown to mollycoddled generations after us, except maybe in emergency. The QFI had to get his talking done during the climb because his voice faded away in the thin air. Stomachs swelled (woe betide anyone who had beans for lunch), teeth ached and the cockpit became very cold. The Meteor was gentlemanly up to about Mach 0.82 and soon recovered from compressibility effects when the excellent airbrakes were extended. If handled too roughly, it could go into a sort of high Mach number spin, from which it would recover in the warmer air about 15,000 feet. (The Vampire's compressibility repertoire included violent porpoising).

At lower altitudes, the Meteor could easily exceed 400 knots. At this IAS, the aerodynamic load on the tail was said to bend the rear fuselage down about one and a half inches. (There are some bits of information pilots do not wish to know.)

After upper air exercises, the short endurance necessitated a steep rapid descent back to base. Very often, the very cold canopy would mist up just as the circuit was rejoined.

Fortunately I never met the only real vice of the T7. This was liable to happen if the airbrakes were not shut before the undercarriage was selected down. The three wheels of the Meteor came down one, two and then three, instead of all at once. This induced a mild snake. If the airbrakes were still out, weathercock stability was so reduced (and the T7 with its longer nose was slightly more susceptible than the shorter-nosed combat versions) that the fuselage could yaw enough to blanket the inner wing. This caused the aircraft to roll and drop its nose. At circuit height, quick recovery action was vital, and of course, the pilot had to realise what was wrong and close the airbrakes immediately. There was a crash at an air display some years ago, due to precisely this phenomenon – which was popularly known as "the phantom dive".

At AFS, we did our solo exercises in the single-seat F4. This was not a particularly likable machine for some reason, perhaps because its short nose, lumpy three-piece canopy and "elephant's ear" shaped fin and rudder made it look ill- proportioned. Like the T7, it had no ejector seat. Pilots who had flown the old F3, which had the original long-span wings and short nacelles, said the F4 had a much better performance. It had a disconcerting habit of tightening up in a turn at circuit speeds. Its successor, the F8 was altogether a nicer flying machine, with more fuel, a better canopy, an ejection seat and a more effective and aristocratic looking fin and rudder.

Such was the concern over the accident rate, by the way, that we students had to write down our QFI's briefing on a little duplicate pad, and stow the top copy in the pocket of our old-style mae-wests. Then if we departed from our instructions, or didn't even come back at all, the carbon copy could be produced at the subsequent Board of Inquiry. What happened, of course, was that when you pulled out your briefing slip in flight, to see what you were supposed to do next, a whole lot of obsolete ones would fall out as well. So you could take your pick.

The F4s at Middleton were filthy, and after all our college lectures about laminar flow and high speed aerofoils, the rough, chipped and scratched paint finish was a bit of a mockery.

Nevertheless, you could wind one up to a fair rate of knots. Belting along one day just below the cloudbase, I blacked myself out, while turning hard and looking over my shoulder to keep some landmark in sight. When I came round, I was in cloud at about 2,000 ft., with all the instruments whizzing round in opposite directions. My Instrument Flying was totally inadequate to sort this out, so my first instinct was to push the stick forward so as to get into the clear below the cloud again. Immediately, the negative G showered me with ancient crud from the floor, and gave the sensation of being upside down. So I rolled hard so as to get upright again. I remember a distinct desire to be somewhere other than the cockpit of a Meteor at that time. I also remember my main thought was "You bloody fool, you've really done it this time"! Anyway, the aircraft shot out of cloud in a shallow dive, and I was able fly home safely, albeit shaking like a leaf.

Later, after I had returned to Middleton as a QFI, I got another severe fright in an old F4, which I had been asked to air test.. Just as the wheels came up on take-off, a terrible hooting noise filled the cockpit. Hastily I landed again and handed the aircraft back to the groundcrew. A rather shame-faced sergeant found the explanation. Cold air for cockpit ventilation in the Meteor came through a pipe, rather like that of a vacuum cleaner, from a hole in the tip of the nose cone. The technicians had replaced this, and neglected to take the wrapping tape off the bulkhead end of the pipe. At 150 knots the slipstream pressure had split this tape and made the pipe into a sort of mega-powered saxophone.

Navigation in those distant times depended very much, apart from a map and the instincts of a homing pigeon, on readings from air traffic control's cathode ray direction finding equipment (CRDF). If this went unserviceable, you had to transmit for a bearing from the old manual DF equipment. By the time the operator got a reading you were five or six miles further on. Some of the older Meteors did not even have a gyro compass, but only a Magnesyn remote reading magnetic one used in conjunction with a separate directional gyro which needed constantly to be reset. It could only be read correctly in straight and level flight because it suffered all the turn and acceleration errors of a basic magnetic compass.

Many Meteors were still fitted with the obsolescent air-driven artificial horizon, which toppled at bank angles common in jet aircraft, even in the circuit. Moreover, it suffered marked turn and acceleration errors, so on take-off it exaggerated the nose-up attitude considerably. This did not matter in daylight, but at night if the pilot held the bar where he thought it should be and did not cross-check with altimeter and Vertical Speed Indicator (VSI), the aircraft would actually go nose-down after take-off instead of climbing. In addition, the rapid acceleration on take-off pressed the pilot back in the seat, giving a misleading sensory impression of a high nose attitude, which had to be ignored. I was having my supper one night when an ominous crump rattled the windows and told of yet another student who hadn't listened to what he was told.

Nowadays, when the RAF is not much bigger than, say, the Israeli Air Force, it is nostalgic to look back and remember how many airfields and aircraft there used to be. Adding all the operational fighter bases to the flying schools, on an average day there might have been a hundred Meteors and Vampires airborne on different training missions across the country at any one time. Thus, it was quite possible for busy controllers to miss an R/T call, or to assume that instructions had been understood, while other aircraft were already calling for attention. Once a controller realized an aircraft had been mislaid, there was not much time to locate it before it was out of fuel. Happily, there were still many old wartime airfields on which an emergency landing was possible. The Meteor was a strong aircraft, which gave a comfortable ride through fences, across main roads, and over a ploughed field, as I found out when my brakes failed during a Wing stream landing at Church Fenton.

Many QFIs had quite low hours on type. A trainee could be "creamed off" at the end of an AFS course, given an intensive course at the Central Flying School, and be back again as an instructor without doing a squadron tour. Some of the older QFIs had come from Dakotas or Lancasters, and had only a few more jet hours than their pupils. My flight commander and my own instructor were killed doing Staff Continuation Training shortly after I left Middleton.

One feature of the time was the number of very senior commanders who were killed in flying accidents. They had been flying Spitfires operationally only a few years before and, in a praiseworthy display of leadership, would pilot themselves in their own Meteors when going on staff visits and inspections. They did not appreciate the importance of continual flying practice, and of having all the emergency drills at their fingertips. One trivial and maybe apocryphal example was the occasion when an Air Marshal supposedly arrived in his own Meteor on a visit, and forgot which side of the cockpit the footholds were. So he scrabbled down the wrong side and fell comically to earth in front of the embarrassed reception parade.

To those of us who flew Meteors, it was all great fun, even allowing for the inevitable selective memory looking back over forty or fifty years. It was the end of an era, when whole squadrons and sometimes complete wings swept the skies on exercises. Thirty or more aircraft from the Leuchars Wing would dogfight with the Linton Wing. The sky would be filled with shining, tumbling silver aircraft with their heraldic squadron markings, the leaders marked out by their coloured noses and tail fins.

Soon all that was to disappear as single aircraft came to cost a measurable part of the GNP, and homing missiles replaced pilot-aimed cannon.

Our generation is now retired. We wonder if our successors get as much fun as we did. Everything today seems to be precalculated and fed into cockpit video displays. We doubt if they would get away with the adventures that we had, intentionally or otherwise, when the world was young and the Meteor was Queen of the Skies. [RHR]

AND DON'T FORGET THE VAMPIRE!

Those of 54 Entry who went on to fighters after leaving Cranwell nearly all flew either the Gloster Meteor, if they were stationed in the UK, or the de Havilland Vampire if they were posted to Germany. Some people thought the Vampire was great, and some of them could well have written a description of it for this book. But they didn't. So this is written by a Meteor pilot…!

The Vampire fighter was a funny-looking little thing with twin booms and a cockpit shaped a bit like a tadpole. It sat very low, so that on take-off you whizzed down the runway with your bottom only inches from the ground. We Meteor men called it the "kiddy car". The tail pipe sloped downwards slightly, so that if the engine was run up against the brakes, it burnt the tarmac. Indeed, a stream take-off by a Vampire Wing was quite a sight as a big cloud of brown smoke hung over the runway behind them.

The single Goblin engine behind the pilot had a rather primitive fuel system, and was prone to make strange rumbling and thumping noises One's confidence was not improved by Pilot's Notes, which told you that some test pilot had actually managed to relight it after a flame-out, but more by luck than design. The Notes also gave dire warning about the poor ditching characteristics of the aircraft. If you had to bail out, it was advisable to roll the aircraft on its back and fall out; otherwise you could be caught by the tail. There was no ejection seat, until much later when the T11 trainer was modified.

Because the tail-pipe sloped downwards, a "wet" start would result in neat fuel running out the back and forming a pool on the ground. If the engine finally lit, a flame might come out and ignite this pool. On one occasion, the cry went round the crew rooms: "Blood, chaps, quick!" and we all rushed outside. There was a Vampire out on the pan with just such a fire underneath it. For a few seconds everyone laughed heartily at one of our mates who was frantically unstrapping and leaping out of the cockpit. Then it suddenly dawned on the onlookers that he was actually in some danger, and people started rushing about ringing bells and grabbing extinguishers. (Fire has an odd effect – people sometimes don't believe it when they first see it.)

In the air, the Vampire was quite nice to fly, although a bit gutless. In a very tight turn or pull-out, it could flick, and at a high Mach number, it was liable to start violent and unpleasant porpoising. Otherwise it had no vices and aerobatics were quite enjoyable. The only distinctive characteristic was that on the final approach, when full flap was selected, there was a strong nose-up change of trim and you had to push on the stick to counter it.

The ergonomics of the Vampire cockpit were typical of its period. The T11 with its side by side seats was worse than the single-seaters because the designers had tried to put twice as much in. There is a story that they made a wooden mock-up, and then threw in as many plastiscene instruments, levers, knobs and switches as they could, to see where they would stick. One author described the result as "the back of the watchmaker's shop!"

Although most of the airframe was metal, the cockpit itself was made of wood, like the Mosquito, and was presumably fastened to the main bulkhead by some sort of glue. You had to put this thought to the back of your mind when pulling "g". However, one day there was an incident at Middleton St. George which gave us some reassurance. Word went round the crew rooms that there was something to see, and everyone rushed outside. A crowd was already standing round a Vampire 5 on the pan.

This particular Vampire had two or three degrees more dihedral than usual. The top surfaces of the wings were rippled, and underneath, a row of large bolts stuck out from the main spar. The tail-pipe drooped a bit too. What had happened, apparently, was that the pilot had been following his leader in a tail chase. Being left behind in a loop, he had tried to cut the corner and lost control. Next thing, he was diving vertically downwards, with the ground expanding rapidly in his windscreen and getting very near indeed. So he had pulled back on the stick as hard as he could, blacking himself out and overstressing the airframe (and his own neck as well), but managing to level out in time.

The engineers reckoned that he had pulled ten or eleven "g" momentarily. The load on the airframe had gone beyond the point of permanent deformation but not quite reached ultimate failure. So it showed that the Vampire was indeed stronger than it looked. The cockpit had not fallen off after all. I believe they jacked it up, glued a new engine and wings on behind, and it flew again.

Another memory is of the time I was taking off in a T11 one winter's day. Just before the nose wheel lifted off, power suddenly died. A lot of steam came out of the cabin pressurisation system and misted up the canopy. Braking to a stop, I found there was enough power left to roll to the end of the runway and then taxy slowly back to dispersal. The engine was muttering to itself and not responding to the throttle. It was actually only running on the top burner cans. The nose wheel had sprayed a whole lot of slush from the runway into the intakes, and the bottom of the engine was full of water! This was proved when the ground crew sat on the tail to tip the aircraft, and the water ran out of the jet pipe.

An episode that was not funny remains a particular memory of the Vampire. An instructor was bringing a formation of three aircraft back to base, and ordered them into echelon starboard for a run in and break. This meant that the student who was number three moved across and took position on the outside of the echelon. Had they remained in vic or gone into echelon port, his aircraft would have been in full view all the time. As it was, his leader was looking ahead and number two was looking at the leader, not him.

Once again the cry went round the crew rooms and we all rushed out on to the grass to see what was going on. The leader and number two had landed, but number three was flying over the tower waggling his wings to indicate R/T failure. We could all see that in fact his aircraft was on fire and trailing smoke, but because his radio had gone, Air Traffic Control had no way of warning him. So he continued round on to the downwind leg, probably wondering why all his electrics had failed.

If he had realised what was wrong, he might just have had time to pull up, invert the aircraft, and parachute out. But he didn't. Perhaps his controls had burned through by then. So from circuit height on the downwind leg, the Vampire suddenly just nose-dived into the ground. No sound; just a column of smoke. Virtually the whole of Flying Wing and Tech. Wing was outside watching by this time. There was complete silence.

Let us end with a bit of Vampire folklore. The very first T11 trainers had a framed canopy rather like the Mosquito. To escape, you had to get out of a fairly small hatch in the roof. We were warned that in the event of a bail out by student and instructor, foreheads would be inspected. Woe betide the instructor who left a footprint on the student's forehead! [RHR]

NEAR THINGS AND CLOSE SHAVES

I have had a fair share of engine vagaries. Over the Egyptian Canal Zone, I was one of four silver Vampire jet fighters of No 32 Squadron flying at twenty thousand feet (about four miles high) in that country's so frequently perfect blue sky. Below was the long straight channel of the of the Suez Canal stretching south from Port Said through little Lake Tewfik, then entering the Great Bitter Lake, on the shore of which was my airfield, Deversoir.

During a vigorous manoeuvre, I whipped into a steep turn and 'poured on the coals', as the phrase was, to *increase* power. There was a loud *plop* noise from my engine, then silence and a rapidly decreasing air speed. Behind me I could see a stream of white vapour pouring from the jet pipe – unburned fuel, as the engine had stopped, or 'flamed out', to use another popular phrase. I straightened out, and closed the throttle and fuel cocks. I had lots of time. To maintain speed and controllability I had to lose height in a descent Sooner or later the aircraft would hit the ground or water, and either would mean certain death if I was still in the aircraft. On the other hand there was no ejection seat in these early jets, and to leave by parachute involved the hazard of striking the tail on the way out, just as fatal, after climbing into the 180 mph airflow. The engine, a De Havilland Goblin, could not be re-started in the air. I made a decision. I would continue to descend – not that I had a choice – but I would do so over the lumpy desert towards my airfield which, at my gliding descent rate, I calculated I could reach with a few thousand feet to spare. Then all I had to do was judge everything nicely so that the inevitable contact with the ground took place into wind, at the beginning of the main runway, at landing speed. There could be two problems. If I misjudged the approach and undershot too low, I would hit the lake, and the Vampire was known *not* to ditch satisfactorily but to dive to the bottom. If I misjudged the approach too high and overshot I would hit a thick plantation of palm trees beyond the runway, which would bring an end to any further problems I might have had.

Throughout the descent I was aware of unpleasantness in my stomach but knew that if I let it dominate, I could not think clearly. I arrived over the airfield at 3,000 feet, reached a position for the final 180-degree turn at 2,000 feet, which was 500 feet higher than normal, put the undercarriage down, flaps down and airbrakes out, even a touch of top rudder for a slight descent-increasing side-slip, then straightened out at the threshold and sank gently on to the tarmac with an enormous grin on my face under my oxygen mask. The air traffic controller had been silent after clearing away all other air traffic to allow me to concentrate. As I began to brake the aircraft and was obviously under control, the Wing Commander Flying, Bertie Wooten (of Battle of Britain fame), who had gone to the control tower to watch, broadcast a terse 'Good show.' My day was made.

It is only right to recount another occurrence from that period which was utterly stupid, much more frightening and which I survived only by the grace of God. While serving with the same squadron, we were asked to give army units which were exercising in the Eastern Desert some experience of tactical fighter air attack. No weapons would be fired, of course, but we would have the practice of finding vehicles and tanks in the sand and making dummy attacks, and they would have the practice of swivelling their guns at us.

I must have flown four packed sorties that day, and it was enjoyable and interesting, but also tiring. We would dive in a stream on our selected targets from about 2,000 feet, breaking off and roaring over their heads at 200 feet or less. On the last sortie and the last attack, as I levelled out low over the troops, I had an uncontrollable urge to show off – a barrel roll over their heads, just to show them. I pulled the aircraft up into a slight climb and rolled. I had not climbed steeply enough: I had rolled too early, and as I came out of the roll, the ground was hurrying up to meet me. At that moment there was nothing I could do to alter anything. The moving finger writes with a vengeance. My stomach was in knots. I kept backward pressure on the stick to a maximum without incurring a high-speed stall, and the desert sand beneath me and ahead came close enough to blur. There was not even time to pray. A second later I was climbing away, feeling oddly chilled in the 120-degree (Fahrenheit) sweaty cockpit, very thoughtful and very thankful. Fortunately for my reputation I had been the last in the stream, and nobody but the troops had noticed. They may have admired it, but they would not have known how close to disaster it had been.

Such frights were brief and followed soon after by a cool shower, a change of clothes and at least one ice-cold beer, to stimulate clear reflection, and perhaps a story while sitting safely on a bar stool. The traditional line-shoot is just an RAF way of off-loading the tensions.

Many years later, on holiday in the USA with my son, Michael, we toured in a small single-engined aeroplane, a Grumman North American Tiger Cub. We took it in turns to fly. When over the foothills of the Rockies, I kept my eyes open for emergency landing areas in case the single engine failed – a habit of mine, but with no real point. Only the rivers might have given us a chance, and they were neither straight nor tranquil. It was Michael who did the landing on the sloping mesa of Sedona's runway (land uphill, take off downhill, regardless of the wind), rather like approaching a sloping aircraft carrier. We explored the vastness of the Grand Canyon, flying below the rim, which is now illegal and should have been then, for good reason: the down draughts could make it impossible to climb out again.

I had had an earlier foretaste of this problem when I was flying in Wales. One of the first flights I had made for Cambridge University was a photographic sortie to Snowdonia, to take reasonably close low-level shots of the rim and slopes of a sinisterly named feature called the Devil's Kitchen, a semi-enclosed crater. It was a bright, breezy day. For years, all my low-level flying had been in operational RAF aircraft with powerful jet engines, which, when the throttle was opened, would thrust you up at a good steep angle to avoid hitting a fast-approaching ridge. I must have forgotten that I did not have two such engines at my disposal. As I entered the Kitchen on its open side, high enough to pass over the sharp rim ahead, I noticed that my air speed was inexplicably falling towards stalling speed. My engines sounded all right. Then I realized that we must be in the grip of a deadly down draught, the wind ahead flowing up the far side of the rim and abruptly down towards us into the Kitchen's depth. Nature abhors a vacuum. Instinctively I had been progressively easing the control column back to maintain height, thus bleeding away the aircraft's speed. While applying maximum engine power, making little difference, I pushed the nose down towards the precipice, now with its rim well above us, and very, very gingerly turned the aircraft about, through a hundred and eighty degrees, at as low a speed as I dared. I spared a thought for the department's curator, sitting behind me and no doubt horrified. When the turn was complete, the ground sloped downwards and away so I could follow it while regaining vital speed. Oddly, what had saved us was the down-draught wind itself, a headwind, of course, which, as soon as I began to turn, helped blow us away from the cliff face. Does one ever learn? Relief was exceeded only by shame at my disregard of basic principles, and the polite, controlled silence of the curator-photographer.

When the spaceship containing my son, Michael, was experiencing an emergency, the media referred to the possibility of "pulling the wrong plug". I then thought of my own frailties, and of an event years ago when not pulling the *right* lever had put me in a hazardous position. I was practising night landings in a Meteor jet. After landing, I opened up the engines and rolled on for another take-off, circuit and landing and so on until final landing. My hands and eyes moved with practised speed: air brakes in – third flap down – undercarriage lever down – three green lights, therefore wheels are down and locked – turn finals – full flap down – at the runway threshold, look at the flattened flare-path V, ease gently back on the control column and let the slowing aircraft sink to kiss the ground with its tyres. Perfect. Open throttles, feel the increasing speed pushing my back, flaps up, ease the aircraft up off the ground into a steep climbing turn towards the beginning of the downwind leg again. Things were going very well, each landing was perfect, the Meteor and I were as one, the whole night sky was ours alone. I repeated this four times and decided that the fifth should be my last. Air brakes in, one third flap, final turn, full flap, crossing the runway threshold at exactly the right speed, bringing up the nose gently to reduce the speed and to sink on to the. . . ! What happened next happened in all its detail over a long period of about half a second. My tyres should have kissed the tarmac. They hadn't. Yet I was exactly right with the flare-path angle for landing with just the right amount of sink. I checked the instrument panel. *No green lights!* My undercarriage was *not down.* I went to full power to avoid the disaster of a wheels-up landing and felt a slight bump on the ground as the thrust took me up and away. I had been very lucky. I landed very carefully, with only a small dent in the aircraft's ventral tank and a very large one in my pride. [C.H.F.]

"THE NEW CAP"

A Cautionary Tale for Young Officers
(or anyone ordering clothing by mail-order)

You are going to get married. You need a new, smart service cap of the fashionable shape made by Messrs. Bates in London.

You are, however, stationed at RAF Leuchars, some distance from London. How do you obtain a cap of the correct size?

Simple. You put a length of string round your head half an inch above your ears, cut off the correct length, and post it to Messrs Bates with your order.

You then receive a reply. "Dear Sir, thank you for your esteemed custom. However, we cannot believe the size of your head…"

You search in the crewroom rubbish bin, find the other bit of the string, and post it to Messrs, Bates with your order… [R.H.R.]

SURPRISE! SURPRISE!

Training at the RAF College did not warn the Flight Cadets of the surprises that lay in wait in the early years of a career in the General Duties (GD) Branch. Surprises were not always unpleasant – indeed, many were valuable and enjoyable and in retrospect quite amusing. Others, of course, could be a pain in the backside!

My first surprise hit me on the day 54 Entry graduated. We were enjoying our excellent lunch in the company of our various guests and looking forward to a relaxing afternoon before preparing for the night's festivities. A heavy hand was laid on my shoulder and looking up I was surprised to see Bob Weighill. "What on earth could he want?" I thought: after all he was "B" Squadron's Commanding Officer and I was in "A" Squadron. My question was quickly answered. "Christie, finish your lunch and get your rugger kit and report to the North Airfield pitch at 1400 hrs for an Air Force trial." And off he stomped. Colin Foale very kindly looked after my guests until after the game, which was not particularly interesting. Surprisingly, I played for the RAF for the rest of the 1951-52 season, which did not please the CFI at Valley since I was hardly around much for conversion to the Vampire.

Conversion to the Vampire was a great surprise! At that time, early 1952, there was no Vampire trainer and so all dual instruction was flown in a Meteor 7. Any resemblance in the handling qualities of the relatively heavy, twin-engined Meteor and the lightweight "dinky-toy" Vampire was purely coincidental. I suppose there was an element of similarity in the handling of jet engines and in high altitude flying, but the first solo in the Vampire was truly a "first-ever" flight on type! Your instructor gave a little help before you set off on that first solo by taking you out to your allotted aircraft and, with ground-crew sitting on the tailplane to raise the nose-wheel off the ground, he said, "Now, see how the ground ahead and horizon appear to you from the cockpit. That is roughly the landing attitude. Off you go!" The first solo passed without incident and the records show no adverse accident statistics for conversion to type in the absence of a dual-control T11. So, the policy was probably right!

After Operational Conversion at Chivenor. I was posted to the Canal Zone with Dougie Burbridge (a National Service pilot) and held in the transit camp at El Hamrah until HQ MEAF decided which squadron we would be posted to- there were only three options available for Vampire pilots – Malta, Deversoir and Habbaniyah. Deversoir was our preference (not that we had a choice) as it was on the doorstep and the Wing had a good reputation. We did not relish another long haul back to Malta and "Habb" was unknown to us. The eventual decision surprised us both. After a couple of nights in transit, so to speak, we were at the cinema when the screen dimmed (much to the disgust of some of the more robust in the audience) and a message appeared saying " Pilot Officers Burbridge and Christie report to Air Movements immediately". We were taken aback since the time was 10pm on a Saturday night! Worse was to come! We were told that we were posted to No.6 Squadron at Habb, to collect all our kit and report to Movements for transport to Fayid where a flight to Habb would be departing soon after midnight. By 0030hrs we were airborne in a "Pig" (Valletta) uncomfortably seated in paratroop seats, in an aircraft whose temperature never got below 115 despite our altitude. After a sleepless journey of over six hours we arrived at Habbaniyah. And what a surprise awaited us there!

Instead of the standard "welcome" by the duty movements officer, Dougie B. and I were asked why we had come to Habb. When we told him that we had been posted to "Six" he pointed us in the direction of the No.6 Squadron hangar and said "You will find the CO over there". We made sure that our clothes trunks would be sent to the Mess and then set off the 4-500 yards to the hangar. Despite the early hour the heat was tremendous but what surprised us more was the hive of activity at and around the hangar. All the aircraft were out on the pan with airmen busily preparing them for flight. In front of the hangar there were piles of kit and seemingly all the pilots in flying gear waiting for the signal that their aircraft were ready! I wondered if this was the usual Sunday morning routine. The CO (Sqn Ldr Pat Kennedy) was pointed out as one of a small group involved in apparently important discussions, so we moved over to report to him. That gave rise to my next surprise – the Air Marshal in the group was none other than George Beamish (AOC Iraq) and next to him was Group Captain J O W ("Doggie") Oliver (SASO Iraq and formerly the Deputy Commandant at Cranwell when George Beamish had been the Commandant). Both recognised me and inquired about my presence at Habb and then moved off. Pat Kennedy then quickly informed us that the Squadron was preparing to deploy to the Canal Zone (to Abu Sueir), told us to get as much kit from our trunks as necessary to last us some 14 days and report back a.s.a.p. to Air Movements for a return flight in the "Pig" which had so recently brought us up from Fayid! We were not amused! Although the Squadron was equipped with Vampires it had a Meteor 7 for instrument flying and target towing and there was therefore a seat available in it to take one of us in reasonable comfort to Abu Sueir. So Dougie and I tossed a coin to decide who was to be the lucky one – I won and poor Dougie suffered the long drag back to the Canal Zone which we had left only a few hours before! The reason for the deployment to Abu Sueir was a crisis in the Egyptian Government but it was soon resolved and we were back at Habbaniyah after three week's detachment.

For three or four summer months in Iraq the temperatures were around 120°F in the shade and aircraft on the ground in the open quickly became untouchable. The daily flying programme then was carried out in the early hours of the day or late evening and night. Nights were also very hot and most residents at Habb moved their beds out into the Mess gardens and slept under mosquito nets. It was not unusual to be wakened in the dark hours by the weird howling of the wild desert pi-dogs and occasionally a pack would race through the gardens too near for comfort. In late October and early November 1952 the Squadron deployed to Mafraq in Jordan for a three weeks exercise with the Arab

Legion (at that time under the command of Glubb Pasha). This presented me with my next big surprise when Pat Kennedy called me into his office and told me that, as I was the junior officer on the squadron, I automatically inherited the secondary duty of OC Road Convoy! I was required to undergo a few hours tuition by the Squadron SNCO MT in order to qualify as an HGV driver. I was also told to study the Exercise Order for the move to Mafraq overland to grasp what this unexpected secondary duty entailed.

Being fully established for virtually independent operations in the field i.e. from minimum prepared desert strips, "Six" held an impressive establishment of vehicles (3-tonners, Land Rovers, motor cycles, Coles cranes etc.), and tentage to accommodate all the squadron personnel and equipment. The deployed "force" included a Field Kitchen (manned by cooks earmarked from the Habb messes, a Sick Bay (manned by a doctor and staff from the Habb hospital) and a Ground Liaison Officer (GLO). This was my charge for the three day journey from Habb to Mafraq!

On 6th October 1952 the convoy set off in good military order, initially on firm tarmac roads following the pipelines, but in the second day we were on well worn camel/truck desert tracks. While on the road which followed the pipeline we encountered some very heavy trucks plying their trade to and from Iraq's neighbours but once on the desert tracks we were alone except for a very few camel trains and the occasional versatile, air-conditioned Nairn bus which, with its large balloon tyres, navigated its way across the desert, back and forth, between Baghdad and Damascus.

The weather in October is pleasantly warm by day but the nights are surprisingly cold, which helped to ensure a good night's sleep (provided one wrapped-up well in the standard issue of "canvas" sleeping-bag of that era!). After serving breakfast the cooks and "cook-house" set-off before the main convoy to prepare lunch at a planned rendezvous~ once lunch was served they proceeded ahead to the appointed meeting place for supper and the stop-over for the night. Between meals en route we brewed our "NAAFI-breaks" ourselves. The technique was simple – a shallow hole scraped in the sand and filled with petrol provided a very effective stove to boil water for tea/coffee and heat-up a can of soup if required. The second day and night followed the same pattern. With a few very experienced SNCOs (old soldiers indeed) I was never called upon for a CO's decision but was kept informed of any potential hitches which might have interrupted the smooth passage to Mafraq, which we reached on the third day, in time to set up camp ready for the Squadron's arrival by air. After exercising with the Arab Legion we struck camp and returned to Habb via the reverse of the route out. All in all this was a great experience for a youngster fresh out of "school" and an enjoyable, pleasant surprising start to one's first squadron tour!

In late 1952 the new AOC had a "cunning plan". He decided to have a pool of junior officers, one nominated from each unit in his bailiwick, from which would be drawn those required to conduct Boards of Inquiry, take Summaries of Evidence, take part in Courts Martial, etc etc. The idea, apparently, aimed at avoiding last minute panics in putting in place all the components required for these administrative or disciplinary proceedings. I was surprised to be told that I was the "earmarked" officer for No.6 Squadron! On reflection I suppose I was the obvious choice, being permanently commissioned from Cranwell.

While we were based at Amman, I was detailed for my first task in this new secondary duty. There had been an MT accident at Aqabah, in southern Jordan in which an airman had sustained a broken leg. I was sent there to carry out an inquiry and, much to my surprise, I was provided carte blanche with a Proctor to fly to Aqabah. The round trip was some three hours so I was not required to stay overnight in that desert strip's very basic tented accommodation. It had been expected that my task would be completed in a day but as fate would have it, I needed three visits to complete the job (most of the witnesses were not readily available because of the need to assemble a search team to recover the bodies from a Valletta which had crashed on the 2500 foot Jabal al Lawz following a gross error in navigation). I presumed that, when I had delivered the result of my inquiry, that was the end of it; how wrong could I be. A week later I was called in and directed to return to Aqabah to carry out a Summary of Evidence. That did not take as long as the original investigation but a few weeks after delivering the Summary and after the "legal eagles" had cast their eyes over my work, came the biggest surprise – I was informed that a Court Martial was to be convened and that I was appointed Prosecutor! The case concerned a corporal driver who had taken some of his mates (and a few crates of beer) on an unauthorised swimming/barbecue run and had had the misfortune to overturn the vehicle with the unfortunate injury to one of the swimming party. He lost his stripes!

All that activity provided me with some very pleasant and enjoyable flying. A Proctor (civil version of the Prentice) was put at my disposal for the flights to and from Aqabah and I took every advantage of the circumstances to explore from the air that historic area between Amman and Aqabah – the pink city of Petra, the remnants of the Hejaz Railway after destruction by Lawrence and his Arab Army, the magnificint Wadi Rum and Wadi Musa. I did a dozen trips in the Proctor and the news leaked out that there were spare seats in the aircraft so I became a popular "tourist" pilot among the personnel at Amman and the Scots Greys based at a small desert strip at Ma'an in southern Jordan. But the most enjoyable aspect for me and my passengers was to take off from Amman, cross the Moab Hills and descend towards the Dead Sea before turning south for Aqabah; I could then descend to approximately 1,200 feet below sea-level! At that height the denser air provided virtual supercharging to the Gypsy Queen with quite a surprising increase in performance!

My final adventure with the investigative "Standing Committee" took me north into the Kurdish lands in the mountains on the Iraq/Turkey border; magnificent, majestic scenery populated by very friendly but extremely tough people. The British authorities had set up a small encampment at Sar Amadiyah some 6,000 feet up in the mountains, for use by the military and civil administrative staffs serving in Iraq as a "Rest and Leave" Centre during the Iraqi hot season. Tented accommodation was fairly basic and holiday activities were very simple – a small swimming pool and carefully supervised pony-trekking (in fact, on mules) in the mountains. The pool was icy cold at that height and so the most popular activity was the trekking out into the countryside for well-organised picnics; all a very pleasant relief from the oppressive summer conditions at Habbaniyah and Baghdad. On one of these recreational sorties a WRAF girl had been thrown from her mule (normally quite docile animals) and had suffered a "broken neck" injury. Fortunately, the incident occurred close to the camp and therefore the camp's RAF doctor was quickly on the scene to see to the girl who was soon transferred to the hospital at Habb. She suffered no permanent damage but service administration rules and regulations demanded a Board of Inquiry which I was nominated to carry-out.

When I learned that I had this task I had a good look at the map to establish exactly where Sar Amadiyah was – some 270 miles as the crow flies from Habb and located in what appeared to be very inhospitable territory. On inquiring about transport I was told that I would fly by Anson to the old RAF airfield at Mosul (Al Mawsil) and then go by staff car to Sar Amadiyah. It all seemed to be fairly simple and straightforward but there was more to the "by staff car" bit than meets the eye! The 200 mile flight to Mosul provided an excellent and enjoyable air view of the variety of terrain north of Habb, initially following the Euphrates with its strips of lush green cultivation along its banks. Here and there you could discern, in the desert areas beyond the cultivation, the outlines of ancient irrigation canals used when the Euphrates/Tigris rivers provided the water which made the rich fertile area known as the "Green

Crescent" in Biblical times. Once away from the river the terrain became reddish-brown desert which gradually gave way to the dusky hills around Mosul, and the great mountains further north. Mosul seemed to me to have been frozen in time; an airbase unchanged since it was built in the pre-war era and which I thought to be like the North West Frontier airfields described in many of the Biggles stories. The car journey started off on a reasonable well-metalled road out of Mosul heading north towards the border town of Zakho. After about 30miles we turned off the main road onto a much less comfortable road heading northeast towards Amadiyah and climbing steadily into the vast mountain range which separates Northern Iraq from Eastern Turkey and northwestern Iran. The temperature was beginning to fall to a more acceptable level as we progressed into the mountains, which were becoming more and more green and lush. After approximately two hours driving, when we had reached about 3,000 feet, we passed close to the magnificent Royal Palace at Sarsank, King Faisal's favourite summer residence. Another hour's driving brought us to the village of Amadiyah and the small RAF outpost where I met half-a-dozen other travellers who would be my companions for the last stage of the journey. Now came the big surprise. I looked around expecting to see a bus which would take the group on the last leg of the journey but, instead, we were guided to a small group of Kurds a few yards away who were tending a dozen or so mules. Some of the animals were pack-mules and already loaded with various stores; the others were fitted with saddles and we soon learned that the mules were to be our transport for the last part of the journey. After a very sketchy briefing from the Duty NCO on how to mount the mule and what was required of the rider to stay in the saddle, we set off in single file at a slow walking pace towards what appeared to be a precipitous mountain face, up which we were told we had to climb in order to reach our destination. Sure enough the path led straight into a cleft in the mountain face and we started the 3,000 foot climb to reach Sar Amadiyah. We had been reassured by the NCO that the mules knew the way, that they were very sure footed and would offer us no problems during the one hour climb. The "pass", as this narrow cleft in the rock face was fondly called, was composed of large and small rocks and much loose shale and, therefore, we progressed by a series of short hops and much slithering. It was not a good idea to look back down the steep "pass" but in any case our attention was more or less fixed on staying in the saddle. At last we were at the camp and able to admire the fantastic setting in which the camp was established but we all suffered to varying degrees from saddle sores and tender rumps! The cold mountain air and a comfortable camp bed under canvas ensured a good night's rest.

Next day I was keen to get on with the Board of Inquiry but it wasn't long before my enthusiasm was dampened. Most of the witnesses had returned to their units and the principal witness was 270miles away in Habb Hospital! I did what I could in the circumstances, put the file away and inquired about the arrangements for my return to base. The main factor was to establish when the Anson would be at Mosul to pick me up. This was not as simple as one might imagine. There was no scheduled service between Habb and Mosul; Communications Flight sorties were made on an ad hoc basis similar to the Anson Flight which took me to Mosul a couple of days earlier. Personnel spending their leave at the camp made the journey by train from Baghdad. Finalising the arrangements for my return to Habb was almost impossible because of the very shaky communication links between Sar Amadiyah and Habb – an obsolete, pre-war field telephone between the camp and the RAF post at the village of Amadiyah, a civil land-line to Mosul and, finally, the military/diplomatic line to Habb via the Embassy in Baghdad. Two attempts were made to provide a flight back to Habb from Mosul but because of the unreliable communications a timely rendezvous at Mosul was not feasible – I was, therefore, advised to take the first available train to Baghdad and finish my journey to Habb by staff car. That arrangement allowed me to spend two very pleasant days climbing and trekking in that magnificent mountainous country which has left me with lasting memories of small "medieval" villages, such as Kani Masi, perched on the mountain cliffs, of gazing down some 2000ft into the Rawandiz Gorge (Iraq's answer to the USA's Grand Canyon?) and of watching in awe the tumbling torrent of the Great Zab river. The return was uneventful (no more surprises!) by first-class rail overnight to Baghdad and by car to Habbaniyah.

I completed the Board of Inquiry by interviewing the WRAF girl in hospital and was pleased to see her on her feet, albeit with her neck firmly braced. She suffered no lasting injuries.

Soon after these adventures I was posted to No 77 Squadron, RAAF, in Korea and then back home to ETPS, thus ending those early days of surprises. However, future tours of duty produced their own unique surprises but they can only be described elsewhere.   [A.McN.C.]

THE DITCHING OF SUNDERLAND RN 302, "CHARLIE"

On graduating from Cranwell I went to the twin-engine conversion school at RAF Swinderby. The Wellington had just been replaced by the Varsity and I was lucky enough to be given a place on the first course on the new aircraft. A two-month Maritime course at RAF St Mawgan came next and finally there was the three-month Sunderland course at RAF

Calshot where we were taught seamanship and maritime law as well as the technicalities of the flying boat. I was then posted to Singapore and my first squadron. The following story is of an incident in which I was involved on this tour. On looking through my Flying Log Book, I see that four of the previous seven operational flights had been cut short because of engine trouble. We had obviously been going through a bad patch!

Number 88 Sunderland Squadron was taking part in a routine Korean detachment, operating out of Iwakuni in Japan, during December 1953. The RAF and American Maritime Patrol Squadrons flew two types of sortie in the theatre; the first was down the west coast of Korea and into the Yellow Sea where the primary tasks were anti-submarine patrol and ship identification and, during the early morning, to take weather observations which were used by operational planners for their daily Sabre flights over the 38th parallel. The other regular sortie was an anti-submarine barrier patrol down the east side and to the north of the peninsula. The US Navy also maintained a Naval Task Force in this area.

On the 27th December 1953, at 0600 local time, RN302 "C" took off from Iwakuni to cover the anti-submarine barrier patrol. These flights normally lasted twelve hours and the aircraft carried a full load of fuel, depth charges and gun ammunition. Flying Officer Dereck Empson, our senior navigator, was our Captain and Flight Lieutenant Jack Oliver and myself took it in turns as first pilot; I was the first pilot on this flight. Pilot Officer Keith Mosley was the second navigator, Flight Sergeant "Art" Mundell was the master gunner, Sergeant "Lofty" Land the first engineer and the remaining crew were Staff Sergeant Mc Millan, Sergeants Glass, Farrell and Nairn. Mc Millan was on loan from the Army and retained his rank of Staff Sergeant. We cleared our guns and checked our search radar before starting on the first search line.

Although the ground war had come to a halt with the cease-fire in July 1953, the USN task force was still in position as there was concern that Russian submarine activity from Vladivostok might materialise down the east coast of Korea. The anti-submarine patrols were kept going throughout that winter.

When we were just two hours into the flight the number four, starboard outer, engine caught fire – the Pratt and Whitney radial Twin Wasp had dislodged a cylinder, causing a total loss of power and intensive fire. Fuel was cut off, the propellor feathered and the remaining fire drill brought the situation under control. We were at our patrol height of 750 feet and cruising speed of 140 knots. Although the

Sunderland could fly quite safely on three engines with that all up weight, it was felt prudent to jettison some fuel quite soon.

We turned back toward Iwakuni and started jettisoning fuel but eight minutes after feathering number four, number two started smoking and rapidly lost power. Fuel jettisoning had only just begun and it was quickly abandoned because of the possible fire hazard, and the two remaining engines confirmed at fine pitch and full power. We had earlier climbed to 1,100 feet but the speed had come back to 105 knots – still on the right side of the drag curve for the Sunderland but with a very thin margin of safety. Drag would increase rapidly if the speed were permitted to fall below 95 knots.

At this point we were just over the northern tip of the island of Tsu-Shima and the nearest sheltered emergency alighting area was at Asau-Wan, some 24 nautical miles to the south. Our weight was in the region of 57,800 pounds and we were no longer able to maintain level flight, so Asau-Wan was out of the question. All was not lost, though, as Tsu-Shima was a long island with many bays and inlets down its east (or lee) side. As we coasted out we were down to 900 feet and it was decided to turn back (i.e.into wind) as soon as possible and attempt a landing close to the entrance of a small bay, Shushi-Wan, where the swell was breaking up nicely. Also, if things went wrong we would be quite close to land fall!! At the point of touch down the surface wind was 310/05 knots and the swell was from 010 at eight feet with 200 to 250 feet between nodes. The Sunderland was designed to land in a maximum of a four foot swell, with a chop of up to four feet on top and a nodal distance of 200 to 250 feet. However, if you could land along the swell the maximum height was, to some degree, academic.

A swell is just a stack of water, or a wave, travelling in a visible direction. If you can land on that stack and stay there whilst you decelerate and convert from aeroplane to boat, then its height is not important. The danger occurs during conversion as your wings are stalled, the rudder effect is reducing and the weathercocking becomes predominant, and all together they could cause you to slide off the swell node. If you slide sideways you may have insufficient engine control to correct this movement. The Sunderland wing floats were not designed to accept violent side loads and could easily break clear, thus allowing the wing tip to dip into the sea. Should this happen, the fuel, all in wing tanks, would run to the lowest point and add weight to the rolling movement and the aircraft could turn turtle quite quickly.

In this event, the drill was to send the crew out through the astrodome hatch to the rising wing – the first man carrying a rope – and hope the added weight would raise the dipped wing.

For the inevitable ditching in Shushi-Wan we were heading into wind but 60 degrees across the open sea swell. Our airspeed was too low and our rate of descent too high. We were now nine minutes into the second emergency. Both pilots were at the controls and the Sunderland bounced two or three times before dropping off the step. On landing the first point of contact between the hull and the sea is "the step" . This area of the hull is heavily reinforced so as to absorb the initial forces of impact on landing and as the wings are stalled during deceleration the increasing weight of the hull would push the step down into the sea, increasing the area of hull in contact with the surface. Deceleration from this point was quite fast. If one bounced on landing the natural tendency was to porpoise and the second impact could then be forward of the step, which was less well reinforced, and the nose section could break off and fold back.

This did not happen to RN302 but the starboard elevator was torn off, perhaps as a result of our attempts to keep the nose up and prevent porpoising, and the No 1 engine (port outer) had broken free and dropped into the sea. With the aid of the one remaining starboard engine we taxied into wind and were able to drop anchor in a small bay actually in Shushi-Wan. Although the wings drooped, the hull creaked and the main spar looked distinctly fragile, our watertight compartments remained sound and, of course, we were lucky not to break our back.

A chopper from the US Navy Task Force 77 answered our MAYDAY call and took six crew members back to Japan. Four remained with the aircraft (the captain, both pilots and an engineer). Whilst the wind blew offshore, everything was safe enough. If the wind came round by more than 100 degrees, to an easterly direction, we could be in trouble as we would be unable to prevent the aircraft from grounding and creating quite an ecological mess, with all our fuel, armaments and depth charges on board. There was no heavy lift equipment available to help so salvage looked to be a non-starter and the remaining option of sinking the aircraft in deep water was outside our authority. The detachment at Iwakuni could not make a decision as to what we should do and so the problem was referred back to Air Headquarters in Singapore.

An American frigate from TF77 arrived to look after us but could not realistically stay for more than 48 hours in the area, and they were greatly relieved when Singapore eventually agreed to allow us to take our old lady out to deep water and scuttle her. The dirty deed was completed at 10.40 hours local time on the 29th December with help from the four-inch guns on the frigate. The four crew members were taken on board the frigate and returned to Japan a week later. We were made comfortable and were well looked after. USN ships really were dry at the time and there was not even a medicinal brandy available in the sick bay over the New Year!! I was never asked to give evidence before a Board of Enquiry, although some time later we were asked why we were in such a hurry to sink the wreckage – did we have something to hide?!!

Note: The three Sunderland squadrons, Nos, 88, 205 and 209, which comprised the Far East Flying Boat Wing, were the only RAF squadrons to take part in the Korean War. To my knowledge, during that period one or two aircraft were lost to typhoons whilst at their moorings at Iwakuni, one crashed on landing there in a storm at night, with the loss of the crew, and one was destroyed in transit between Hong Kong and Iwakuni when it flew into high ground on Taiwan. "Charlie" was the only aircraft lost on operations. [N.A.I-S.]

A QFI AT CRANWELL

Less than four years after graduating from Cranwell I found myself back again, but this time as a Qualified Flying Instructor fresh from the Central Flying School. Despite having spent more than six years at Cranwell as an Aircraft Apprentice and a Flight Cadet, I was happy with my posting.

Travelling by rail, I arrived at Grantham to catch the connecting train to Sleaford. Needless to say, I was in civilian clothes and while waiting on the platform saw that there were a number of young men in civilian clothes also waiting for the train. One of them approached me and said "Have they got you as well?" and in response to my "Pardon?" he asked if I was going to Cranwell. I agreed that I was. He then told me, with some satisfaction and an air of superiority, "Of course, I could have come last term but they made me Captain of Cricket at school so I stayed on for the summer." It then became obvious that all these young men were about to become cadets. On arrival at Sleaford there was an imposing Flight Sergeant waiting with transport and his salute when I made myself known caused the cricketer's jaw to drop. I have reminded him of this at various times over the years, including after he reached air rank.

By chance I was posted to "B" Flight, the flight in which I had begun to learn to fly in 1950. That had been on the Percival Prentice flying from the South Airfield but by 1955 the Prentice had been replaced by the Percival Provost (with a piston engine and not to be confused with the Jet Provost) and basic flying training was located on the North Airfield, with the South Airfield reserved for the Balliols which had by then replaced the Harvards of the advanced wing. As things turned out, it was the last term for the Balliols as they were replaced by Vampires in the January of 1956.

The CFS course had been in two parts with the basic on Provosts at South Cerney followed by the advanced on Vampires at Little Rissington so I had not flown a Provost for three or four months. Another new instructor had arrived at "B" Flight with me from Little Rissington and we were given a Provost and a copy of Pilots' Notes and told to re-familiarise ourselves. We signed for the aircraft, climbed in, remembered how to start it and flew around the local area before trying a couple of circuits and landings. On our return to the flight office we were given three cadets each as pupils and I flew my first instructional flight that same day, with Flight Cadet Ryan. Having three pupils was interesting in that one cadet was from each of the three terms in the basic year so as well as starting from scratch with one Flight Cadet my other two were more advanced and I was faced with a good variety of lessons to deliver rather than having to plough all the way through the course and then start all over again from the beginning.

Although a "Qualified Flying Instructor" (QFI), I was only a B2 and, unlike B1, A2 and A1 instructors, was not permitted to send a cadet off on his first solo flight. Instead, I had to satisfy myself that he was competent and then ask the Flight Commander to give him a solo check or detail a B1 or higher to do it. My three cadets were all reasonably competent and the junior, Ryan, achieved solo standard without difficulty. I found it very interesting and rewarding to teach the basics of straight and level flight, climbing, descending and turning and then stalling and spinning before getting on to circuits and landings, with a basic introduction to forced landings as well. After that we continued with stalling and spinning and went on to aerobatics, forced landings, precautionary landings, instrument flying, night flying and formation flying. It was an absorbing and enjoyable term, and good to be flying round familiar territory and, at night, recognising the familiar beacons at Waddington, Coningsby and so on.

The grass airfield at Spitalgate, just outside Grantham, was in use as a relief landing ground for circuits and landings and instructors sending cadets solo would watch their charges from the runway controller's caravan. At night the runway was marked out on the grass by two lines of gooseneck flares. These were a little like shallow watering cans with wicks coming out of the spouts. They were filled with paraffin and were lit, just like primitive oil lamps. Naturally, they exuded some heat and at night it was interesting to watch them and see mist develop over them. When this happened, the cadets would be called in to land, pick up the instructor and get back to Cranwell before it became impossible to do so.

When the Balliols were replaced by Vampires some QFIs already qualified on that aircraft were required and I was transferred to "H"

Flight of No 4 Squadron on the advanced wing on South Airfield. This pleased me as, my first flying tour having been on De Havilland Hornets in Malaya, my only jet experience up to then had been on the CFS course. Coincidentally, the basic wing transferred to Barkston Heath and flying on the North Airfield ceased.

As a Flight Cadet I had been a member of the same "H" Flight, but the flight offices and crewrooms had moved from the old wooden huts to one of the permanent hangars. Several of the instructors had Vampire experience but the others had to get some flying time on type and get the Vampire qualification entered in their logbooks. My first few days in the flight were devoted to getting back in form on the Vampire T11, the trainer with side by side seats, and also flying the single seat Vampire FB9 which was to be used for solo flying and was the same as the aircraft formerly equipping fighter squadrons. At that stage the Vampire T11 did not have ejector seats but it did have the canopy which lifted completely rather than the earlier small hatch in the roof which must have made it difficult to escape in an emergency.

One of my cadets was MJF White, who had been with me on the Provost in "B" Flight and at the start of the next two terms I picked up the other two cadets I had trained on the Provost; but I had other cadets as well, of course. Advanced training was different from basic in several obvious ways. Most obvious was that we were not starting from scratch with basic principles but were first of all aiming to convert reasonably competent pilots to fly the Vampire and to make them familiar with the characteristics of jet engines and the higher speeds, heights and general performance they would have to cope with. Nevertheless, conversion followed much the same pattern as ab initio training in that the pupils had to be shown stalling, spinning and general flying before going on to circuits and landings. As before, pupils had to be approved as fit for solo by a B1 QFI. In the main, cadets who had done reasonably well in basic flying experienced few problems in reaching solo standard on the Vampire – but there were exceptions.

The flying syllabus at Cranwell required about 250 hours, so by the end of the course most Flight Cadets were really quite proficient and in my opinion were more proficient than I and my colleagues had been when we graduated. I put this down partly to the flying characteristics of the Vampire being less demanding than the Harvard in some ways and partly to the standard of instruction which I believe had improved over the previous four or five years. There was a rigid system of continuation training, careful supervision and frequent checks on the ability and proficiency of the instructors. All Flying Schools had "Standardisation Squadrons" to carry out checks on instructors and pupils alike to ensure that proper methods were being used and to examine instructors for Instrument Ratings and upgrading from B2 to B1.

The Vampire syllabus included high speed flight and high level aerobatics. As to the first, speeds were not so high as to be supersonic but were enough to show cadets the onset of buffet at high Mach numbers and the effect of this on controls. They then experienced this for themselves solo in the FB9s. High level aerobatics taught careful handling at low indicated but high true airspeeds at height, over-controlling usually resulting in a spin or incipient spin. Some cadets were very good indeed at aerobatics at high level and Ryan could perform a creditable stall turn with the top at over 40,000 feet. Formation flying was practised and towards the end of the course some cadets could be trusted, solo, to keep in formation on a climb through cloud and could also carry out some aerobatics in formation. Cadets were also introduced to a few simple aerobatics at night.

Spinning in the Vampire was sometimes authorised and sometimes forbidden. This was because there had been fatalities caused by failure to recover from spins. We were lectured about 'B/A ratio' and the use of in-spin aileron. Eventually the T11 was cleared for spinning but only dual and with recovery to be completed by 10,000 feet. The FB9 was never to be spun and cadets were not to spin solo in the T11. However, one instructor in "H" Flight was concerned because his cadet seemed more than a little apprehensive about spinning and aerobatics so he came to a rather drastic decision to ignore the Flying Orders and he sent the cadet up solo in a T11 with orders to carry out several spins. The instructor followed in a FB9 to see that he had been obeyed. As luck would have it, all went well and it did wonders for the cadet's confidence. Later in his career the cadet became a QFI and also led an aerobatic team.

Instructor Training (IT) or Staff Continuation Training (SCT) as it was sometimes known, was carried out when the cadets were otherwise engaged. Some of it was indeed formal training as the instructors had to keep up their Instrument Ratings and keep themselves ready for standardisation and re-categorisation tests. Often, though, SCT was an excuse for some fun. One day when there was a low cloud base so that everyone on SCT remained low and local, I entered the low flying area and spotted another Vampire carrying out a tight turn so I got on his tail only to find that he was on somebody else's tail and so on. Then I became aware that there was a Vampire behind me and I counted 10 all in a turn trying to turn inside the man behind. In 1956 – 58 there were many active airfields in Lincolnshire and East Anglia and another popular piece of SCT was to take a formation of four Vampires over Norfolk and look for some of the local fighter aircraft such as Meteors or

USAF Sabres and have a dog fight, usually getting back to Cranwell with the absolute minimum of fuel and then, after a coffee in the crewroom, getting down to the more sober business of producing more pilots for the RAF.

There were no aids to navigation in any aircraft used for training at Cranwell other than the compass, basic flight instruments and the pilot's watch and map. The only aid on the airfield was a Cathode Ray Direction Finder (CRDF) that displayed on a cathode ray tube the bearing of a received radio transmission. This enabled an aircraft to be guided down through cloud and onto a line of approach to the airfield. It was not a landing aid. Nevertheless, there was also a manual DF station at Digby and the Air Traffic Controllers had it arranged that when an aircraft called for a bearing or course to steer, the manual operator would also take a bearing and pass it to Cranwell tower so that when the aircraft was finally approaching the airfield the controller had a cross bearing which gave a range and enabled the controller to advise as to what height the aircraft should be at. This was somewhat rough and ready and also unofficial but it had some value. On one occasion the Vampire wing was rehearsing for a flypast which entailed landing and waiting at Barkston Heath. The weather deteriorated and the cloud base came down but we took off in pairs at two minute intervals and all returned safely to Cranwell using the CRDF and manual DF.

Lincolnshire weather has a reputation in the RAF and it was a constant consideration at Cranwell. Sometimes it changed rapidly during the day and I can recall looking out of the crewroom window and seeing a bank of fog advancing eastwards at a fast walking pace after having formed on the escarpment, Lincoln Edge, a few miles to the west. A system of black and white flags was flown in the signals square outside the Control Tower, a white flag meaning no restrictions, a black flag meaning no flying at all, and a black and white flag meaning dual only. This latter category was then sub-divided into other restrictions such as "only two aircraft per flight" or "one per flight" etc. After a few days of black flag everyone longed for an improvement and at the first sight of this instructors would be pressing to be allowed to fly a weather check. Usually it would be the duty QFI in the tower who would ask for a check and would obviously ask his own flight to do the necessary. The lucky instructor chosen would then have the pleasure of taking off into, usually, still fairly low cloud and then popping out of the top of it like a cork out of a bottle. The transition from the gloom below cloud into the brilliant blue of the sky and the whiteness of the cloud below was something always to be savoured, particularly after days of inactivity and gloomy weather. Indeed, that magical transition is something enjoyed by pilots flying in every role "... shaking off the surly bonds of earth". On the report of the weather checker depended the colour of the flags and the progress of flying

The "H" Flight crewroom was a very friendly and, indeed, jolly place because we had a good bunch of chaps. After a few months with Vampires and the inevitable changes because of postings in and out, we settled down with a mainly young group of instructors, most of whom had a fighter background. Two older men were Paul Pritchet, who had flown Spitfires and Tempests at the end of and just after the war; and Bob Mackie, an Australian who had been awarded the DFC flying Spitfires on Photo Reconnaissance during the war. On pulling his leg about his accent, Bob told us that on returning home after the war his father greeted him with "Jeez, Bob! Where'd you get that flaming Oxford accent?" Ever after that we called him "Oxford Mac".

Our crew room was like that in a fighter squadron, with people in and out all the time and, if there was a lull because of bad weather, a lot of pilots all together. In contrast, in the crewrooms of eg transport, maritime or bomber squadrons, some crews are usually away from base and others are busy planning so that it is rare for many to be together and there is not the same camaraderie – although some may dispute that. There was always some sort of banter and chat going on and a few practical jokes. To many these things would appear childish and this reminds me of the small boy at the air display who was sitting in the cockpit of a fighter plane and had been allowed to put on the pilot's helmet. Completely overawed, the boy said to the pilot "I want to be a fighter pilot when I grow up!". The response to this was "Well. Make your mind up, son. You can't do both!"

In addition to the banter there was also serious talk about all manner of subjects such as developments in training and how individual pupils were progressing. It was a daily occurrence for QFIs to be preparing their brief for the next lesson and then go into the briefing area to teach their pupil with the aid of blackboard and chalk. Came the time when F Gordon Agnew arrived to become OC 4 Squadron; Jock Agnew had come from the Examining Wing of the Central Flying School, and thus was not only a "trapper" but an A1 instructor to boot. At first he seemed an awesome character and appeared to enjoy the trapper reputation. He would suddenly appear in the crew room and, naming one of the instructors, say "I want a brief on maximum rate turns in 15 minutes!" Or else he would ask one of the trappers' old chestnuts such as "What is the longest piece of metal in the aircraft?" (Answer, "the winding of the generator" – a particularly useless piece of information but just part of the give and take of the trapping set-up.) Jock Agnew improved greatly with time and we developed a great respect and, indeed, liking for him.

The crewroom itself was not very large, with a table and chair and a number of arm chairs. The inevitable kettle was on the window sill with a few mugs and somewhere there was a cardboard box with jars of coffee and milk powder as well as a quantity of things such as Wagon Wheels and Penguin bars. These were the energy foods it was thought that we needed and so they were issued free of charge. Between the crew room and the flight commander's office was a sort of hallway where there were filing cabinets containing the Forms 5000 relating to each cadet. After every single dual flight the instructor had to write a report and file it in the cadet's folder (RAF Form 5000). Sometimes the QFI would be a little bored with either having to write a report or even with his pupil and so some rather irregular phrases would creep in such as "After a few spins Bloggs parked his custard again" (meaning that the poor cadet seemed prone to be airsick) or "he levelled out at carrot knots and tomato thousand feet" – another reference to airsickness, those vegetables always seeming to be prevalent in such cases, and staple items in the cadets' diet. Once I saw "Bloggs is not fit to drive a corporation dustcart". This caused the Squadron Commander to demand, quite reasonably, to have explained to him why, in that case, Bloggs was being allowed to fly one of Her Majesty's valuable aircraft. The Forms 5000 were reviewed regularly by the Flight and Squadron Commanders and, of course, also contained reports on every flying test. In this way a very close eye was kept on each pupil's progress.

By the spring of 1956 our Flight Commander was Clive Francis who had been a Flight Cadet in 47 Entry. He was a "press on" and, indeed, forceful character and it was he who delighted in leading a four over Norfolk to see what sport might be found. Clive also formed and led an aerobatic team and seemed determined that "H" Flight should be as much like a fighter squadron as possible. His determination was tested to the full when flying one day on Staff Continuation Training.

After a short time our T11s were fitted with ejection seats and also leg restrainers. These were two lengths of webbing anchored to the floor of the cockpit and which were threaded through metal "D" rings on straps around the leg of the pilot, just below the knee. The ends of these webbing restraints had loops through which the lugs of the shoulder harness straps were placed before being secured in the parachute harness quick release box (QRB). The idea was that on ejecting, as the seat rose the restrainers would pull the legs together so that they would not splay out in the airstream, with the risk of damage to the hip joints and pelvis. As the seat rose higher the anchor points would break and release the restrainers from the cockpit floor. Unfortunately, we had not been told to ensure that the restrainers were placed under the QRB before inserting the shoulder strap ends. In Clive's case, it transpired that his restrainers passed over the outside of the QRB. It came to pass that during the SCT flight in question some emergency arose which made it necessary to abandon the aircraft. The other pilot ejected and landed safely. Clive ejected and as he descended through 10,000 feet the barometric device operated to move the release lever of the QRB as it was supposed to do in order to allow the pilot to fall away from the seat so that the parachute could open. In this case the lever moved only enough to jam itself on the restrainers. Clive then spent some agonising moments clearing the jam and in the end the seat fell away, the 'chute opened and, after only a few seconds, Clive's feet touched the ground and he saw that the seat had landed just a few yards from him.

Clive was succeeded by Brian Ball (49 Entry) who had won the DFC flying Meteors with the Australian 77 Squadron in Korea. He took over the formation team and had the same sort of outlook on flying as Clive but was less flamboyant. Nevertheless, he had a good sense of humour and was greatly respected.

Another instance of the danger of incomplete knowledge came when one of my cadets managed to put out the flame in his engine but carried out a successful relight procedure which ought not to have worked! On the Vampire FB9, the single seat aircraft, there was a rotary time switch to work the high energy igniters and we were under the impression that to relight the engine one closed the High Pressure fuel cock, rotated the time switch and when it had ticked back to the start, opened the HP cock slowly. After this incident we found that we ought to open the HP cock while the switch was ticking and the HE igniters were cracking (which could not be heard in the cockpit in flight). With hindsight this was obvious, but we had not known. The cadet must have slightly jumped the gun and caught the engine with the last crack of the igniters. As a corollary, the Squadron Commander told me to take my cadet up in a T11 and find out exactly what he had done to flame out the engine. Accordingly we climbed up to about 10,000 feet and I told him to show me. "I was practising maximum rate turns and breaks, Sir, like you showed me" As regards the "breaks" I had told him to fly at speed and then put on a lot of bank and pull the stick back. Flying dual he had repeated this satisfactorily but when I called "Break Starboard!" during this trip he put on about 60 degrees of bank, and jerked the stick back hard into his stomach so that we flickrolled merrily up and up. The T11 accepted this but the FB9 had not.

As a matter of interest, the cadet was an Iraqi by the name of Munther al Wandawi. He was a good pilot, an intelligent young man and was likeable and popular, with a well-developed sense of humour. So far as I was concerned he would have been a credit to the RAF or any other air force. Just before the 1991 Gulf War I saw Wandawi on TV news speaking as the Iraqi ambassador in Paris! So, he was indeed a man of many talents.

During my time as a QFI at Cranwell there were some accidents but I believe that the accident rate in training was better by that time than it had been only a few years before, eg in the Meteor Advanced Flying Schools of the early '50s. A month or so after I arrived the Provosts were flying one night when the weather deteriorated quickly and one aircraft was left trying to get down on to the north airfield. After several attempts and missed approaches it struck a tree and both instructor and cadet were killed. Not long after training started on Vampires, Bill Worsley (55 Entry) of "G" Flight, was killed together with his cadet. I have an idea that he had spun out of a stall turn and did not manage to recover. In 1958, Don Murchie, a popular instructor in "H" Flight was killed in a flying accident. On another occasion, from the crewroom window we could see a crash take place at the end of the runway.

Bill was a man we knew well and so was Don and we were extremely sorry that they had, as the saying went, "bought it". However, we did not all collapse and find it impossible to go on without "counselling" and "grieving" and I and my generation find it strange to see how the media now hype these things up and, in hushed tones, talk of whole towns "coming to terms" with some unfortunate situation such as a murder. Perhaps it was because we were mixing with men who had fought in the Second World War when there was no opportunity to drop everything and grieve so they just got on with the job in hand. Also, we had all been in squadrons or flying schools when friends had been killed and the same ethos applied. Further, we lost three friends from our own Cranwell entry within a few months of graduation and of the 31 of us who graduated seven have been killed – a high casualty rate for peacetime. There were three fatalities in No 33 Squadron during my first flying tour. The rest of us were sorry to lose friends, were happy that we had survived, carried the coffins at the funerals, had a few drinks and, dare I say it, a few laughs afterwards and then carried on. We were not heroes and neither were we callous. I prefer to think that we were simply realistic and knew that nothing said or done could change the situation and so life just had to go on.

There were other Old Cranwellians back on the staff as QFIs and as Cadet Wing Officers ("housemasters") and it was good to see the return of Brian Meadley and Tony Dawes in the latter capacity, as Flight Commanders of the Junior Entries. However, although I believe they envied us because we were flying, we did not envy them their job which required them to be, as the Army would say, "Regimental" at all times. We scruffy instructors were actually an embarrassment when, as we did one day when the weather precluded flying, we visited them in their offices. Soft flannel aircrew shirts, and trousers tucked into flying boots, did not accord with their dress code. I recall amusing ourselves by going through the card index of punishments meted out to cadets for a variety of offences. Two offences which stick in my memory were "Whilst on drill parade, smiling at the incompetence of his fellows" and "During Squadron Commander's room inspection, having black laces in his brown civilian shoes".

When not actually flying there were always other things to do, briefing one's cadets, writing reports and, of course, secondary duties. These might include a variety of tasks but mine was to be holder of the inventory of engineering tools. With a number of airmen each supplied with a kit of tools all on the same inventory this was sometimes a real nightmare when a routine inventory check was required. The large items such as starter trolleys and tow bars were easy to account for but there were hundreds of small hand tools such as files and screwdrivers. Luckily, the Station Equipment Officer, a Squadron Leader, was both sympathetic and helpful and many a surplus item of one type was "converted" to a deficient item of another type by means of a Form 21. This ingenious "conversion" system was, I am sure, employed throughout the service and would no doubt now be described as "creative stocktaking". This reminds me of an inventory problem I met years later as OC 103 Squadron in Singapore. Some of the Squadron's helicopters were used for Search and Rescue and the SAR inventory included an item listed as "Bolts, copper". I asked to see these copper bolts and to have their purpose explained. The bolts could not be found and even the old experienced SAR aircrew NCOs did not know what do with them if they could be found. Finally it transpired that "bolts, copper" was a transcription error for "bolt croppers" used for cutting in rescue operations!

As flying instructors we were expected to play a wider part in the life of the college by eg attending dinner and guest nights, attending church parade, turning out to watch sports (wearing a hat, of course) and taking part in sports. I was never much good at games and although I had played rugby for RAF Butterworth in Malaya I did not feel up to the more intense and serious approach to rugby at Cranwell. Instead, I had a stab at fencing. Not the elegant kind, but bayonet fencing. I do not know precisely how I got into that but seem to recall that Flight Sergeant Bendelow, a PTI from our cadet days and still in post at the gym, persuaded me because he needed someone to make up numbers. The bayonet was not a popular way of fencing and I believe it was a relic of the Army of the late 19th and early 20th centuries. The fencer wore a very heavy padded jacket something like that worn by a baseball catcher, heavy gauntlet gloves and a heavy and substantial helmet made of thick hide and with a face guard of a heavy mesh. The word "heavy" is most appropriate. The weapon was a dummy rifle with a "bayonet" in the form of a steel rod which slid like a piston against a spring in the barrel of the rifle. The act of fencing was strenuous, to say the least, because of the weight of the weapon and the protective clothing. Bendelow then had me take part in the inter-command fencing championships at St Athan but I was not awarded colours for Flying Training Command. During that competition they even got me to fence with the foil because someone had fallen out.

Later I was persuaded to try putting the shot and, with rather more success, I was in the Flying Wing Tug o' War team. This was a baby of the Chief Flying Instructor, Group Captain Brooks, who was determined that we should win. To help achieve this he had us out training in the early mornings and also took us to dinner at Woodhall Spa. This was very enjoyable but by no means good training. Other than that, I swam in the command Sea Survival competition between Flying Training Schools, and we won! Groupy Brooks thereupon took us to the bar in the mess at lunchtime and insisted we celebrate with the trophy filled and refilled with Dragons' Blood – a concoction of Guinness, champagne and brandy. I did not make it to the Flight party in the Red Lion at Caythorpe that night. Next morning the Group Captain came to the crew room to see how we were and confessed that he had had trouble with his horse the previous afternoon. Having found the need to dismount several times he tried to re-mount but found it necessary to climb on a wall to do so. Unfortunately, the horse entered into the spirit of the thing and put its forefeet up on the wall as well.

The Red Lion at Caythorpe was a popular pub for Flight parties, as it had been in our cadet days. This was before the breathalyser but, of course, there were still laws about drink driving. However, one night after such a party I was driving my Morris Minor Traveller (very carefully) behind the 1938 Austin 7 driven by one Mike Tarrant when his front passenger door opened and a young QFI, Hugh Bever, he who sent his cadet spinning solo, stood on the running board, holding onto the roof and striking sparks off the road with his heels. In that manner we processed to the college main gates and the Austin drove onto the sacred

Orange. With what purpose the passengers had in mind after an evening of good ale I will leave to the imagination.

Commanding the Vampire Wing of the College was Wing Commander Ian MacDonald who, like Jock Agnew, had been a trapper. He was what is now referred to as "laid back" and was a popular figure. I flew with him to recategorise from B2 to B1 and all we did was fly to Hatfield for a meeting he had to attend and then back to Cranwell. His briefing was "I'll just sit there fat, dumb and happy while you fly it and tell me what you're doing." Recategorising to A2 was a different kettle of fish and involved an overnight stay at CFS at Little Rissington and a thorough grilling on the ground before and after two sorties. I had neither the wish, nor enough ability, to become an A1 instructor and those who had both inevitably returned to CFS as instructors or trappers. My friend John Hardaker, also from "H" Flight, went that route and, sadly, was killed when his parachute failed to deploy after ejecting from a Hunter during an examining visit to an OCU.

To get back to Mac, after one of our rare Station Parades he went up to each of his squadron commanders in turn and told them "Your squadron was the best!" There was also the story about Mac and the planning of a flypast for a College parade. It was decided that the formation would have to be overhead the Orange just as the Advance in Review Order had been completed and with the order for the General Salute about to be given. Mac, it was said, sat patiently listening to all this and then the College Secretary said "I don't understand how you are going to be overhead at the precise moment". Mac replied "The band is on the steps of the college and the bass drummer wears a leopard skin. Right?" College Secretary: "Yes. But what has that to do with it?" Mac: "Well. Don't you see? We have a radio in the front hall with a cable running down the steps, over the shoulder of the bass drummer, under his leopard skin and to a microphone inside the drum. When we hear the third beat we all fly over".

Ian MacDonald was sympathetic to us QFIs and allowed some of us who had not flown the Meteor to have some familiarisation training (one dual and two solo flights) when we represented to him that as Duty QFIs in the ATC tower we were expected to advise cadets flying those aircraft. This had come about when a small flight of Meteors was established for the benefit of those cadets who were too tall to fit into the Vampire. Mac also arranged for a few of us to go to Rissington to familiarise ourselves with the Hunter. The excuse for that was that some of our cadets would go to the Hunter after graduation and we ought to know what they were in for. I went down with another QFI and after a skim through the Pilots' Notes the previous evening, the instructor concerned briefed us in a car on the way from Rissington to Kemble, where the Hunters were based. So far as I was concerned, and the same applied to my colleague, he gave further briefing as I sat on a kitchen chair in front of a lifesize photograph of the Hunter F4 cockpit and then, still talking, took me to an aircraft, strapped me in, pointed out the various controls and dials, pushed the starter button, gave a "thumbs up" and left me to it. Then followed six flights in the F4, including a "boom" or supersonic flight. There was no dual control Hunter T7 trainer.

All this indicates the sort of spirit in which our training system operated in those years. Most of the instructors were post–war, including Cranwell graduates, but there was a leavening of those who had flown in the war. We were instructing on jet aircraft which had been part of the front line not long before and it was really quite an exciting time and a lot of fun. I found the experience rewarding in many ways, including the fact that my own flying skill improved considerably. However, nobody was really keen to remain on training as we all wanted to get back to operational squadrons. The V Force started to expand in 1956 and we could see mighty Vulcans flying just up the road at Waddington. Volunteers were invited to apply and several instructors went to fly the Vulcan. I thought about it but dismissed the idea after a few minutes. I did, though, volunteer with many others to reinforce the squadrons of Venoms engaged in the Suez operations. To our disgust, the only pilot chosen from Cranwell was the Commandant's ADC – and he did not actually go.

My time for posting came in 1958 and I was given my first choice, namely Photographic Reconnaissance, flying Canberras (it has been interesting, in 2004, to see on TV the same Canberra PR9s being used over Iraq as I was flying in 1960!) At the time I was pleased to move on but I have often looked back fondly on my very enjoyable time as a QFI back at Cranwell.   [F.D.H.]

Postscript: Some 45 years later, when taking a grandson round the Fleet Air Arm Museum at Yeovilton, I saw that they had on display the fuselage of a Vampire T22 (the Naval equivalent of the T11) with an invitation to sit in it. I found that my head, without a helmet, almost touched the canopy and that the instrument panel seemed to be very close to the eyes. Even without a flying suit and life-jacket there was very little room and I wondered how I could have taught and, even more so, how cadets could have learnt to fly in that cramped space. But I did, and they did!

THE OTHER SIDE OF THE COIN
A "HOUSEMASTER" AT CRANWELL!

Following my second flying tour – as a Vampire QFI at RAF Oakington – I knew that a ground tour was coming. Sure enough, I arrived at Cranwell in July 1957 to take up my post as OC No 2 Flight, B Squadron – No 2 Flight comprising the two junior entries. The OC Junior Entries, as we remember him, was being replaced by three Flight Commanders, one for each of A, B and C Squadrons. And who should occupy the next door office as the Flight Commander of A Squadron but Brian Meadley! The routine was very similar to that of eight years previously so I found myself doing all the same things that I did as a cadet, although from the supervisory standpoint! I had to watch drill daily, give lectures, take charges, hold interviews and attend dinner nights.

The day would start at 7.15 am to watch my squadron drilling. We all remember dinner nights and twice a week I had to pack my car with my dinner jacket for the dinners at 8.00 pm. After watching drill parades I had to inspect bedspaces and kit layout, then I would watch other aspects of their training – and who will ever forget swimming, dinghy drill, PT and road drill? Who, also, will ever forget the Orderly Room daily? Only this time the boot was on the other foot and I had to deal with cadets charged for the customary offences – from untidy kit, poor drill or "smiling on parade". The gravity of some offences often bemused me and I couldn't always get in the mood to deal with them. But deal with them I had to. Other exciting activities we will all remember include watching sport, attending Church Parade every Sunday and participating (fully) in every Leadership and Survival Camp in the Cairngorms. At times I think I would have preferred to have been a cadet!

I also had to be available in my office at lunchtimes for interviews requested by cadets. Their reasons varied, but were in the main personal problems. Sometimes the queue for interviews and charges would stretch down the corridor and join the queue waiting to see Brian! I always remember one interview when the cadet was almost in tears. He was worried over some of his poor exam results, an instructor was being heavy on him and he wanted to withdraw from training. He brightened up considerably when I told him that I had suffered the same problem as a cadet (true) and that I would speak to the instructor. He didn't suspend and became a future very senior air officer! So perhaps it was all worthwhile after all.   [A.D.R.D.]

LAME DOGS

My career as a QFI did not start very auspiciously. My very first student on Meteors had a nervous breakdown.

Being proud of my new status as a QFI, and having had no previous students with whom to compare him, I did my best to nurse him along. He had been a second pilot on B29 Washingtons, and I did not realise he was terrified of the Meteor. I thought all student pilots climbed out of the aircraft soaked in sweat and unable to speak.

Then one day we were on an asymmetric approach to Croft airfield (now a racing circuit). An embankment carrying the main Edinburgh to London railway line crosses the approach path. We were getting far too low and I had to take over. The rudder footload was terrific and took all my strength to hold. Fortunately we made the runway.

The reason for the almost impossible footload was that my student had panicked, and was desperately pushing the wrong pedal, so that I had been fighting not only the live engine, but him as well. Men in white coats led him away sobbing, while my flight commander gently explained that I should have reported his problems and had him checked long since.

A few years later, I was instructing on the Vampire T11. I had a student who was a bit clumsy and slow, but who made what I thought was adequate progress. Being a more senior QFI by that time, I was able to authorise him for solo myself, without a second opinion. The day came when he seemed to me to be ready. I sent him off and informed the Duty Instructor in the tower.

Ten minutes later the DI telephoned to say something odd was up, and would I come to the tower. I found him peering through binoculars at my T11, which was standing at the marshalling post. Apparently it had been there for some time, and the pilot was not answering R/T calls. The NCO in the caravan reported that he could see no one in the cockpit. I went out in the Air Traffic Control Landrover to see what was going on. The aircraft was standing there with its engine running, and right enough, no pilot could be seen. Braving the howling Goblin engine, I managed to climb up and open the canopy.

The student had been slumped over the controls, but now sat up, looking dazed. I got in and taxied back to dispersal. After I shut down, he explained that he could remember setting out for his flight, but at the marshalling post everything had gone blurred and he thought he had fainted.

Again, it was a case of someone terrified of flying who had forced himself to subdue this fear and actually cope with flying training as far as jets. In the Vampire, with its side-by-side seating, he had good kind

Uncle Robbie beside him, patiently showing him how to do things and ready to take over if he couldn't manage. Then came his solo. While doing his take-off checks, he saw the empty seat and the shock hit him! No good kind Uncle Robbie! It was too much, and he passed out.......

He was taken off flying, and remustered as an intelligence officer.

As for me, I gave up helping lame dogs over stiles after that. What most lame dogs actually need is a kick in the backside and a good haircut.   [R.H.R.]

THE BOYS ARE OUT LOOKING...

I was still a fairly new boy on my first Meteor Squadron based in Germany. Autumn was closing in and with it came worse weather, which did not always behave as advertised by the met man. (Does that German met man still say that 'the vind is weering?')

I was flying a low-level cross-country navigation exercise. In those days we had no other navigation aids than a map on the knee – very satisfying when it was successful, but, well, you can guess the alternative.

On the last leg home the weather steadily deteriorated. The cloud base got lower and lower and more indeterminate – the visibility too got worse and worse and was aggravated by a grey, miserable, misty drizzle. I continued to keep track of my position as best I could, but eventually I had to admit to myself that I was uncertain of my position (the standard euphemism of the time for 'lost').

Soon the cloud base was just above the tree tops (the smaller ones anyway) and the drizzle grew darker and more menacing by the minute. It was possible to call base and get a course to steer, but it was considered *infra dig* to do so, so I continued gaping from map to ground and ground to map in the hope of spotting somewhere recognisable. Nothing recognisable showed up and the fuel gauges seemed to be moving relentlessly faster and faster towards the zero mark. Infra dig or not, the time had come to call for a steer. It was then that I learned that the radio was not working; quite dead in fact. This was the opposite of serendipity – the humiliation of having to call for a steer without the benefit of actually getting one. On the other hand, at least nobody knew that I had been reduced to that desperate measure. Not that there was time to ruminate over Nature's fickleness.

During our training, the RAF had drilled into us that when things got difficult the thing to do was to make a plan and stick to it. I made a plan and stuck to it. Knowing that I must have been somewhere near base, I resolved to start a square search for it and that if I had not found it when my fuel was down to ten gallons per side, I would either climb up and eject or carry out a forced landing in a field. It took only a few more minutes for the gauges to register ten each – minutes in which the airfield failed to materialise. So this was it – but which to do? There were only seconds in which to decide, but it took only half of one of those to decide to land in a field. Though I had done the parachute course, I had never jumped in cloud, and did not relish the idea of doing so now. In hindsight, of course, perhaps it would have been better to have climbed up into cloud and ejected. But as mentioned before, I was a new boy.

A line of trees appeared out of the mist and the field beyond it would be as good as any. Keep the gear up but put down about a third flap. Clear the trees – good – close the throttles and select full flap. Put her down. Just as the aircraft was about to touch, the edge of a forest suddenly appeared out of the gloom. To hit it at this speed would be eye watering to say the least. So open the throttles for a missed approach. Before the engines had a chance to increase rpm and develop some thrust, the underside of the engine nacelles touched the ground. But it was still better to go through with the go around, which had now become a touch and go. The aircraft slid on the nacelles for some yards and then got airborne again. At least the low fuel state gave a low take - off weight! Over the woods and another field in sight. Very short of fuel now – land in the next field regardless. This time there was enough distance and the aircraft touched down and came slithering and sliding to a fairly rapid stop.

As briefed for this situation, I quickly left the cockpit, ran a few yards and threw myself on to the ground to avoid the worst of the imminent explosion. After a few moments I cautiously raised my head and opened my eyes. Somewhat disappointingly there was no blinding flash nor the sound of an explosion. But there was the sound of jet engines. "How slick", I thought, "The boys are out looking for me already!" It then dawned on me that the sound was that of my own engines – in my haste I had not taken the time out to close them down. So they were still running and drawing in tons of soil and expelling huge black clouds. Hoping that no one had noticed, I went back to the cockpit and shut down the engines and made the ejector seat safe.

It was at this time that the farmer arrived, looking very anxious. He took me to his farmhouse and we telephoned Gutersloh and told them what had happened and where we were. He then proposed that we have a beer, a course of action that met with my total approval. After several more he produced a bottle of schnapps and suggested that we change to that. Schnapps is an acquired taste. I acquired it.

Then my Squadron Commander arrived – the excellent Bob Pugh. He was a fine commander, in particular in the way that he trained and encouraged new pilots on their first tour. He was most concerned about me until he was satisfied that I was not hurt. I assured him that I was not even bruised, and apologised for breaking one of his aircraft.

"Ah! The aircraft," he said. "I suppose you know that you will have to pay for the damage. They will stop it out of your pay."

Considering the miserable salary we were paid in those days, it was clear that it would take decades to clear the debt. Then he grinned broadly at me, and for the first time in my young career, I realised that squadron commanders were capable of having a sense of humour. The farmer invited him to join us for a glass of schnapps, and the relish with which he did so suggested that he had already acquired the taste.

The aircraft was recovered and was flying again in two weeks, which it certainly would not have been had I ejected, so perhaps I got something right.

If by chance you should read this, Bob, my warmest regards to you – it was a pleasure to serve under you. [B.M.]

HI-FLITE – ACROSS THE ATLANTIC IN AN F84

During my tour of duty with the USAF at Shaw Air Force Base in South Carolina I had graduated from the RF84F to the mighty F101 Voodoo which I flew for the first time in December 1957 and bust my first ten tons a few days later. But in February 1958 the Voodoo's fuel piping developed a snag with the Marmon clamps. As the fuel flow in afterburner at ground level was some 72,000 pounds per hour, it was rather important that there was uninterrupted flow to the J57 engine.

So we were grounded for a few weeks while a retrofit was made and installed and I was asked if I would like a temporary duty job ferrying F84Fs from the repair base to the launch base for Hi-Flites, a well-used system of ferrying aircraft to Europe for various allied air forces. I jumped at the opportunity and three of us set off from my squadron at Shaw to Mobile in Alabama, where the airfield seemed to me to be totally covered in F84Fs, the venerable fighter version of my old friends the RF84F, an unarmed reconnaissance machine as opposed to this heavily armed animal.

Finally, when we had shipped all these aircraft to Warner Robins we three were asked if we would like to do a Hi-Flite to Europe and once again we jumped at the opportunity of something new.

Ferrying a single-engined single-seat aircraft across the Atlantic Ocean never became "old hat" and we ferried our machines as they became serviceable to Harmon AFB in Newfoundland where we joined up with 21 other F84Fs and waited for the right tail wind with a certain amount of trepidation and old fashioned smelly fear! The range from Harmon to Lajes in the Azores is 1,485 nautical miles and the dry tanks range of the

"Superhog" was 1,450 nautical miles with two 450 gallon drop tanks so a tail wind of sorts was rather necessary and we got down to the tedious business of waiting.

"Let's go fishing". I suggested.

"Where?"

"On the beach. We can get poles from the sports store and frozen prawns from the commissary for bait."

The three Shaw men set off and we found a comfortable fishing stand on the wing of a crashed F89 Scorpion which was lying in a tangled mess in line with the runway.

Minutes later we were hauling in magnificent flounders of about three to four pounds each and having made a fire of driftwood we baked a couple, and delicious they were, too. Since we had landed very nearly 100 pounds of fish we decided to donate it to the Transit Mess and we found a pole and a length of wire and transported them back like a lot of safari bearers.

A small boy came past on a bicycle along the shore.

"Flatfish. Huh?"

"Lots of them".

"Prefer cod, myself".

"They're not biting".

"They are now."

Fifteen minutes later he pedalled past in the other direction with a huge cod tied to the handlebars.

"Cod." He said.

The Transit Mess was delighted to get our fish; theirs was always flown in, frozen, from the ZI and at supper lots of people had fresh flounder fried in butter, but they charged the three fishermen for the chips!

Early next morning we heard the cry "It's GO, guys!" I looked out of the window into the February morning of gloom and grey fog and thought that someone in authority was losing his grip. We were all chattering over breakfast at a significantly higher pitch than normal, then donned our immersion suits and trooped off to briefing. Flight logs and plans were issued, emergencies discussed and frequencies checked.

"Duckbutt Bravo will be along your route with a NDB and you will overfly him until you have tracked outbound on your way to Lajes". The Duckbutt was an SA16 amphibian with a beacon on board which would be stationed half way along our route to give us guidance. Or so the plan was.

Twenty four machines started up and taxied slowly to the take off point. Patches of fog were still swirling around but it was clearing rapidly.

"Hi-Flite leader ready for take-off!"

"Hi-Flite leader cleared for take-off as briefed. Sections of fours, one minute intervals. Wind easterly 7 knots, Good luck fellas!"

"Hi-Flite leader rolling.!"

With two 450 gallon drop tanks the F84F was no great accelerator but we were safely airborne in plenty of time and popped out of patchy fog into bright blue and the long climb to cruise altitude began.

There was little of the good natured chat usual in large Balbos, the apprehension level was too high; then leader called

"Hey, guys. I have the Duckbutt far to the left."

"So have I, leader."

"Me too. What the hell's going on?"

"Duckbutt Bravo this is Hi-Flite leader."

"Go ahead."

"You're 'way off to our left. You should be right ahead."

"Checking the beacon and our position."

"Duckbutt. Are you sure you're on station?" This was long before the happy days of GNS and the navigators had to depend on all the witchcraft and wizardry of which only navigators were capable.

"Damn right!"

"Well, with this angle and rate of change of angle we're not going to make any dry land."

"Hi-Flite leader, my navigator reckons you are 200 miles south of track".

"Jesus! We're past PNR and the Azores is the only dry land possible."

"Shit!" Many voices joined in the chorus with variations on the theme. Mouths were getting so dry that further sensible discussion was nearly impossible.

"Hi-Flite leader. Duckbutt Bravo."

"Yah."

"A confession here. Navigator has recalculated and we are 200 miles off position."

"Goddam all navigators!"

"Shoot the bastard!" "Hang him!" and the radio got very jammed with expletives of every blasphemous nature.

Half an hour elapsed.

"Leader, I have Lajes beacon on the nose."

"Right on the nose?

"Yeah."

One by one came the call "Me too!" and a few minutes later – "Land Ho!"

"Hey fellas, that's a volcano!"

"So? It's dry!"

And soon Terceira Island and Lajes hove up. The engines started to run smoothly again! "Salt water mag drop" was a celebrated phenomenon over open sea even with jets which didn't have magnetos. A very Anglophile Colonel met us.

"Hi there Limey. Good trip?"

"Bit of a bollocks with the Duckbutt, Colonel, but leader will tell you all about that."

"Doesn't need to. The Duckbutt captain has been demoted and the navigator has been fired."

"Christ! That's quick!"

"What would Her Majesty say if we drowned you?"

"She's never heard of me."

"But you've been counted!"

Two days of warm sunshine and marvellous food and excellent port at two shillings the bottle cheered us up and we waited for a plus one tailwind for our next jump to Deols AFB at Chateauroux, in France.

The day of the requisite tailwind dawned and we were hustled into briefing and once again began the great procession of groaning, squealing F84Fs to the take-off point and away we went, six neat sections of four aircraft and this time I was No.2 to the leader. We climbed up to 30,000 feet and began the slow drift upwards as the weight dropped because of fuel consumption. Leader slid close to me, waggled his wings and tapped his mike as the indication his radio had quit and I was now the leader.

"Hi-Flite this is No2. Leader has radio failure. I lead now."

"Redcoats are coming!"

"Yahoo, Limey! Hope your homing instincts are good." And such like light banter clogged the radio.

Some time later –

"Leader, we should see Vigo by now."

"I know it."

"No tailwind here. I think a headwind."

"I know that too."

Vigo eventually appeared far distant on the right and far behind schedule. Our "Brain" – and there's always one in a crowd – called:

"I figure we have a 40 knot headwind

"This is going to be close, people." I said, "Bordeaux for us."

Half way across Biscay came the cry from tail-end Charlie –

"Bingo! 700 pounds with the warning light on." Some 8,900 pounds of fuel had gone.

"Bingo!"

"Bingo!"

"Bingo!"

One by one they called in.

"Leader here. Clear the air" pause, "Mayday. Mayday. Mayday." And I filled in the details of our predicament.

"Hi-Flite leader, this is Navy XYZ" – probably a nuclear submarine. "We are relaying your Mayday. There's help on the way."

"Hi-Flite leader this is Air Force 121. We have radar contact. How many ships in your formation?"

"Twenty four".

"Say that agin slowly."

"Twenty four. Two fower."

"Jeeze!" Then a pause to digest this approaching calamity.

"Leader, this is Air Force 121. Bordeaux is in thick fog and well below limits."

"Lovely! Bloody lovely bloody French!"

"Not now. Limey."

"Leader this is No.6 section. We are low on fuel we will make one pass at Bordeaux and then bang out."

"Leader this is Navy. If you all have to jump, do it close together and we will guarantee rescue."

"Good lad."

"My pleasure. Sir."

Number six section descended to the coast at Bordeaux.

"Six leader. OK fellas, one pass then up and bang out."

Minutes passed, very slowly.

"Hi-Flite leader. Six here. We're on the ground!"

"Weather OK?"

"Weather shit," said the trembling voice. "We'll get to the beer before you!"

But they didn't, since the French arrested them and initially chucked them in the brig, causing a few ruffled feathers in NATO corridors.

We all tested our pet theories. Some stayed aloft and made crash dives at the Deols runway. Some switched off their engines and relit at 10,000 feet. Two crazy fellows of Polish descent came in for a break and landing and ran out of fuel on short finals. The whole thing was a major lip-biting exercise and nearly all ran out of fuel at various places on the taxi track and dispersal. I switched off with the fuel gauge on zero and strangely the engine thumped to a sudden stop. Engineers explained to me later that my oil system had failed and I had been running on molten bearings for God knows how long.

There was our Anglophile colonel again, this time with a very large case of cold beers and he tossed two into the cockpit. Then he drove off in a jeep to every aircraft wherever it had stopped and tossed two beers into each cockpit. The Americans are a kind and thoughtful people.

My stomach for Hi-Flites had hit rock bottom and it wasn't very long before I was assigned to another – but now with two engines and air-to-air refuelling and this time I reached my destination at Nouasseur, Casa Blanca, non-stop from the USA with 6,000 pounds of fuel remaining in a single seat fighter aircraft. That's more like it!

R.P.J.K.

SURVIVAL AND EVASION

RAF Arctic Survival Course

In March 1954, RAF Bruggen received a signal from Headquarters 2nd Tactical Air Force seeking two pilots to attend the RAF's Arctic Survival School course in Ehrwald, Austria, to the northwest of Innsbruck. Another pilot on the squadron and I were "volunteered". During the two weeks before the course started I took the opportunity of going to the gym to strengthen my knees and ankles in preparation for the skiing that was to be part of the course.

The course comprised two days lectures on survival practices and techniques, followed by two days and nights in the nearby woods, each pair of aircrew being given a parachute and some emergency flying rations. Part 3 of the course, namely skiing instruction, followed. The slopes and lifts were about a mile away from the school and students had to ski there cross country before starting lessons – 20 minutes to the slopes, two hours skiing, 20 minutes back to the school for lunch and then the same procedure in the afternoon. The ski lift was a continuously moving, spaced out anchor/chair lift. With skis parallel you had to grab the moving anchor as it came to you, stuff it between your legs and around your bottom, hold onto the bar and, keeping the skis parallel, brace your legs and allow yourself to be taken up the slope. Initially we would put too much weight on the anchor, slide down on the ground and the hook would catch in our jackets and tow us up the slope on our bellies! We soon got the hang of it but it was hilarious at the time.

The remainder of the skiing was not so funny for some who literally fell by the wayside with broken ankles, one broken leg and, often, sheer exhaustion. I was glad of that fitness training in the gym. So there were not many of us left for the end of course timed race from the top of the piste to the finishing line which, if reached, earned us a bronze, silver or gold award.

Après-ski activities in the local Gasthaus, another ski trip away, awaited those still able to stand by the evening.

Escape and Evasion Exercise

In August 1954 another signal from HQ 2nd TAF sought two volunteer aircrew to participate in a Royal Norwegian Air Force Escape and Evasion Exercise. I again "volunteered" with a colleague. After an uncomfortable trip in an Anson (memories of the Junior Entries and the little brown paper bag) we arrived at Gardermoen Air Base, about 50 miles north of Oslo, to join a large number of Norwegian aircrew for the exercise. We were paired off, each of us being with a Norwegian pilot. Dropped at night with map, compass and no money, we had to reach a pre-arranged rendezvous about 80 kilometres to the south on the fifth day. Being paired with a local turned out to be particularly beneficial for me.

With police, Army units and others looking for us, and radio broadcasts about the exercise, our policy of hiding up by day and travelling by night paid off, as many were captured that first day. With the option of taking the rail, road or river routes we initially chose the river. However, the local inhabitants were not very co-operative, since the few boats we found were securely fastened. So we travelled by road at night, and if we saw any vehicle headlights we dived into the nearest ditch or hedgerow. On one of these leaps I tore a large strip down my trousers on thorns or barbed wire. As the nights were pretty chilly up in Norway, I needed to get the pants repaired so we risked calling in a house early the next morning. The old lady was most solicitous and gave us a cup of hot coffee. While she was sewing up the tear there was an announcement on her radio about the exercise and that the population should look out for us and report any sightings to the authorities. I didn't speak any Norwegian but I got the message by the looks on their faces. However, she was clearly on our side, smiled at us and, suitably refreshed (and repaired), we thanked her and pressed on.

Oslo was a revelation. Showing great initiative, my partner soon contacted friends there and, with a night to spare before having to arrive at the RV, we went down town suitably kitted out in civvies. I was thoroughly enjoying the night club cabaret when an incident nearly gave me a heart attack! Two men came to our table saying they were police and marched the two of us outside to take us to the police station. For us, they said, the exercise was over. I was about to make a run for it when we were in the street but was just prevented from doing so by my partner. He had arranged the "arrest" as a practical joke! Luckily, I have a sense of humour and saw the funny side, and was relieved to return to my beers and enjoy the rest of the evening. My colleague made up for the prank and, showing even more initiative, fixed a car to take us within walking distance of the RV, which we made on time. My squadron mate also made it to the RV and we cheered him in as he pedalled furiously on the bicycle he had stolen early in the exercise. This was one means of transport we had not considered but, of course, hadn't needed. He was livid when he learned of my cushy ride and night out in Oslo.

Even today I feel slightly (but not a lot) guilty when I look at my "Escape Diploma" presented to me by the Base Commander at Gardermoen.   [A.D.R.D.]

A "WHAT MIGHT HAVE BEEN" WITH THE OTHER 54

In 1955 I was with 46 Squadron (flying Meteor NF 12s and 14s) at Odiham, a base we shared with 54 and 247 Day Fighter squadrons (who were busy changing from Meteor 8s to Hunters). This story concerns 54 Squadron and my involvement with them when ITV tried to get some film of the squadron aerobatic team doing their stuff.

My log book entry for 3rd November 1955 reads: *NF 14 – "E" – Self – Mr C******* – air to air photos, Hunter formation, FOL (ie. Flame out landing) –1hr10min – 10min actual IF.*

Within that one line lies a mini-drama, and a maxi 'what might have been'...[4]

Mr C was from ITV and the plan was to get some film of 54 Squadron who had formed the first Hunter formation team; just four Hunters led by Dick Immig (a Captain in the USAF on exchange posting). As I had previously flown a similar sortie with an Air Ministry photographer (Mike Chase) who had got some good pictures of the team I was detailed to fly the Meteor with Mr C.

At low level the weather was marginal with visibility of about a mile below a layer of stratus, base about 1,000 feet and some 2,000 feet thick, but above that it was clear and OK for the job in hand. The formation leader had overall responsibility for the whole mob which comprised the four Hunters in the team, my NF 14 with Mr C aboard, and a Vampire T 11 which was also planning to take some photos.

We joined up overhead and as soon as the fuel state allowed (I must have had some in the ventral tank to start with in view of the total time of the sortie) we tried the first loop but without success as far as the film was concerned. Mr C was not experienced in these things and asked if I

---

[4] The major drama that might have been concerned my Mr C. When we got back to dispersal, the ground crew who went to assist him unstrap found that he had, in fact, undone all the buckles and he told them he had done so early in the sortie so as to make it easier to handle the camera! So, I wonder, what would I have done if we had followed the Vampire and been instructed to bale out, and if, at that stage, I had told my passenger to follow the briefing he had been given and go, and he had replied "Oh dear! I have undone all my straps!!"

could somehow avoid his camera getting too heavy to lift when we pulled into the loop! We went on trying several manoeuvres until my fuel was getting low and I felt it was time to confirm we were somewhere near base. I disengaged from the formation, got a fix, and to my consternation found we were some 40 miles away. I shut down one engine to fly for range and set course for home, fervently wishing that I had my trusty navigator, Don Roberts, in the back seat instead of Mr C. At this stage there would have been no big drama but for the intervention of the duty gremlins. Firstly the Hunters and Vampire went on aerobatting so they arrived overhead, short of fuel at about the same time as me, and at that point the Odiham GCA went on the blink.

I don't remember the initial details of the approach but I do remember in stark detail being instructed to change to a Farnborough frequency for a GCA in time to hear them tell the Vampire ahead of me that they could not assist him and he should therefore climb out on the heading they gave and abandon the aircraft. A querulous voice from the back said "was that for us?" and in the smoothest tone I could muster I said "No, don't worry I know where we are".

In fact, from the last fix I had had, and after some hasty DR (demented reckoning!) I thought I could safely let down in a gentle starboard turn, and being short of any better ideas, that's what I did. To my great relief, as we broke cloud the first thing I saw was a big white building which was the distinguishing feature of Basingstoke. From there I followed the road back to Odiham and with insufficient fuel to do a circuit was able to land downwind.

The final score for the exercise was: One Vampire T11 abandoned, one Hunter pilot ejected, one Hunter damaged on landing at Tangmere, Formation leader plus one landed at Farnborough, yours truly landed back at Odiham.

And as far as I know there was no film and no photos![5]   [R.H.B.]

HELICOPTER TRAINING – OF A SORT

At the beginning of February 1957 I joined No 16 Course at the Empire Test Pilots' School, at Farnborough. Seven months later the Chief Test Flying Instructor said I was to be given helicopter training. Apparently the Royal Aircraft Establishment Farnborough and the Aeroplane and

---

[5] Footnote 2 – This debacle was seen in due course as a precursor of an even bigger cock-up which occurred a few weeks later at the Day Fighter Leaders' School, West Raynham. I was told they prided themselves on using their fuel to the last drop on every sortie and this time went too far. In poor weather they got caught out and finally the formation leader is alleged to have given the ultimate despairing call "every man for himself". Hunters were spread all round East Anglia but I forget the final score.

Armament Establishment Boscombe Down each wanted another helicopter pilot in January.

In the RAF of the 1950s there was less emphasis on conversion training than there is today. This was particularly so at the ETPS as it had to produce test pilots who could readily fly new and unproven aircraft. At the start of the course students were given a pile of Pilot's Notes so that they would be ready to fly any of the school's aircraft when appropriate. That was the theory although the reality could be somewhat different. I recall a murky afternoon in mid-October being suddenly told that the Gloster Javelin was awaiting my pleasure, and having to take a keen candidate for the next course in the rear seat to read the Pilot's Notes to me. I couldn't even have started the engines without his aid.

So when it came to my helicopter conversion I suppose I should not have been surprised that it was on the skimpy side. The ETPS had two Westland Dragonfly helicopters, ready for the fray. My training did not include any ground school instruction, only pre-flight briefings. Moreover I was very busy with other course work as well as spending much time on the south coast courting a lovely Wren stationed at the Navy's helicopter school at Lee-on-Solent. Thus I never got around to studying the important principles of rotary wing aerodynamics.

My training consisted of six dual flights, totalling four hours, spread over eight weeks. These were given by the CTFI who had only limited helicopter experience himself, no doubt gained in a similarly relaxed manner. I was not taught autorotations properly and did no power-off approaches. On my first solo I suddenly realised that I was far from competent and recall having the greatest difficulty descending without overspeeding the rotor. The approach to the small landing area was a nightmare.

One month, and eight flying hours, later came the final exercise of the course. This was the Preview Assessment, in which all the important handling and performance characteristics of the Dragonfly had to be determined. All went well until I came to the section involving the behaviour following a power failure. On this flight I was accompanied by a Flight Engineer to record results. I was briefed to fly at 2,000 feet and 50 knots, then to close the throttle leaving the collective pitch constant to check how quickly the rotor speed decreased, but not to go below 150 rpm.

It was here that my ignorance of helicopter aerodynamics caught me out. Following fixed wing practice I decided it would be safer to have more height and speed, so I levelled out at 5,000 feet and 70 knots with a rotor speed of 195 rpm. The first two tests were uneventful so I decided to work down to the minimum of 150 rpm. At 158 – wham! The helicopter pitched up sharply and rolled to port into a steep spin, with rotor speed fluctuating wildly even though I was trying to control it by varying collective pitch (also wildly!).

I feared the blades would either hit the fuselage, cone upwards or fail through excessive centrifugal loading. As full right stick and rudder had no effect at all, I moved the stick in stages around the cockpit until, when it was fully back and to the left, the helicopter suddenly ceased spinning and I regained control. The height was now 2,000 feet. Happily, no damage was caused but I now knew something about the effect of stalling a helicopter's rotor. Belatedly studying Pilot's Notes I learnt that the minimum permissible rpm was 170.

After joining the Experimental Flying Department of the RAE in January I managed to get a proper helicopter course at – yes – Lee-on-Solent. It started half way through my honeymoon so I took my Wren bride back to the station she had just left. We rented a flat in the town and the CO said that as we had lost half of our honeymoon I could treat the course like a flying club and only come in when I was needed! Happy days! [D.A.C.]

REFRESHING TIMES

On a QFI tour at No. 5 FTS, RAF Oakington, one day, quite out of the blue, came a request for two RAF squash players to go to Norway to give demonstrations in their first squash court, recently built, and to coach some Royal Norwegian Air Force aircrew. A colleague and I flew up there in a twin-engined Dakota – it turned out to be a long and cold flight in an unheated aircraft. On landing at Rygge air base on 27 January 1956 after a 5½ hour flight the outside air temperature was minus 25 and the air was so cold that it was almost painful to breathe. We found that the squash court was so cold that we couldn't give demonstrations as the ball hardly bounced at all. We managed to get some heating laid on and lined up six balls on a radiator. The Norwegians had never seen the back wall of the squash court in use before, but now that we were using a hot ball, they did! However, as our game progressed, the ball became colder and we had to change in mid-game to a fresh, warm ball. A strange procedure but it worked! Another five hour flight in the freezing Dakota before I got back to Oakington.

The RAF policy in the mid-50s was that some operational aircrew could return to their old squadrons for a short period of "Refresher Flying", to be carried out 6 to 12 months from their leaving the squadron. I had left Bruggen in November 1954 and I was thrilled to learn that I was to return there in mid-September 1955 for 10 days operational refresher training. On a particular flight, returning from the air/ground range, one of the F86 Sabre's external drop tanks did just that – it dropped off! Apparently it didn't hit anything or (anyone) and nobody bothered me about it on my return to Bruggen.

Another one-off event while at Oakington was the arrival of a Refresher Course of senior officers that passed through our hands for refamiliarisation with flying after being on one or more ground tours. I well remember a "student" Group Captain who was allocated to me who was hoping not only to go solo but get an instrument rating as well. I think that his last flying had been on Hawker Hart biplanes! Unfortunately he couldn't cope with the speed and acceleration of the T11 Vampire. It all happened too fast for him and we had many circuits and bumps sorties before I was persuaded to allow him to go solo. Thankfully, he got down in one piece but he never made his Instrument Rating Test. Actually, I felt sorry for him, as I myself would experience the problems of returning to flying after a long lay-off with ground tours. [A.D.R.D.]

4.   Secondary or Extraneous Duties

As may have been seen already, there were many other things for young officers to do, as well as fly; after all, it was the "General Duties" Branch to which the pilots belonged. Some of these extra tasks were of a very temporary nature, such as checking an inventory, overseeing a pay parade or auditing accounts, some were not, such as being officer in charge of a club or sport , and some were sad duties. Here are just a few examples:

THE CONVOY

You have only been in Germany for a fortnight, but Wingco Admin has already nobbled you for a practice convoy.

It is a cold foggy morning at Wildenrath. Twenty enormous Magyrus trucks have been brought out of the reserve compound, and now stretch for about a quarter of a mile along the road. Each is driven by a nervous C Class driver, summoned from a safe job in some cookhouse, clothing store or orderly room. At the front is a minibus for you to drive, accompanied by Nobby Clarke, a navigator from the Communications Squadron. Nobby has the route pencilled on a map. An RAF policeman on a motorbike leads the way.

At your signal, twenty mighty diesels thunder into life. You are off, into the foggy, featureless German countryside. Neither you nor Nobby have much idea where you are, or where you are going, but all you have to do is to keep the motorbike in sight. At every crossroads more 'snowdrops' stand ready to wave you through. Twenty enormous Magyrus trucks obediently follow. All is well.

After an hour or so, the police signal you to stop for a scheduled refreshment break. The twenty trucks pull up behind you. With a loud bang, a German minibus runs straight into the back of the last truck. The front of the bus is all smashed in, but there is not a scratch on the Magyrus. You drink your tea, while the snowdrops sort it out with the local Polizei. The hapless German driver is blamed for everything, by everyone. Then you are off again.

Nearly home, in the town of Wassenberg, there is suddenly no sign of the escort. Never mind, Nobby Clarke has the map and directs you down the right road. Except that Nobby is not the sharpest knife in the cutlery drawer, and it is a wrong turning and not the right road. You realise that you are now taking everybody along a minor country road that leads to the back of beyond. Furthermore, there is an unmanned border crossing about a mile ahead, so the back of beyond, towards which the road leads, is somewhere in Holland.

Panic! What to do? You dismiss the idea of twenty C Class drivers trying to do three-point turns in their enormous Magyrus trucks in the narrow road. What about getting the whole convoy to reverse back into Wassenberg town centre? Equally impossible. Then you see a solution!

Just ahead is a small filling station. With instant decision, you turn into the forecourt, drive round the back of the pumps, and out again on to the road, going in the opposite direction. A German is standing there filling his Mercedes. You have a snapshot picture of him with his mouth open and the pump nozzle spilling petrol, as one after another, a quarter mile of enormous Magyrus trucks follow you.   [R.H.R.]

IN CHARGE OF A PIPE BAND

One day during my Singapore tour, the Adjutant rang me up and asked if I would like to go to Hong Kong for a week in charge of the Far East Air Force Pipe Band as the normal officer in charge of it was unable to go. I jumped at the chance although I knew nothing about playing the bagpipes. We had a great time and were well received by the local residents and the RAF at Kai Tak.

There were three memorable occasions which stand out in my mind. The first was a visit to the Tan Toc Sin Hospital where the band played to the children who were suffering with spinal TB and were mostly bedridden. They loved it and so did the young nurses, who flirted with the men in the band.

The second memory was the band playing on the Star Ferry over to Hong Kong Island. The ferry operators cleared the car deck and the band marched up and down playing away, much to the delight of the passengers. We had dinner that night on one of the floating restaurants in the harbour. One of the sergeants in the band got up and played his bagpipes to the assembled diners and received a great ovation.

The third occasion was when I was interviewed on Hong Kong Radio. I was asked the inevitable question "What does a Scotsman wear under his kilt?" I seem to remember I glossed over that question and invited the band to play on the radio.

The band completed its tour by playing at a guest night in the Kai Tak officers' mess, which was attended by the Governor. I was briefed to ask the Governor what tune he would like the band to play; the answer was "Bonnets over the Border" which luckily the band knew, as I had briefed his ADC on the band's repertoire the previous day.   [R.S.H.]

ATTENDANCE AT COURT

One of the airmen from Technical Wing at Wildenrath is due to appear in the magistrates' court in Roermond on a motoring charge. Wingco Admin instructs you to attend the hearing as the CO's representative, to answer questions on the guy's Service record, conduct and so on. Next morning, dressed in your Best Blue and armed with the required information, you drive to Holland and find the magistrates' court.

It is a long, rather dark room with rows of sort of pews. The accused is sitting right at the front. You take a seat further back and wait. Finally, a door opens at the far end and several people enter, wearing black gowns and white "Geneva bands", like Presbyterian ministers. They huddle round a table and have a long confab. You can't hear what they are saying, but it is all in Dutch anyway. Then they pick up their papers and go out of the door again. Nobody has taken any notice of you at all.

After nothing else happens for a bit, you catch a court usher who speaks English, and ask when the case is going to begin. "Oh", says he, "That was it. It is finished. The court is in recess now." "What do you mean? What happened?" "Well, the prosecutor demanded a year in prison, but they just sentenced him to three weeks in the end."

Ye Gods! An RAF airman sent to prison in Holland! What will be the repercussions? Will he be thrown out of the Service in disgrace? Will it be an international incident? How the hell are you going to explain this when you get back to base?

As soon as you get back, you report to the Wingco Admin, in full expectation that the sky is going to fall on you. Three weeks prison sentence! And you did nothing about it. What is he going to say?

"No problem" is what he actually says. "We'll take it off his leave entitlement. He'll have to go and work on a Dutch prison farm during weekdays, but they'll let him out every weekend anyway. Do him good. Thanks. Was there anything else you wanted to discuss while you're here?"

Strewth! [R.H.R.]

"BUT, SIR, THAT ISN'T MY ONLY PROBLEM!"

(Or, 'Getting to Grips with Reality')

When I arrived on my first squadron, straight from AFS and the OCU, I was somewhat surprised by the warmth of my reception from the Squadron Adjutant. However, I soon realised that this was because he felt that he had long enough in the post, and having had sight of my documents from Cranwell, he saw me as a ready-made successor. Only a few months later I was appointed Squadron Adjutant in his place.

However, although flying was my main *raison d'etre*, I was naively confident that my College training made me well able to cope with a spot of administration as well, and I looked forward to the challenge.

It was not long before the hairy old Flight Sergeant Discip told me, a twenty one year old pilot officer, that an LAC wished to come and talk to me. As I had already expressed a "my door is always open" policy, I agreed, and felt that this was really getting down to business. I had all the Cranwell ground school behind me and I was armed with copies of Queen's Regulations and the Manual of Air Force Law.

When the young airman arrived he seemed a pleasant chap but he was obviously very worried. So I indulged in some light-hearted chatter to try and put him at his ease. When, finally, I asked what he wanted to discuss, he promptly explained that he had made his girl friend pregnant. This came as a mild shock to me bearing in mind that in the early 1950s attitudes towards sex were far different from what they are today. However, I soon thought of various courses of action, the simplest being marriage since neither he nor the girl were married. So, I told him that we could soon settle the matter. But he then said "But, Sir, that isn't my only problem!"

" Oh!?", I said. He then explained that he had also made the girl friend's mother pregnant!

This felled me, and I couldn't for the life of me think of any of our College lectures that covered any such eventuality.

After further discussion with the lad, I promised to give the matter further urgent consideration. Having already built up a good working relationship with the OC Admin, I tore along to see him and described the situation. A wide smile appeared across his face and it seemed to me as though he thought it was an everyday occurrence, and he told me to leave it with him.

I never heard the final outcome, but I do know that a sudden posting to 'foreign parts' came through very quickly. [D.J.B.K]

THE KEYS! WHOSE KEYS? THE QUEEN'S KEYS!

As a secondary duty at Wildenrath, I had charge of a disused hangar. There were about thirty keys, some that were labelled and some that were anonymous, some that were duplicates, and some that didn't belong in the first place. There were outside door keys, fire door keys and office keys, all mixed up.

I spent a whole morning going round trying them in the locks and identifying them. Then I put tags on them. Keeping only the keys for the CO's office and for an outside door, I put all the rest in a tin wastepaper bucket, and hid it in the desk. Thus I could let myself in again using just two keys, and get the rest from the CO's office if required.

One day, 14 Squadron hangar was to have a new floor laid, and everything was to be shifted temporarily to my unoccupied hangar. No problem. I proudly handed my two keys to the wing commander, explained where his lads could find all the others, and went off flying.

Upon my return, I found all hell had broken loose. The window of the CO's office was unfastened, and the bucket of keys had disappeared. Mountains of equipment were being piled in front of the hangar, while aircraft were being towed down to the pan. Meanwhile a team of German locksmiths were drilling and chiselling out all the locks and fitting new ones. Nobody was happy. Avoiding the hierarchy of 14 Squadron, I vented my fury on OC Station Police, who promised to get his best detectives on to the case forthwith. It was not a good day.

A week or so later, the SNCO i/c Police came sheepishly into my office. He looked remarkably grubby and sweat-stained. There was mud on his white belt and gaiters. He held a tin wastepaper bucket in his hand. In it were some filthy keys. He explained.

One of his corporals had been patrolling one night. Round the back of my hangar, he had found a window he could prise open. Overcome by his own cleverness, and seeing the chance of crowing over some officer, he had climbed in and looked for something to take away as evidence. Looking in the desk, he had seized upon the bucket of keys, and proudly taken them back to the guardroom, where he had put them in a locker.

Next morning he had gone back to the UK on leave, completely forgetting to tell anyone the keys were there. While he was away, there was a big bull session in the guardroom for the forthcoming AOC's Inspection. Somebody had found the bucket, assumed the keys were old ones that nobody wanted, and again without telling anyone, had thrown them out.

The dishevelled SNCO before me had just spent several hours in charge of a team of SPs, all digging in the station rubbish tip, with orders to find each and every key, whereof he would fail at his peril...

Many, many years before, as a mere AC2, I had been pulled up by the SPs in Piccadilly Circus for not having a weekend pass. Yea verily, is it not indeed true, that revenge is a dish best eaten cold!

As for the keys, they were no good anymore because all the locks had been changed. So they went back onto the rubbish tip again... [R.H.R.]

FOOD CONTROL

During the Second World War, bands of guerillas in Malaya had been armed by the British to fight the Japanese after the capitulation of

Singapore . Most of these guerillas were from the Chinese section of the population, as opposed to the Malays and Indians, and they were almost all dedicated communists. They had links with the communists in China and received a great deal of political education from that source, but much of their military training came from British officers left behind after the capitulation in 1942 or delivered clandestinely afterwards by sea or parachute. After the war, what had become an army of guerillas agreed to hand back their weapons but as well as the "official" ones they had acquired many weapons abandoned during the retreat in 1942 and which the Japanese had failed to impound. So although on the face of it they had disarmed, they still retained possession of a considerable armoury, which they concealed in the mountains and jungles.

During the years immediately following the war the communists instigated civil unrest and riots. In 1948 they felt that their time had arrived and so they began an armed campaign, attacking public officials and police stations, setting ambushes on country roads, raiding rubber plantations and killing planters and their families. In response, a state of "Emergency" was declared and the British armed forces became involved, together with the Federation of Malaya Police which expanded rapidly to include a para-military Police Field Force. The Malayan Emergency continued from 1948 to 1960 and over the years many thousands of British soldiers and marines took part in operations in the jungle and the RAF supported the land operations in various ways.

Transport aircraft of the RAF parachuted supplies to army units on patrol in the jungles and in due course there were helicopters to move troops and supplies and evacuate casualties. Some aircraft were equipped with loudspeaker systems so that voice broadcasts could be made to the communists, by then known as Communist Terrorists, or CTs. The voice broadcasts and leaflet drops were part of what came to be known as Psychological Warfare. Additionally, the RAF supported the land operations with photographic reconnaissance and by attacking the CTs from the air, with bombs, rockets and cannon fire. A number of types of aircraft took part, including the Hornets of No 33 Squadron, based at Butterworth in the north of Malaya, on the west coast immediately level with the island of Penang.

From 1952 to 1955 I was a member of No 33 Squadron and took part in a number of strike operations. These were usually against targets which were merely map squares of jungle. Only rarely was the target a clearing and it was very rare indeed to see anything tangible. However, occasionally reports were received of bodies found by the army following up and very often the airstrikes were found to have helped influence a CT to surrender. It was shown that a graph of surrenders followed a graph showing the intensity of air operations. Air attacks also had the effect of causing the CTs to move when they realised that their locations were known to the security forces.

At first the CTs established some large camps where they trained and even grew some crops for food. The disruption caused by land and air operations made it difficult for them to continue with secure longterm camps and hampered their chances of growing their own food. Obtaining food was a major problem for them and as they could not rely on becoming self-sufficient they had to come out of the jungle for supplies. Their best method was to apply pressure on the Chinese section of the population living and working on the edge of the jungle. Pressure included various acts of blackmail, theft and violence and in some cases murder. Some of these people were working in estates or mines but many were "squatters" who had carved plots of land out of the jungle to grow food. Effectively they were what we would term smallholders. There were over 400,000 of them in Malaya and partly because of racial links and partly because of their vulnerability, they were a source of hope for the CTs who, by threats and promises, obtained recruits and food from them.

It became an aim of the Director of Operations to offer these squatters and workers protection against pressure from the CTs by moving them to New Villages surrounded by fences and providing defence in the shape of the police and Home Guard. Squatters were removed in dawn raids by the army and police and sometimes force had to be used to achieve the aim. In most cases the compulsory moves took place without more than the minimum of distress and the British soldiers, unsurprisingly, did things to ease the way such as gently lifting children and old women into the trucks. It has been written that the kindly and humane treatment they received from the British soldiers came as a surprise to the squatters and helped greatly to influence them in what had become a battle for hearts and minds.

It was also decided to reduce the food available for the CTs to steal or confiscate by keeping stocks at a minimum in these "New Villages" and in any place likely to be vulnerable to the approaches of the CTs. In this way the squatters were also made less of an attractive target for coercion. To this end, frequent and unannounced inspections were made to check that stocks of food were no higher than needed for a few days only.

I seem to recall that the Station Commander was asked by the District Officer at Butterworth to supply a junior officer now and again to accompany an inspection visit, or the scheme may have been the brainchild of our Ground Liaison Officer but, however it had come about, one day in 1953 I found myself with the Assistant District Officer, a Police Lieutenant, a number of police constables, a few Chinese interpreters, and a police armoured car, on the way to a village on the jungle fringe about 20 miles from the airfield. Except for the ADO and civilian interpreters we were all armed but this was nothing out of the ordinary as we aircrew carried sidearms on duty throughout my tour and kept our pistols and ammunition in our rooms in the mess.

On arrival, the police set up blocks on the roads and tracks around the village to prevent anyone coming in or going out and the ADO met the headman to explain what was going to happen. Then we started to go through the houses, with policemen keeping a close watch to ensure that food was not being moved from house to house or to some hiding place.

The houses were just huts with attap thatched roofs, very simple and, indeed, primitive. There was no electricity, no gas, no running water and no internal sanitation. Nevertheless, the houses were clean, a few magazine illustrations adorned the walls and the household gods were in evidence with a stick or two of joss burning. There was very little in the way of furniture and the highest material aspirations of these hard-working but poor people would probably not have risen above a bicycle, a Tilley lamp to light the dark evenings and a cheap radio set for news and entertainment. Although they had the basic essentials of a roof and enough to eat, these were not people on whom Providence could be said to have smiled, certainly not by the standards of today, 50 years later. They had so little and had to work so hard that it was not difficult to understand that some would be attracted by promises of a Communist Utopia and a redistribution of wealth. One could only feel sympathy for them as we outsiders rooted around among their pitifully few possessions. I think, in retrospect, that a reason for inviting officers such as myself to take part was to see fair play by making sure the police, almost entirely Malays, were not too heavy handed in their dealings with the Chinese villagers and squatters and their families.

The householders were required to produce all their food and the constables searched to see if anything was hidden. The food stocks were primarily bags of rice, tinned goods, such as fish and condensed milk, and fresh vegetables. There were usually some sweet biscuits and I assume the Chinese were very partial to these as there were Chinese biscuit factories to be found all over Malaya. An assessment was made of the amount of rice and fresh food the household could retain, depending on the size of the family, and any balance was to be confiscated. In respect of the tinned foods, a few tins were allowed to remain whole for consumption over the following day or so but the rest were punctured with a spike so that they would have to be used virtually at once, the climate not being conducive to the keeping of food, and refrigerators not figuring among the meagre possessions of these poor folk.

There were, as might be expected, arguments about the quantities of rice which could legitimately be kept and objections to tins being pierced but I do not recall any vast quantities being taken away or damaged, just enough to make the point. I suspect that by that time it had become known that it was best to keep within the limits and the objections and remonstrations were made more or less for form's sake and perhaps in a spirit of optimism. Where food was confiscated or destroyed, one would hope that compensation would have been paid, as it was in relation to the forced moves to New Villages, but I was not aware whether any was paid or payable in respect of the operation in which I participated.

Training at Cranwell at that time was aimed at producing officers for the General Duties, Secretarial and Equipment Branches. As a member of the GD branch I had been trained for what was at that time my basic task of flying Hornets to attack the CTs in the jungle, CTs who could well have been related to, or be friends of, the villagers, but my training had not extended to taking part in a food control operation. The experience, though, was certainly something to remember. I do, indeed, value the memory of it and I suppose that such a task could conceivably be covered by the heading of "General Duties". [F.D.H.]

A VERY SLOW MARCH

In the fifties, we were all very familiar with the procedures and ceremonies of Service funerals because, sadly, we had plenty of experience. When I was serving with No.2 Squadron at Gutersloh in Germany we lost C—— and my Squadron Commander tasked me to take care of the arrangements. I made a list of things to do and got started.

I called the MT section to ask for a low loader to be used as a gun carriage.

"What?" the MT officer exclaimed, "Another? The Station Adjutant asked for one only two hours ago!"

"No, not another – please disregard."

I called the armoury to ask for rifles and blank ammunition for the firing party.

"What?" the Armaments Officer exclaimed, "Another? The Station Adjutant asked for this only two hours ago!"

"No, not another – please disregard."

I called the nearby Army Barracks to ask for their buglers who played a beautiful and moving Last Post.

"What?" the Bandmaster exclaimed, "Another? Your Station Adjutant asked for them only two hours ago!"

"No, not another –please disregard."

It was evident that the Station Adjutant considered all the arrangements to be his responsibility and that he was most efficient. I confined myself to taking care of C......'s affairs and effects and drilling the Squadron airmen in slow marching, reversing arms and resting on the arms reversed. I also practiced my own sword drill because it was my job to lead the cortege

The day came and all started well. The funeral procession marched from Sick Quarters, where C..... had lain since they recovered him, through the station to the Guard Room by the main gate. There we were to fall out, board buses and travel the twelve or so miles to Cologne cemetery. One detail remained – one that I should have already checked. No matter, the detail I needed could be obtained from the Station Adjutant and he was only a few yards away. I crossed the road, went into Station Headquarters and thence to the Adj.'s office.

"Hello" he said cheerfully, in spite of the sombre occasion, "Everything going all right?"

"Yes, and many thanks for making all the arrangements. Just one thing – what grave plot number have they allocated us?"

"Oh I never get involved in the cemetery end of things. I always leave that to the Squadron!"

I looked through his window at the scene by the Guard Room. There was the gun carriage with the coffin draped in the Union Flag. There were the parents, the girl friend, the Squadron Commander and the whole Squadron, some senior officers and other mourners and the transport, all ready to go.

"No grave?" I asked, hoping that perhaps I had misheard or that he was playing a black joke on me.

"No grave." he confirmed.

For a second or two I visualised what my Squadron Commander (the formidable Bob Weighill) would say and do to me if I told him that we had better postpone the whole thing. But only for a second or two. There was a wing of R.A.F. Regiment based on the station and one of its officers, John Strickland, whom we thought was a frustrated pilot, visited the Squadron whenever he could and we were all friends together. I quickly telephoned him and explained the problem.

"Leave it to me!" he cried, "Just give me as much time as you can!"

As I crossed the road on my way back to the Guard Room two Regiment Land Rovers each containing half a dozen strong Regiment men, the lead one driven by John, went round the corner on two wheels and raced off.

The funeral vehicles travelled in convoy and I took my seat by the driver of the leading one. I insisted that he drive very slowly, give way to all other traffic and even took him round a couple of diversions. When we finally got to the gates of the cemetery, I took as long as possible to get the Squadron airmen properly paraded and gave them another very thorough inspection.

John had arranged for an official of the cemetery to be there to tell me where the plot was. I tried to look as if I was discussing most important things with him, and spun out the conversation as long as I could. When I could stall no longer I gave the order to slow march and we set off. I marched as slowly as I possibly could and took exceedingly short steps.

I turned the final corner not knowing what I would find. Something seemed to flash through the air, but I could not make out what it was – it was gone in an instant. But there, to my considerable relief, was C.......'s final resting place. It was not quite as deep as usual, but only I noticed that. The rest of the ceremony was completed without further complication.

I found out later that the Regiment lads had been digging till the last possible second and that as my leading foot came round the corner, the last of them took a header over the low hedge and they were all lying on the far side of it throughout the Service. John, if you should by chance read this, my warmest regards, and thank you again. C...... was a great chap with a warm sense of humour and I can not help thinking that he was looking down at us and laughing his socks off.

A moral to the story? Yes, and I have never forgotten it. If you want something done properly, do it yourself.   [B.M.]

5. Later Years in the Service

This part deals with later times when members of the Entry were more senior and in a variety of posts, flying and non-flying

TARGET MARKING WITH THE CANBERRA

No.139 Squadron, when I joined as training officer in the late fifties, had a unique role as target markers for visual bombing by the Canberra and V Forces. This role was already becoming obsolete, since the shooting down of Francis Gary Powers in his U2 had demonstrated that low level attacks using entirely different methods would be the only viable tactics in future. Readers may recall that Powers was flying a U2 "spy 'plane" at very high altitude when brought down by a Soviet missile.

Anyway, how the squadron operated was as follows. A marker team of four, or sometimes six, Canberra B6s took off at timed intervals, some loaded just with flares to illuminate the target area, and the others with a mixture of more flares plus coloured target indicator bombs (TI). These were the same as those used by Bomber Command in the war on Germany twenty years earlier.

The aircraft carried two navigators, but since one of the ejection seats had been removed to make room for a sideways looking radar, one of the navigators had to sit on the rumble (Rumbold?) seat next to the pilot. Between the two of them, they had to arrive at a predetermined Initial Point (IP) at exactly the right time, and then direct the pilot on a timed run to reach the target. The first aircraft to arrive dropped their flares so that, if all went well, the actual markers saw the target below. The marker leader then dive-bombed it with a TI. Depending upon the accuracy, either he or Marker Two backed it up with other TIs as necessary.

While these were burning, the "Master Bomber" called up the "Main Force" and told them which colour to bomb. (This Main Force was often an entirely imaginary one, or at best, a couple of Canberras from Cyprus if the target was El Adem range!).

The angle of dive was thirty degrees – not really steep, but it seemed horribly so in the Canberra, especially at night. Furthermore, doing it at night with brilliant flares burning both underneath and above you was simply asking for disorientation, as was proved when one of the flight commanders went splat one night. On the way down, the navigator in the back would call out the height from his altimeter. The pitch and volume of his voice was inversely proportional to the nearness of the ground. I think I can say that it was the most dangerous thing I ever did in my flying career.

It was not particularly easy to get a direct hit either, because the poor angle of downward view over the Canberra's nose meant that if you kept the target in view all the way to bomb release, you were actually undershooting. So just before you finished your dive, you had to pull the nose up and guess, as the target disappeared, exactly the right moment to release. I persuaded our engineers to fit a GM2 gunsight in the squadron's T4 but, again, it could not be depressed enough to solve this problem.

In order not to overstress our Canberras, we were told to empty the integral wing tanks before dive-bombing. Later, when the aircraft were fitted with g-meters for LABS bombing, the boffins instructed us to ensure the wing tanks were left full as long as possible, so as to reduce the bending moment on the wing roots. Exactly the opposite of what we were doing before!

When not carrying out marker exercises, the squadron carried on with the same training as the other Canberras. To keep the squadron flying hours up to target, we were told not to land under three hours, except in emergency. The briefing would be Gee-H, visual bombing and/or Staff Continuation Training. If the radar became unserviceable and the visual ranges at Holbeach and Wainfleet were fully booked, you just flew about for three hours in acute discomfort, doing practice diversions to any airfields that would accept you. Gee-H was transcendentally boring, combining as it did the maximum of concentration with the minimum of satisfaction and excitement. No real bombs were dropped, but theoretical points of impact were measured by radar on the Gee-H ranges, so it was all a matter of disembodied voices, with nothing to see, then round and round again, for what seemed like hours on end.

It was on one of these night sorties that an alarming and potentially serious incident happened. I had an Air Training Corps cadet on the rumble seat. Immediately after take-off we called Wainfleet, knowing that there would be a queue as usual, then climbed to 40,000 ft to orbit and wait to be called in by the range. My navigator suddenly realised that our passenger was slumped forward, and what could be seen of his face was a funny colour. He hastily unstrapped and went to see what was the matter. The cadet had been sick in his oxygen mask, and while we were busy, had been quietly choking to death. We had to do an immediate emergency descent and a straight-in approach, while the SMO awaited us at the end of the runway. Fortunately the cadet's airways were cleared in time and he survived.

Another story from 139 Squadron was eventually published in Flight Safety literature but, as far as I know, was never resolved. We had been detached to Malta for a month. I shared a room in the Transit Mess at Luqa with a navigator from another crew. For some reason, I had to return to Binbrook for a couple of days, and on getting back to Malta, found the nav's personal kit being sorted from mine and packed away. He was missing, together with the rest of his crew.

A marker team had set out at night while I was away, to go to El Adem range. This particular aircraft had checked in after take-off, but had never been heard of again. The Mediterranean had been searched by Shackletons and other NATO aircraft and ships, but absolutely nothing was found, and the search had finally been called off.

It was a year before anything further happened. Apparently an Arab came into a French Foreign Legion fort in the Sahara desert in Algeria, wearing sandals made out of rubber tyre treads. When questioned, he told of a wrecked aircraft miles away, buried in a sand dune. The French realised its markings were RAF, and reported this to London. The fuselage code letters identified it as the missing 139 Squadron Canberra.

A Board of Inquiry was reconvened and went out to Algeria. At that time, a civil war was going on, so they were flown out to the site escorted by other helicopters with armed escorts. Right enough, the Canberra had its nose buried in a sand dune, but the wings and tail were mostly accessible. I think they found remains of the crew. There was nothing to explain the crash – the aircraft seemed to have been in a gentle descent when it hit. No conclusions could be drawn from the brief examination before the armed expedition had to leave again.

I think the only recommendation was that aerial photos should be taken periodically, to see if the desert wind would uncover any more of the wreckage, but as far as I know, nothing came of this. The whole affair was as mysterious as the Marie Celeste. It is difficult to imagine what emergency could have explained the circumstances. Even if there had been a total electrical failure, there were two experienced navigators on board, a stand-by magnetic compass, hand torches, clocks, ASIs, charts, even the moon and stars. Yet their heading towards the crash site bore no relation either to their planned heading towards El Adem, or to a return to Malta. Furthermore, they must have maintained this inexplicable heading for a long time, to be so far into the Sahara. What on earth were they doing? [R.H.R.]

SWING HIGH, SWING LOW

It was a dark, overcast, unpleasant winter's day on the east coast of Scotland. My Javelin squadron was preparing for a special night exercise and as many of the aircraft were in for servicing, it was decided that the flight that I was on should go off for dinghy drill. I thought that this was a jolly good idea and I looked forward to being driven off to a heated indoor pool, having a pleasant swim and a paddle around in a dinghy, followed by hot coffee and sticky buns. However, we were driven off to the coast where we were to board an Air Sea Rescue launch, taken out into the North Sea, dumped overboard, and were expected to get into our dinghy and set it up with all its bits and pieces before being hoisted out by helicopter.

All started well and the chopper duly arrived out of the murk. I got into the sling and was being hoisted up when the link on the sling, above my head, broke open, and I was set up for a free-fall.

Fortunately I already had one hand on the line and within nano-seconds it was joined by the other one. I wasn't at all sure that I could cling on until I was hauled up to the helicopter door, so had to decide whether I should let go straight away whilst I was at a comparatively low height or stay with it and risk falling involuntarily from a greater height. Not knowing the best way to fall I decided to hang on. I shouted up to the winchman, but he was quite unconcerned. Finally, on being hauled in, he seemed surprised that I was very reluctant to release my grip on the line until every part of me was inside the chopper.

I tried to explain to the crew what had happened, but either they could not hear me above all the surrounding noise or they just didn't want to hear it.

Back at base I reported the incident, but it was all hushed up because "we don't want to cause trouble for the SAR flight which is in the same Flying Wing as us, old boy".

I still wonder which **is** best way to fall into the sea from a great height – like a dart, but hands and head first, or feet first, or perhaps like a ball??

When I see a stuntman in a similar situation in a film I have some sympathy, but they get paid a lot more than I was.   [D.J.B.K.]

ENCOUNTER WITH A TIGER

During my tour at Seletar in Singapore 1962/64 I went on detachment to Kuantan in Malaya with the Beverley squadron (No 34) and Twin Pioneers (No 209 Squadron). One of my tasks was to inspect the Bulk Fuel Installation (BFI) and dip the tanks each morning to check the contents.

On one particular morning I noticed some large footprints in the soft ground round one of the tanks; I took little notice, thinking it might be some animal. However on the next morning at about 0615 hrs when I was doing my daily check, I walked round the back of the BFI and there facing me was the biggest tiger I have ever seen! We stared at each other for a while. I remained rooted to the spot as I thought that if I ran away he might come after me. In the end the tiger just turned away and disappeared into the jungle and I hot-footed it back to the camp. Naturally I dined off a few cans of "Tiger" that evening. For the rest of the detachment, I took a member of the RAF Regiment with me armed with a rifle but we didn't see the tiger again. [R.S.H.]

FOOD, GLORIOUS FOOD!

In 1999 I was leafing through some old copies of the Cranwell Magazine and I believe it must have been in one of these that I saw the following tale. I do not know what the copyright position may be but I offer the author my apologies, particularly as I am writing from memory.

One evening the teller of the tale was working in the cookhouse in East Camp (presumably as a defaulter) when the cooks were preparing breakfast for the following morning. Suddenly, one of the cooks rushed over to a steaming vat of porridge, leaned over and began fishing around with his ladle. After a few seconds he straightened up and was seen to have a cat on the ladle, covered in porridge. Expertly flicking the cat off the ladle and towards the open door the cook muttered "Stupid cat! It did exactly the same thing last night!"

This brought back recollections of a number of other incidents involving food but I will merely relate a few moments I recall from days in Borneo during the Indonesian Confrontation.

Our Whirlwind helicopters were based at Kuching to support army operations in the First Division of the state of Sarawak. Having received tasking orders by signal during the previous evening we would usually set out from Kuching at about 0730 or 0800 hours and might be away until 1600 or 1700 hours or even later. During that time we would have been flying between company locations and various landing sites, moving men and supplies, doing what had to be done and refuelling from drums of avtur stored around the place. Often it was simply not possible to calculate how long crews might be away from base. Strangely, we never took any food with us. I cannot remember any official reason for this and no doubt rations would have been available if we had asked. However, I think we simply became accustomed to being looked after by the army.

Almost everywhere we landed the soldiers would offer us at least a drink of the lemonade made up from crystals and usually termed "jungle juice". I was told that early on, before they had got used to the novelty of RAF helicopters, the Gurkhas used to offer mugs of rum, but jungle juice or tea were the usual refreshments. I remember one occasion when, working all day with the Durham Light Infantry at Balai Ringin, we shut down for a break after a few hours and the RSM, a very large man, approached and asked quietly and civilly if we would like something. When we indicated our grateful acceptance he turned slightly away from us and in a real parade ground voice roared "Private Gallon! Double away and fetch the gentlemen a drink!" No doubt it was the name of the soldier which has made this stick in my mind because a rather small soldier appeared within a few seconds, running, and carrying a large cookhouse dixie which must have held, literally, several gallons of jungle juice.

At a battalion headquarters in the little town of Bau there was a permanent staff of locally employed labourers who virtually ran the landing site. The senior one had been given an RAF beret and was always known as "Number One at Bau". Not only could he be relied on for tea, coffee or jungle juice but he supplied us with "egg banjos". I have never been able to establish the connection with banjos, for these popular food items were merely two slices of bread with a fried egg in between. Number One would hand them up to the pilot while the rotors were turning if there was no time to stop. Payment was never required and I assume that Number One had a good contact in the army cookhouse. Egg banjos were also the stock in trade of the Pakistani vendors, always known as "Pop", who had permission to set up mini-canteens on the airfield and elsewhere. Coffee and tea from Pop always came very sweet and milky in pint glass mugs. Obviously, Pop's goods had to be paid for.

Landing and closing down at a Gurkha location at the right time could mean a good chance of a curry and so perhaps it is really not surprising that we did not ask for RAF flying rations. However, this ploy misfired on one occasion. After a long and busy morning I landed, well into the afternoon, at Padawan, which was home to a company of Gurkhas with whom we were on particularly good terms. We were ravenous and looked forward to a good plateful of Gurkha bhat; at the very least some rice and dhal, we thought. Unfortunately, the Gurkhas were all out on patrol but Padawan was also home to a detachment of Royal Artillery with two 105mm howitzers. So, I approached the young Second Lieutenant in charge of the gunners and asked if he could offer any refreshment. He pointed out that it was mid afternoon and his men had eaten more than two hours ago, but he promised to see what he could do.

There were four of us, from two Whirlwinds, and we followed the subaltern through the sandbags into the gun position and seated ourselves around one of his guns. The gunners' cookhouse was also within the same sandbagged bunker and as we sat and chatted to this very pleasant young man we could hear some clattering and banging going on. We waited, but no appetising smells accompanied the clattering and banging, only some muttering and grumbling from the cook whose afternoon we had presumably ruined. At length, out came the cook, a surly sort of individual, who produced two tin plates, one piled high with thick doorsteps of bread and jam and the other piled with slices of luncheon meat. Disguising our disappointment, not to mention our distaste, and hunger getting the better of us, we tucked into this watched by the young officer. After a while he could contain himself no longer and said "Heavens! That looks so good it makes me feel hungry. I think I'll have some myself!"

One kitchen supplied all the messes at Kuching. The food was not greatly appreciated and many of us went into town virtually every evening to eat in the open market where the local food was cheap and delicious but sometimes had unwanted effects on the system. One morning when flying I was subject to an urge which would not be denied so, landing at a company base at Tepoi, I closed down and jumped out. Tepoi and Padawan were only a few miles apart and both were about a mile from the border with Indonesia. On making my requirements clear I was shepherded through the barbed wire into the company fort, which was built around the summit of a small hill, and shown the way to the top where the Company Commander had his quarters. Clearly, the Gurkhas decided that I should have the facilities provided for the sahibs whereas in my state anywhere reasonably private would have been adequate. I ran up what seemed a very long path with steps made of ammo boxes and sand bags. At the top of the hill I was ushered to what in the 18th century was termed the "seat of ease" (and a better euphemism could surely not be found). It was amazing!

Directly beneath the seat was a shaft lined with empty fuel drums with the tops and bottoms cut out and falling to a pit about forty feet below. The convenience was spacious and situated to the side of and just below the summit of the hill. It was not brick-built but constructed of sandbags and corrugated iron with what I can only describe as a huge unglazed picture window. The view from the seat of ease was to the west where range after range of the mountains of Indonesia receded to the horizon, the colours changing from shades of green to shades of blue gradually getting paler and greyer with the distance. It was all so tranquil and beautiful that it was hard to realise that men were ranging those hills intent on war. I believe it must have been one of the most magnificent views possible from such a facility and the experience was almost worth the pain!   [F.D.H.]

FEASTS AND FESTIVALS

The month long fast of Ramadan began not long after my arrival in Sharjah and its ending was marked by the Eid al Fitr, a time of rejoicing and feasting. In the morning of the great day we three Wing Commanders put on our best uniforms and went to pay our respects to the Ruler of Sharjah in his majlis in the centre of the town. The Ruler, Sheikh Khaled al Qasimi, sat in the centre of a row of chairs along a wall facing the entrance doors and with rugs at his feet. He was flanked by important men, we assumed, but when we had saluted and greeted him some of these men made way for us to take their seats, in accordance with Arab etiquette. The Ruler's coffee maker then came along carrying a silver coffee pot and probably a dozen or more coffee cups. These were like wide but shallow eggcups, without handles, and were nested in a pile which ran from his left hand up his arm to his elbow. The coffee maker poured a few drops, literally not much more than would fill a teaspoon, into the cup in his hand and offered it to the person to be honoured with coffee. The receiver would drink the coffee, which was flavoured with cardamom, and hold the cup out whereupon a few more drops of the beverage would be poured. This would be repeated for a third time and then good manners required that the cup be shaken from side to side to indicate a sufficiency, and returned to the coffee maker who would place it on the top of his pile, shake the cup at the bottom of the pile into his hand and then repeat the ritual with the next man.

Coffee was all very well, and so were the trays of sweets, but when the trays of sticky and glutinous *halwah* (akin to Turkish Delight) were offered, this was different matter. I smiled and declined, but one of my colleagues did not and so had to scoop out and eat a handful of the sweet stickiness and cope with a very sticky hand afterwards.

In the afternoon, we wandered into Sharjah town in civilian clothes and joined the throngs circulating in the souq and in the open spaces. In one place we came on a group of Bedu dancing and singing, and stayed to watch and listen. There were about 20 of them forming three sides of a square, with their left arms round the waist of the man on their left and their right hands waving their camel sticks in unison as they chanted. These sticks are like short thin walking sticks and are used to guide and control their camels. A drummer was beating out a slow rhythm while the dancers performed a slow shuffling step and sang. As they danced, anyone who felt moved to do so fired a shot, or several shots, into the air. Then there arrived a Landrover containing a man of substance, judging by the quality of his garments topped by a cream coloured jacket of European cut. He alighted from his vehicle, whereupon his servant handed him a chromium plated AK47 assault rifle. By this time we had decided that with all this live firing going on the safest place to be was as near to the firer as possible, so we moved nearer as he raised the rifle and fired a complete magazine into the air. That done, he handed the weapon back to his servant, got back into his Landrover and drove off. The whole event was captured on a tape recorder, but unfortunately not on camera. No doubt to fire off so much ammunition was a sign of affluence.

From time to time the Station Commander would receive an invitation to the palace of the Ruler of Sharjah or the Ruler of Dubai, Sheikh Rashid al Makhtoum. Usually the invitation would be for the CO and two or three other officers and almost always it would be for the evening. Thus we would wear mess kit rather than khaki, and never civilian clothes. The meal would always start at 8.00 pm so we would have to arrive by 7.30 and go into the reception area where we would be presented to the Ruler and then circulate among all the other guests, mainly Arabs but including European residents such as engineers and bankers and the British policemen running the Rulers' own police forces. The coffee ritual would take place and soft drinks would be offered but, of course, there would be no alcohol.

The Arabs have a reputation for being casual as regards their attitude to time and this may be so in relation to business affairs but at a Ruler's dinner the Ruler and his entourage would surge from the reception room into the dining room dead on 8.00 pm. This was a large room and furnished in European style with tables and chairs to seat about 200 people – that is to say, men. These were all male affairs. There were occasions when European men were accompanied to the palace but their ladies were then taken off to the women's quarters where they were entertained in much the same way as the men except that they were treated to a whiff or two of incense, some of which was wafted up under their skirts.

On entering the dining room the Ruler and his most senior guests sat at the top table and the rest of us were left to enter and find seats as there were no seating plans. The food at the Ruler of Dubai's dinners was supplied by Lebanese hotels and was very good. The tables were set with plates and cutlery and huge trays of rice, white, yellow and spiced. Then there were equally large trays bearing roast sheep which might be stuffed with a goat which in turn might be stuffed with a chicken. All along the tables were smaller dishes containing savoury gravies and sauces and things such as curried chicken legs.

To start the meal one took a helping of rice by the simple method of picking up a plate and pushing it into the side of a heap of rice. To get some meat to go with it one would be expected to use the right hand and pull off a piece from the carcase. However, the Arabs were very hospitable and anxious to display their ways to European guests and so one would be treated to a choice piece of meat pulled off by a neighbour or even by a man several seats away on either side of the table and thrown or flicked onto one's plate with skill and accuracy. In addition, there were serving men walking round the tables to replenish and who would lean over, tear at the carcase and approach with handfuls of meat. The contents of the smaller dishes could be had with a serving spoon and, as Europeans, we could eat with spoons and forks but most of the Arabs ate using only their right hands, forming a small handful of rice into a ball to flick into the mouth with thumb and forefinger and picking up morsels of meat. Let me say that I never once was offered or even saw the proverbial sheep's eye – I am glad to say. Sheeps' eyes for dinner are a myth, although one presumes that someone somewhere must at some time have been offered one for the myth to be created – perhaps it was done as a joke. But in addition to mutton, lamb and chicken I have eaten goat and young camel at those feasts.

After the meat and rice came the sweet courses, with fruit, dates, jellies and blancmanges. It was interesting to see an Arab opposite me eating a pink blancmange with his hand – something one would discourage children from doing!

The form was to leave the table as soon as one had eaten enough. There was no lingering for conversation at those tables. As one man left then another would take his place and so it would go on with the lower orders replacing their betters until, so it was said, people came in off the street to finish off the generous supplies of food. This might almost be said to be a simple method of social security.   [F.D.H.]

MAGNIFICENT LABS

Early British atomic weapons were huge, and only the V-Force could carry them. Towards the end of the 1950s, however, the Americans supplied a smaller "tactical" bomb, which would fit into the Canberra's bomb bay. The role of the UK-based Canberra light bomber force was originally to drop conventional bombs from high altitude, either visually or by radar, using Gee-H but this became an ill-advised procedure after the Russians shot down Gary Powers in his U2. The problem was how to deliver the new small atomic bomb at low level and escape without being blown up yourself.

In those days, before solid state circuitry had been invented, nuclear weapons were full of fragile electronic components, which would break on hitting the ground, so they had to explode in the air. It was not possible to have a delayed-action fuse which would let your bomb just lie there, waiting until you were safely distant. The answer was "toss bombing", officially known as the Low Approach Bombing System, or LABS for short. The Americans seem to have invented this, and we used their instrumentation.

After a Canberra had been modified and test-flown by RAE Farnborough, I became one of an instructional team which introduced LABS to the operational squadrons and trained the first aircrew. The mark of Canberra in use at that time was the B6, with the T4 available for initial aerobatic practice. Later, LABS was also introduced in the B(l)6 and B(l)8 in RAF Germany. Modifications included the fitting of fatigue meters, baffles at the rear of the bomb bay, non-toppling artificial horizons, and of course the LABS computer itself, which worked on a gyroscope.

The training syllabus, naturally enough, started with a number of practice manoeuvres at a safe height in the T4 dual trainer, followed by some more in the B6. This could be carried out from home bases in Lincolnshire. However, for live bombing we would detach to ldris in Libya and use Tarhuna range (this was before Gaddafi took over, of course). We had the range to ourselves, and no one complained about low-flying.

Before a bombing exercise, the navigator would work through a planning form, entering wind speeds, temperatures and so on, to come out with the exact pull-up point and heading required. As far as I can remember from so long ago, we ran in at 420 knots and 250 feet, and pulled up at 3.5g. Triggered at the IP, the LABS computer timed the necessary run and indicated when to pull up. When the aircraft reached a preset angle of climb, and therefore the corresponding height, the bomb was automatically released. It continued upwards and forwards like a howitzer shell. Meanwhile, after a half loop, the aircraft was rolled out into a shallow dive towards home.

The bomb went up to about 4,000 feet, and travelled a couple of miles in the original direction before going off, so with any luck you would survive the blast. In practice, we were fairly safe anyway because we were just using 25 lb. smoke bombs, not the real thing, thank goodness.

The Canberra was quite aerobatic in a rather elephantine way. It barrel-rolled nicely, even at 40,000 ft, and could do interesting stall turns at 160 knots with full flap down, so the LABS manoeuvre was well within its capabilities. It just needed a certain amount of pilot muscle. The question of airframe fatigue life had to be considered though, and we were told to keep our integral wing tanks full and run down the fuselage tanks, so as to reduce the bending moment on the wing roots

As part of the fatigue calculations, all the aircraft had to be accurately weighed, and the variation was surprising. One B6 in particular was nearly a ton and a half heavier than average. It was one of those built by Shorts under sub-contract, so maybe they had used some left-over bits from Harland's Belfast shipyard! Alternatively, since it was a squadron commander's aircraft, maybe the oak panelling, cocktail cabinet and leather-upholstered ejection seat had something to do with it.

When the squadrons began to convert, we could only do so much simulation in the T4, then we would have to demonstrate in their own B6s. This meant either QFI or pilot sitting on the "rumble" seat (actually Rumbold, I believe). To save having to land and swap over, it was not unknown, unofficially, for us to change seats in the air. It was a bit like swapping drivers in a mini-car without stopping, with one holding the control column while the other squeezed under his arm. I gave up the practice. One day I had just got out of the driving seat and my student had climbed in when one of the engines suddenly flamed out, for no apparent reason. It was rather quiet on the intercom for a while afterwards.

We QFIs on the instructional flight had interesting moments trying things out for ourselves before the squadron conversion programme began. One instructor, on his first runs over the desert at Tarhuna, could not get his Canberra down low enough and fast enough, even at full throttle. At least his altimeter and ASI said so. Although it was difficult to judge height visually over the desert, he was startled when he got to the IP to find himself level with the top of it; a pyramid of oil drums only forty feet high! It was reckoned afterwards that he that had got so low that his aircraft was flying in its ground cushion. Goodness knows what error his static vents were picking up, and what speed he had actually reached. When he returned to base, the baffle in the bomb bay was still hot; such had been the turbulence and vibration.

On another occasion, a bomb door fell off at 400 knots about fifteen miles from the range (they were designed to be removable on the ground by the withdrawal of some big pip-pins). We were somewhat taken aback when the desert rescue team went to recover it, and got themselves bogged down in the sand and ran out of fuel before getting there.

One morning over the desert I let my navigator have a go at a LABS manoeuvre (at that time pilots in a T4 did not have ejector seats, and you could slide the instructor's seat back on rails. The nav was then able to wriggle into it and slide it forwards again.) At 420 knots the aircraft needed a lot of nose-down trim. You had to pull against this as you rolled off the top at much lower speed. I did not think to warn him about this before we began, so he relaxed the back pressure and allowed negative g when we were upside down. His parachute and dinghy fell out of his empty seat in the back, and the lanyard triggered his emergency oxygen bottle. What was more exciting, though, was that both engines flamed out. Fortunately they relit, (just as well, in view of the Desert Rescue Team's previous effort!).

A couple of years later, by the way, we were again in the legendary situation: "upside down, with nothing on the clock but the maker's name", thanks to LABS. I was to give a demonstration at a well-known Norfolk airfield, one Battle of Britain Day. There was no LABS modified Canberra available so I took an ordinary B6 since it was only a simulated attack anyway, and did not require a release computer. No sweat....

At the given time, we thundered towards the airfield and pulled up. Meanwhile, on the airfield below, the Wingco Tech was blowing up a patent concoction of oil and old ammunition to create a realistic mushroom cloud, to the gasps of the vast audience. Unfortunately, two things happened on the way up. The artificial horizon toppled, being an early model. Secondly, we shot into cloud. So I had to finish the manoeuvre and recover from being upside down, blind, with only primary flight instruments and a mere couple of thousand feet from the ground. This was not made any easier by the misleading way the Canberra's vertical speed indicator initially responds to pitch changes. I don't know if the audience was impressed by the LABS maneouvre – little did they know how much more spectacular it nearly was.

Out in the desert, once the sun got up, the air used to become very bumpy. Our flight commander was what might politely be described as a press-on type. One of the ground crew asked to ride with him on a bombing sortie. Before long he was horribly airsick. Whether the boss cared or not, or even noticed, we could only guess. Anyway, after he had landed back at base, someone asked where the passenger was. At first, it was a complete mystery, until we saw a trail of slime across the tarmac, such as a snail makes. When this was followed, it led to a moaning body, face down under some palm trees, waiting for death to end its misery!

It was during a sortie at Tarhuna with a squadron crew that I had an experience that I claim to be unique amongst RAF aircrew. When you were monitoring a trainee crew through a bomb run from the rumble seat, you were frustrated by not being able to see enough over the nose. So I used to stand up until we reached the IP. On this occasion, I was too busy concentrating on his accuracy to realise what was going to happen, until suddenly the pilot started his pull up.

It was too late to sit down once the g was on, making me weigh about 500lbs. I would simply have folded like a jack-knife on to the floor as soon as I bent my knees, and hurt myself. The only thing to do was to try and maintain a geometric lock in my knees. It worked, although I wondered afterwards if my legs had gone pear-shaped. Anyway, I claim to be the only RAF pilot to have taken 3.5 g *standing up!*

How accurate was the LABS method? Surprisingly so, considering all the factors that had to be taken into account, and the unusual trajectory of the bomb. Direct hits were not unknown. After a bit, we QFIs who flew on many runs alongside squadron pilots found we could often forecast where the bomb would land from watching their instruments and the accuracy of their flying. Errors in airspeed, response to the pull-up signal and g-loading on the way up would give an under or overshoot, while any heading error or deviation from wings level would throw the bomb left or right of the target. Overall, the bombing results compared reasonably with conventional methods.

I had doubts, though, whether LABS attacks in a real war would have been a good idea, at least from the crews' point of view....

Imagine troops positioned round some obvious target such as an airfield. There is an air raid alert, and next they see an enemy bomber coming at them, head-on at low level. Suddenly, about a mile and a half away, it begins to pull up and show its vulnerable plan view. What's it doing? You don't wait to make sure. There are just a few vital seconds to knock it down, or else a nuclear bomb is coming your way! You wouldn't just stand there waiting for it to happen, would you! Everyone is going to drop everything, and let loose at it with every weapon they can lay their hands on.... even pelting it with rocks if that is all they have! A good time to be somewhere else....

I heard an RCAF pilot admiring the courage of the mad Brits who would even contemplate trying such an attack. As the French general said when he saw the charge of the Light Brigade, *c'est magnifique, mais ça n'est-pas la guerre...* [R.H.R.]

STARLIGHT AND HAWKEYE

"Please come to the radio, sir. Battalion HQ need to speak to you." These were the words with which the young soldier wakened me and, coming to my senses, I wondered for a brief moment how it was that I was in jungle green and stretched out on a makeshift table made up of ammunition boxes in a bunker inside a company fort about 400 yards from the border with Indonesia.

It was at a place called Serikin, a company location of the 2nd Battalion 10th (Princess Mary's Own) Gurkha Rifles whose Battalion HQ was at the small town of Bau, southwest of Kuching in Sarawak. The time was around midnight and the date the 21st of November 1965. The war with Indonesia, known euphemistically as "confrontation", was at a very active stage. There had been a number of enemy incursions in the area and just four days earlier Bert Fraser, of my squadron, had been shot down and killed when he inadvertently overflew the border at Stass, only about 10 miles north of Serikin. I was in command of No 103 Squadron, equipped with Whirlwind helicopters and based at Seletar in Singapore but with most of the squadron serving in Borneo on rotation. Including our detachments of two Whirlwinds at Simmanggang, one at Balai Ringin and one at Lundu, we had 12 aircraft based at Kuching, which was the RAF's base for operations in Sarawak, at the western end of the island of Borneo, Labuan being the base at the eastern end. Only a few months before I had been what is sometimes known as a "Whitehall Warrior" but, having completed the helicopter course at Ternhill, there I was out from Seletar, and not even asleep in the mess at Kuching but in a very warm room in a bunker at Serikin.

There were forts like this all over Borneo at that time, surrounded by several fences of barbed wire and made of wood, corrugated iron and sandbags – thousands of sandbags. They relied for resupply largely on our helicopters and on airdrops from Argosies, Hastings and RNZAF Bristol Freighters as most were not accessible by road or track. The room I was sleeping in was actually the office and storeroom of the company quartermaster, a Lieutenant (QGO), that is to say a Nepalese soldier who had become a Queen's Gurkha Officer after rising through the NCO ranks.

I had arrived a few hours earlier, not long after sunset, with the task of evacuating some wounded who were expected back at the fort that evening. As I have indicated, things were busy at that time and we were in support of operations by units of 99 Gurkha Infantry Brigade based in the town of Kuching and more usually known as West Brigade. The soldier who had woken me up was British, a gunner from the section of Royal Artillery manning the 105mm gun howitzer at the fort.

Late that afternoon we had received warning from the tasking cell at West Brigade that a Whirlwind would be required to pick up casualties from Serikin which, as I have said, was only a few hundred yards from the border with Indonesia. I decided to take the task myself and detailed a crew and Whirlwind. The task required "Full Precautions" which meant two pilots, preferably two crewmen, flak jackets and 7.62mm GP machine guns. In the event I dispensed with the GPMGs and merely retained our personal weapons, in my case a Sterling SMG in preference to the Webley .38 revolver. As second pilot I took a Sergeant Pilot, Mal Buckley and as crewman, Flight Sergeant Bill Cox, a very reliable crewman with a lot of Search and Rescue experience. Then we waited. After that we waited again, with messages coming in from time to time giving revised times when the patrol with the casualties could be expected to arrive at Serikin. Eventually we were told to go to Serikin and wait there. By that time it was dark but Serikin was easy to find. From Kuching we flew to Bau, overhead the Battalion HQ of 2/10 GR, and from Bau along a route over flat ground to the head of the valley which had Serikin at the other end. The valley was fairly wide but with a sharply rising ridge of hills on each side. Luckily, it was a place with which I was familiar, despite my short time in the region.

There was no moon but the sky was clear and bright with stars so it was easy to see the crest of the ridge on each side of the valley and so to keep straight towards the company base. Inside the fort's fence was an area used as a helipad. The soldiers had placed a light at each corner of this pad and the approach to land was not difficult. Over the last twenty feet or so I used the landing lamp to make sure there were no obstacles and in the knowledge that this made us easy to see. Against this I reasoned that if Indonesians were listening and watching then they knew full well exactly where helicopters landed and would therefore most probably have it covered with a gun on a fixed line if they were interested – or if they were near, and I had no reason to think they had troops near the border at this point.

As we landed I could make out the small green marker lights slightly above and to the side of the outer defensive positions and which were intended to prevent anyone further inside from firing into the backs of their friends. On landing, I shut down and went inside the fort which was typical of company bases in Borneo. It consisted of interconnected bunkers made of corrugated iron and covered with earth and sandbags. There were rooms for stores, for signals, for the command post and so on. Inside I met the Lieutenant (QGO) who had been left in charge while the company commander, Captain Maunsell, was out leading the patrol which comprised most of the company. There were only a few Gurkha soldiers left behind, including the cooks, and the Royal Artillery detachment. The Lt (QGO) was fairly tall for a Gurkha and spoke good English, as would be expected of a man who had spent years in the army and risen in rank and status. During the course of the night we had a long conversation and it turned out that we both had families in Singapore, he had three children there and I had four.

He told me that the patrol would not arrive for a while so we sat and talked, my crew having found themselves somewhere to sit and some tea for us to share. The Gurkhas could not feed us as they were awaiting resupply and had only some eggs and rice which was earmarked for the patrol. Luckily, Bill Cox had brought a pack of dehydrated rations for us to share. As the evening wore on into night the sky became overcast with what appeared to be thick cloud. Still no firm ETA was forthcoming for the patrol and it was on the cards that it would be a long wait so I decided we should get some rest, hence my being asleep, stretched out on ammo boxes amid stocks of army socks, singlets and jungle boots and the like.

At the radio the caller identified himself as "Moonray", second in command of the battalion, and addressed me as "Hawkeye". Strictly speaking, Hawkeye is the army signals code for the Army Air Corps but as there was no codename for the RAF it had to do. Moonray told me that Kuching reported the weather as being unfit for my return during the night and that my orders were to remain at Serikin until next morning. Needless to say, I had a few questions to raise about this but Moonray made it clear that these were the orders he had been required to pass on. I asked what was to happen to the casualties and he said he would try to get a Landrover ambulance to Serikin, although he realised that the tracks were very bad and had been made worse by recent rain. At that point I had no option but to sit tight and, of course, we had noticed the build-up of cloud over Serikin ourselves.

It would be wrong to say that we settled down for the night because all three of us were deeply unhappy at being ordered to get some sleep and wait for morning. Having been tasked to bring out casualties, that was what we wanted to do. So we stood around and talked and kept looking up at the sky to see if we could detect any improvement. The night wore on and the waiting continued but eventually we received word that the party with the casualties would arrive before long.

At last they made their way in through the wire. One casualty was walking but the Gurkha with the major injury was on a stretcher with the medical officer walking by his side and holding up a drip bag, and an orderly holding a hurricane lamp; the picture in my mind is still vivid. At this point I must mention that the army signals codename for a medical officer was "Starlight". The walking casualty had received an Armalite bullet through his elbow and it had gone straight through the flesh, leaving a mark like a bee sting. However, he was presumably suffering from shock and was talking loudly, indeed shouting and waving his good arm, as he went into the cookhouse area to sit down to some rice and fried eggs. His companion was in no condition to shout or talk and the MO said he had taken a bullet through the front of his thigh which had tumbled, shattered the femur and in exiting had taken off a large area of the back of the thigh.

I spoke to the MO and explained that I had received orders to remain until morning. The MO said it was imperative to get the wounded man to hospital as soon as possible. He said he supposed that he would have to send him in the ambulance. After a while the Landrover ambulance arrived with two RAMC men who reported having had a terrible journey from Bau. The track had been washed away at some points, was treacherous and, to say the least, bumpy. The Land Rover ambulance was not an ideal vehicle as its bodywork was, to the average eye, too big for the chassis and therefore somewhat clumsy. When I asked what the chances were the MO replied that the journey by land would most probably kill the soldier, but if he were to wait until morning he would die anyway, so what could he do?

I was very unhappy about this and so were the crew. There we were, all prepared to take the casualty to hospital and with a serviceable helicopter, but ordered to stay put. To us it did not look well for the reputation of the RAF, and I hated being placed in the position of having to say that we had to obey orders. In conditions of darkness and cloud it seemed ironic that "Hawkeye" "Starlight" and "Moonray" could not between them do something to help.

At Serikin the weather did not seem all that bad and we could see the occasional star in gaps in the clouds. So far as we could tell the cloud base was above the hills each side of the valley. Now it was my turn on the radio. I went to the gunners and told them to get battalion HQ urgently. I asked what the weather was like at Bau and found that it was much the same as at Serikin. Next I asked Bau to call the Brigade HQ at Kuching and get them to speak to RAF Kuching. Having established that chain of communication I asked for a weather report. The answer was somewhat vague so I told whoever was at the end of the chain at Kuching to go outside, look up at the sky and report what he could see. There was cloud, at a height unspecified but no rain. The visibility was quite good.

On that basis I said that I had decided to try to get to Kuching, that RAF Kuching and the hospital in the town should be told to stand by and that I wanted the runway lights to be switched on at the airfield. My reasoning was that it was safe to take off from Serikin and if it proved impossible to get to Bau then I could return to Serikin. If all was well overhead Bau then I could head for Kuching and if there was no way through then we could go back to Bau. All this depended on being able to keep below cloud; there could be no question of going into cloud as there were no navigation aids and no radar cover.

Accordingly, I told the crew and Starlight of my decision and we prepared the Whirlwind for the flight back. The badly wounded soldier was placed on the cabin floor on his stretcher, still attended by Starlight with the bag of saline drip. The walking wounded, by now fortified by his meal, came too. Lifting off, I went into forward flight, turned sharply to go back up the valley and was relieved to be able to make out the crests of the ridges on each side, darker than the sky beyond. At the end of the valley I turned port towards Bau and climbed a little to make sure we would be above the hills and outcrops near that town. Then we could see the lights of Bau and flew overhead the Army camp and landing pad so that they could tell that we were on our way and report to Kuching accordingly. From Bau I turned northeast towards Kuching and could see occasional dim lights on the ground. It was possible to keep a safe height, albeit not one calculated in the prescribed way with safety margins added, and still be below cloud, and by now we had radio contact with the airfield. After a few minutes we could see the lights of the airfield and from overhead the runway it took only a couple of minutes to reach the town. Fortunately, I had landed at the hospital only a few days previously in order to familiarise the staff with receiving helicopters by day and night and so it was easy to find and the RAMC staff had sufficient lights to mark the landing site. Safely on the ground, hospital staff came forward to take charge of the two wounded Gurkhas, Starlight still with them and still carrying the drip bag.

By now it was 3.00 am. The job done, we returned to Kuching and found groundcrew waiting. I signed the F700 and we went to bed.

Some while later I was told by the CO of 2/10 GR that although the soldier with the shattered leg would never again be a fighting infantryman, he was expected to recover sufficiently for duties as a clerk or cook.

Later again, we were very interested to find that the operation in which the Gurkhas had been involved had resulted in the company commander, Captain Kit Maunsell, being awarded the MC and Lance Corporal Rambahadur Limbu the Victoria Cross.   [F.D.H.]

DASHERA FESTIVAL

Among my souvenirs is an invitation card, which I was honoured to receive, from "Gurkha Major Balbahadur Tamang MVO MM, all QGOs and other ranks 2nd Bn 10th Princess Mary's Own Gurkha Rifles" to attend Dashera Festival at their barracks on the island of Blakang Mati, just off the south coast of Singapore, on the 21st October 1966. On the back of the card is a programme requiring me to be on the Main Square in a lounge suit at 2000 hours for "Kalaratri", at the Pujaghar for "Kalaratri Puja" at 2359 hours and next morning at 0945 at the Pujaghar again for "Mar". This invitation resulted from an incident in November 1965 in which, in a Whirlwind helicopter, I had brought back from a frontier post at night two Gurkha soldiers wounded in an action after which another man in their company was awarded the Victoria Cross.

Not for nothing have the Gurkhas been described as "bravest of the brave".

On the 21st October 1966 I took a taxi from Seletar to the ferry and crossed to Blakang Mati where transport to the Officers' Mess was waiting for me and the other guests, several Army officers. My mistake was in not getting a full briefing beforehand. I knew, of course, that the Gurkhas are Hindus and that Dashera is their major festival of the year. I knew that there would be religious ceremonies, including animal sacrifices, that the battalion's weapons would be blessed, that there would be a party and that there would be plenty to drink, but I did not realise that there would be a feast as well. Consequently, and foolishly, I heeded advice to eat something before leaving for the barracks, where I arrived in the evening for the event at 8.00 pm.

After leaving my overnight kit in the room I was given in the Mess, I was conducted to the barrack square where most of the battalion had already assembled with their families under awnings erected all round the square. I was shown to my seat beside the Colonel who, it being the Gurkhas' own show, was also a guest. We were garlanded and the Gurkha Major appeared and ordered drinks for us. Here I should explain that the Gurkha Major was the senior Queen's Gurkha Officer (QGO) in the battalion and that the QGOs ranked from Lieutenant (QGO) to Major (QGO) but were subordinate to the most junior British officer. At about that time there were also a few Gurkha Commissioned Officers (GCOs) who ranked as British officers and were in all respects treated equally. Since those days, I believe, the number of GCOs has increased and, indeed, I suspect that the title is no longer used and they are granted commissions in exactly the same way as the British officers. The Gurkha Major was the Colonel's adviser on all matters Gurkha and a very important man. He was also the organiser of Dashera.

Shortly after our arrival the horde of children running about on the square were chased off. The music which had been playing over the loud speakers stopped, the crowd of women and children on the far side of the square parted and on came the first act of the concert, girls and boys of the school dancing to a song sung by two Gurkha lady schoolteachers. These children were aged between eight and twelve by the look of them and were in Nepalese national dress, the boys in white caps, black jackets and white trousers gathered in at the ankles and the girls in saris, decked out with ornaments and with rouge on their cheeks. They danced delightfully and everyone applauded.

Then came on another troupe of dancers who appeared to be young men and girls aged about 18 to 20. They were dressed in the same fashion as the children and, again, danced gracefully and beautifully.

Where did the girls come from? I wondered, because I knew that the women were not allowed to mix with the men and this was obvious from the fact that all the women and children of the soldiers' families were on the far side of the square while the men were on the front of the square and at the sides – strictly in order of rank and seniority, I had little doubt. Looking closer at these rouged and lipsticked lovelies, I noticed standard issue basketball boots appearing from under the hems of the highly coloured saris and it was explained to me that the youngest soldiers are detailed to play the part of nautch girls on these occasions and are dressed, ornamented and painted accordingly. They don't like it, but tradition requires it.

From the beginning there had been plates of food placed before us. First there were curried chicken legs and after these disappeared, relays of plates of curried lamb and other delicacies just kept on coming as did the drinks, which included that Gurkha favourite, rum, as well as whisky and beer and everything usual in a bar. Of course, being a guest of the Gurkha Major and being seated next to the Colonel Sahib might be said to have contributed to this generous hospitality but my other experiences of being entertained by Gurkhas told me that we would be given the best of attention regardless of such distinctions.

The dances went on and there were some comic turns. It is possible that people seeing Gurkhas would think them rather inscrutable, enigmatic and dour in appearance but they are extremely cheerful and good-humoured people. They are highly disciplined, very respectful and deferential but without a hint of servility. It is very difficult to describe this quality but it is evident on spending a little time with them. Anyway, the comedians put on an act which was uproariously funny, at least to those who spoke Gurkhali. Even the linguistically challenged of us could see, though, from their antics and tumbling about, that these were the battalion clowns. I assumed that the jokes were mainly at the expense of the NCOs and officers of the battalion.

More food, more drink and more dancing. By now, at about 11.00 pm, the dancing had changed and instead of rehearsed performances by those in costume the dancing was by anyone who chose to go on the square, and mix in with the "girls" and young men; but we sahibs had no choice. Three hours of whisky and beer etc tends to improve one's outlook on dancing even if it does not enhance the ability but, in any event, the soldiers were very persuasive, even forceful, but, as I have said, respectful with it. Suffice it to say that this sahib and the others were placed in the lines of dancing soldiers, with arms linked on shoulders, and we danced. It was a very simple step, which was just as well. It was a bit like Greek taverna dancing. We did a few steps to the right, one step to the left, one back and one forward, or something of that nature, and gradually and slowly progressed to the right, moving round the square. I was told that this was a dance peculiar to the Limbu tribe of Nepal, most of the soldiers of the 10th having the name "Limbu" incorporated with their other names eg Lalbahadur Limbu or Rambahadur Limbu (he who had been awarded the VC).

After this, we were allowed to resume our seats and more refreshments were pressed on us as midnight approached. About ten minutes to midnight everyone started to move towards the Puja ground, which was a small area of grass about a hundred yards or so from the square. In the centre of the Pujaghar was erected a stake, painted white and with a few Hindu marks on it. Just before the hour struck a black goat was led on by two men dressed all in white and taken to the stake under the supervision of the battalion priest, or "bhoum". The rope round the neck of the goat was passed through a hole in the post and pulled tight by one man so that its head was against the post while the other man held the goat by the body and soothed it. The bhoum spoke some words and another man in white approached with a large kukri. He raised the kukri above his head and, using both hands, brought it down so that he cut off the goat's head in one stroke. There was a loud cheer and a party of riflemen at the side fired a volley. It was a very eerie experience and somewhat sobering in its effect on the uninitiated – including me.

From this macabre scene we returned to the barrack square and the party continued as before. I have no idea of the time of going to bed but I remember waking up in broad daylight, looking out of the window and seeing a crowd of soldiers, many still dressed as nautch girls, dancing and singing outside the mess. Clearly, they had had a lot to drink, as had we all, but they were not behaving in a drunken way. Some of them entered the mess and "persuaded" some of us to join them again in the dance. It was not such fun in the light of day! Eventually we managed to get back in and prepare ourselves for the rest of the festival.

From the mess all the officers and guests went back to the Puja ground and were shown to chairs under an awning where, once again, we were plied with whisky and sodas and beer, or whatever took one's fancy, in elegant silver goblets and tankards from the officers' mess. Our rows of chairs faced onto the Puja ground with the sacrificial stake in full view. To the left was a party of riflemen in uniform and on the right was a sort of stockade of branches, decorated with palm leaves, within which were stacked the battalion's weapons – rifles, machine guns, mortars and anti-tank weapons. Nearby was the battalion pipe band and all around were the off duty soldiers in their best civilian clothes. Of course, being Gurkhas they were all dressed exactly the same and were immaculate even though it was the morning after the night before or, in most cases, a continuation of the night before.

At midnight the sacrificial goat had been black and I was told that it was so important to have a black goat that any white bits had to be blacked over with boot polish. In the morning, to my surprise, the first things taken to the stake for slaughter were some "animals" made of cucumbers with sticks for legs! At the stake the heads of these animals were solemnly lopped off with a kukri by the men in white. These were specially selected soldiers who, we were told, had had to submit to a period of ritual purification before carrying out their tasks. Thus they had been denied participation in the revelries of the night before. After the vegetable figures came some chickens and then ducks. All were taken to the stake and beheaded and each time there was a cheer, a volley was fired and the pipes and drums struck up for a few bars. After the fowls, the animals were brought on, goats first and then, at the end, two bullocks. As before, each falling head was greeted with the cheer, the volley and the pipes and drums. At some point during the morning the weapons were blessed but I cannot remember how this was done. All this time we sat sipping our cold drinks from goblets and tankards beaded with condensation. Somehow the ritual execution, or slaughter, did not seem as repulsive to us, as witnesses, as it might appear to readers.

I have described how the animals were led to the stake and their leading ropes passed through the hole and pulled tight while a man held and soothed the animal. He did this to get the neck straight and still and, as may be imagined, the bullocks were going to be a more difficult proposition. They were brought on by a team of about six or eight soldiers dressed in PT shorts and singlets. The rope was passed through the hole in the stake, half of the party took hold of the rope while the other half took hold of the beast's tail. They then heaved as for a tug o' war until the bullock was stretched out straight. Up to then the kukris used had been the standard issue weapon as carried at the belt, or slightly larger, but now the two headsmen were armed with kukris with blades of about three feet in length. There was a hush as the first bullock was prepared. The kukri was raised on high and then brought down so that just the one blow was enough for decapitation. For the bullock the cheer seemed particularly loud, and it is said that it is bad luck if more than one blow is required. Certainly, it would be bad luck for the unsuccessful wielder of the kukri who would, I should imagine, then be an object of scorn. Again followed the volley and the pipes and drums. Then the second bullock was dispatched in the same way and with equal success.

By then it was nearly mid-day. We dispersed and I made my way back to Seletar to sleep for the rest of the day. Nowadays this ceremony would undoubtedly be viewed as politically incorrect but I doubt whether such an attitude prevents it from continuing to be celebrated each year. Yes, the ceremony could be said to have been barbaric but it had been carried out this way for centuries and I have to say that it did not seem out of place in its context. So far as I was concerned, it was an unforgettable experience and I felt privileged and honoured to be invited to witness it.   [F.D.H.]

TIME TO SPARE? – GO BY AIR!

The following story is certified true. Only the name of the pilot concerned has been changed to protect his identity. He probably became an air marshal later on – and could afford to sue.

At the time, most of my squadron was away in Cyprus on detachment, but some of us were minding the shop back at Binbrook. Every week, our old Canberra B2 used to do a mail run out to Cyprus and back carrying exchange crews, spare parts, letters and so on. It didn't have the range to do this in one hop, so was routed via Idris airfield near Tripoli to overnight and refuel. (This was before Gaddafi). It was due home this particular day.

Meanwhile the CO gave me the job of taking one of our aircraft down to a Maintenance Unit at Wroughton in Wiltshire for a major overhaul. "I will fix somebody to come and collect you", he said, "But at the moment, until the flying programme is sorted out, I can't tell you who it will be." So I dug out my navigator, and in due course we arrived without incident at the M.U., about 45 minutes flying time from base.

Typical of most of these places, it was manned by cheerful civilian technicians, who plied us with the inevitable cups of tea before we got down to the paperwork involved in handing over one of the Queen's aircraft to them. This was when we discovered we were expected to take all the safety equipment back to base with us. This comprised the parachutes and dinghies from three ejection seats. It made quite a mountain of gear by the time it was all removed from the cockpit and piled by the hangar door.

Still, if it had to be, we supposed we could manage. We settled down to enjoy the sunshine and wait for our lift home.

Long years of service had engrained in my navigator a deep mistrust of any arrangement to be picked up by another crew. After a while I began to feel uneasy myself. It was getting on for one o' clock, and we had had nothing except cups of tea since early breakfast. It is at times like this you realise that a mere forty minutes' flying time actually represents about 250 miles between yourself and home.

Just then however, Air Traffic rang to tell us our long-awaited lift was in the circuit. Obviously the pilot was in a hurry, as he taxied at great speed after landing, and swung on to the apron with tyres squealing. I was a bit surprised to see that it was the old B2, only due back from the Mediterranean that morning.

The scream of the engines prevented any questions or answers. My nav dived into the second navigator's seat in the back, I heaved all the parachutes and dinghies after him, and then squeezed in myself with a couple of groundcrew pushing from behind. There was only the little folding seat left for me, beside the pilot, with my feet on the pile of safety equipment and my knees under my chin. The pilot unhooked his oxygen mask and shouted something at me that I couldn't hear, but I recognized him as a newcomer to the squadron whom I didn't know very well.

Once I had succeeded in getting my lap-strap done up and my R/T lead plugged in, I was able to talk to him. Immediately I gathered it was not his day, to say the least. In fact, the CO had just given him a hell of a rocket, and told him to find a bag somewhere in Southern England. That is, unless he wanted to do Orderly Officer for the rest of his miserable life. Not surprisingly, he was wound up to a high degree.

The full story did not emerge at once but, briefly, it was as follows. Our friend, whom we shall call Henry to save his embarrassment, had stopped at Idris overnight with his crew as instructed. Early this morning he had packed his bag and left it by the front door of the mess while he nipped over to Sick Quarters to get something for his gippy tummy. When he returned, his bag had vanished. His navigator had no idea where it might be, and a frantic search ensued. Not only did the bag contain Henry's own kit, but also, more importantly, the precious squadron mail!

Then one of the mess staff had a thought. "There was a lot of baggage in the lobby. I thought it all belonged to the passengers travelling on the Beverley, so put it all on the truck to be loaded." It was too late! Outside came the roar of four mighty engines as they struggled to drag the great pantechnicon into the air. It was already en route to England, with a stowaway bag on board. Apparently, its destination was RAF Lyneham.

Henry's Canberra could easily have caught up with the Beverley, of course, but he could hardly have asked it to heave-to in mid air so he could board it and retrieve his bag. He decided the best thing was to get back to base as soon as possible, and telephone Lyneham so that somebody could find the bag and hold on to it, pending arrangements to collect it.

When Henry got home, the CO told him exactly what he thought of him, and his ancestors, not to mention his cousins and his aunts. Then he gave Henry strict orders that as soon as the B2 was refuelled, he was to go to Lyneham himself for the bag, whereof he would fail at his peril. Then, remembering us, he told Henry to collect us as well (thus, to use an unfortunate metaphor, killing two birds with one stone).

So here we were, not going home, but en route to Lyneham first.

We arrived there without too much difficulty, and were parked on the apron several hundred yards from the huge terminal building. "I'll keep the engines running", Henry shouted at me, "Would you nip out and pick up the bag?" There wasn't much choice. If he shut the engines down, we would need a groundcrew team with a fire extinguisher to start them again. In any case, Lyneham probably did not have the right starter cartridges, so we would have had to unscrew the camera hatch to get at the spares stowed in the rear fuselage.

On the other hand, if the engines were kept running, someone had to sit in the pilot's seat and look after the brakes. I accepted the inevitable, being next to the door anyway, and struggled out on to the tarmac. Nobody seemed to be taking any notice of us, so I had to thumb a lift on a passing tractor over to the main Customs and Baggage Hall.

Lyneham was like a military international airport, geared to deal with hundreds of passengers at a time. The unscheduled arrival of a breathless figure in flying kit caught the staff unprepared. After I had been passed from one official to another about four times, and explained to each of them that I had Nothing to Declare, that I hadn't got Form so-and-so, that it wasn't my bag anyway, that I had nothing to do with the Beverley, and that I wasn't trying to smuggle my aircrew watch, it dawned on me – there had been no phone calls at all from base about this wretched bag.

Far from just picking it up and going home, I was breaking a virgin trail.

At last I found someone who knew something. The Beverley had indeed called at Lyneham, but only for Customs clearance. All the passengers and luggage had then been reloaded and taken on to Boscombe Down. Hastily I telephoned Air Traffic, asked them to clear us to Boscombe and rushed out, no doubt leaving everyone convinced that I was the idiot who had lost the bag in the first place.

By the time I got back to the Canberra, it had been standing in the sun for about twenty minutes. The cockpit was stuffed full of people and parachutes. The round perspex canopy acts like a greenhouse anyway, with only a tiny clear-vision porthole you can open for ventilation. (You can't run the air conditioning on the ground because the heat exchanger burns out.) So although I was dripping with sweat, my state was as nothing compared with those who had sat waiting. I told Henry the wild goose had fled, and we took off again in chase. He was so hot by this time that he had to keep taking his hands off the controls to undo his oxygen mask to wipe the sweat off his face. I tried to keep him calm.

Now it is to be understood that Boscombe Down in those days was an awesome place to ordinary squadron aircrew, with secret aircraft, test pilots, warnings of visitors by "prior permission only" and so forth. It was not the sort of place you just casually arrived at, without first establishing radio contact, getting precise instructions and doing what you were told. The only radio frequency we had in common had about ten other people talking on it at the same time. Henry kept missing what was being said to him, and every time he should have transmitted, he had his mask off to wipe his face. It looked as though we were going to be right on top of the place before we got permission to join.

Too late, we already *were* on top of the place! Just then, a Vulcan shot past going in the opposite direction, and I realised with horror we had assumed a left-hand circuit, and it wasn't, it was right-hand. Now, when you are sitting on a little folding seat, not wearing a parachute, a pile of gear is blocking the door anyway, and your life is in the hands of a man who has an ejection seat, you have to be a bit careful not to rattle him. So, in a voice only about one octave higher than normal, I gently made a few helpful suggestions to Henry. We landed safely.

Soon we were surrounded by efficient groundcrew in white overalls, and Henry was driven off to the other side of the airfield to find his bag. The other three of us sat on the grass and cooled off while the Canberra was refuelled. I found myself looking at my navigator, and he looked at me. We both had the same unspoken thoughts. It was too far to walk home. We didn't have the train fare. We were stuck with Henry and his aircraft.

Could we take it from him and fly it back ourselves? Unfortunately, his name was in the authorisation book as captain. Would it be mutiny under Air Force Law? After all, he was not actually mad like Captain Queeg, just a bit overwrought. Well, very overwrought, actually. Perhaps when he got his bag back he would relax, and after all, the trip home was straightforward. Surely nothing else could go wrong. We shrugged and accepted the situation.

So for the fourth time that day, we clambered into the cockpit, and set off into the wild blue yonder, with the precious bag added to our encumbrances. Henry's navigator gave him three five zero to steer at three hundred knots, which he acknowledged. Shortly afterwards, I had difficulty reconciling the ground with my map. In such a case, it is wise to assume that the ground is telling the truth, and you have got the map wrong. A quick check gave the answer. We were steering three zero zero and flying at three fifty knots, not the other way round. Furthermore, we were steaming straight through a prohibited area.

Some more kind and helpful suggestions to Henry got us out of that, and we had a fairly steady and uneventful flight for the next half an hour, apart from cramp, heat exhaustion, starvation and thirst. Twenty miles out from base, we called for let down and joining instructions. Home at last!

But what did we hear? The other two squadrons, which were still full strength at base, had been on a Bombex, and eighteen aircraft were in the pattern for let down and radar approach. We were number nineteen, and had to orbit for another half-hour before our turn.

When we finally climbed out of the Canberra in dispersal, no one could even speak...   [R.H.R.]

MAKING THE FILM 'THE BATTLE OF BRITAIN'

The film of the Battle of Britain, including the events that led up to it, was released in London in September 1969. It was originally intended that it would be released in September 1968, in time for the 50th Anniversary of the Royal Air Force. Unfortunately, however, the proposed backers lost interest, and it took a year for new backers to be found.

The producer was Harry Saltzman, well-known for his series of James Bond films, the co-producer was Benjamin Fisz, who flew with the Royal Air Force in the war as a member of a Polish squadron, and the film was backed and distributed by United Artists, an American film company. The director was Guy Hamilton, who directed at least one of the James Bond pictures, as well as a number of other well-known films, and he was assisted as aerial director for most of the flying sequences by David Bracknell.

The film was based broadly on the book "Narrow Margin" and the official histories of the battle. It purported to be completely unbiased and to show each side of the story without frills or embellishment.

The line-up of stars taking part in the film was most impressive, and most of them took fairly small parts as mythical Station Commanders and Squadron Commanders. For instance, Kenneth More played the part of a Station Commander and Michael Caine, Robert Shaw and Christopher Plummer were Squadron Commanders. Among the main characters in the story were Sir Lawrence Olivier as Lord Dowding and Trevor Howard as Sir Keith Park. There were also well-known continental actors playing the parts of the various German Staff Officers and Squadron Commanders, from Goering downwards. Apart from the obvious characters mentioned, the film dealt with factual history built around fictional characters and all squadrons and people manning them were fictional.

The film lasted for two and a half hours and there were forty minutes of flying sequences.

Apart from the studio work done at Pinewood Studios, airfield locations and sets were built in Spain, where the German scenes were shot, Duxford, which had four different sets built on it, North Weald, Hawkinge and Bovingdon. Flying also took place from Debden, Panshanger, Sywell, Lydd, and Montpellier in southern France.

Model shots were made on the south coast and, when I left, a model unit was scheduled to spend a fortnight or so in Malta, in search of good weather. We operated for the most part from Duxford, with some time spent at Debden and Bovingdon.

The primary camera aircraft was a converted B25 Mitchell, with camera positions in nose and tail, and also two waist positions. It was very well equipped, including closed circuit television with a playback facility for use by the director. Also used extensively for camera work was an Allouette helicopter, which had a camera mounted in the port passenger position. These two aircraft were used for most of the air-to-air shots; the B25 for large formation work and the helicopter for smaller formations and for filming particular manoeuvres.

The Heinkel 111 bombers, 2-seat Spitfires, 2-seat Messerschmidt Me109 and one Mk9 Spitfire were also used to carry cameras at various times.

A total of twelve Spitfires took part in the film; this number included two dual Spitfires and three belonging to the Royal Air Force Memorial Flight at Coltishall.

One Spitfire Mark 2 had in fact taken part in the Battle of Britain and until the last fortnight or so still had the original engine. This engine gave up eventually, luckily with no more than a slightly apprehensive pilot to show for it, and the aircraft was re-engined with a Merlin 35 and later added to the RAF Memorial Flight.

There were three Hurricanes, comprising one belonging to Hawker Siddeley, one belonging to the RAF Memorial Flight and one which had been rebuilt in Canada and which now belongs to a Mr Samuelson.

Sixteen Messerschmidt 109s were used, including one dual aircraft. They were all Spanish built and had Merlin engines. Thus their nose shape was not quite the same as the aircraft used during the actual battle.

They were the newest aircraft in the film, the Spanish Air Force having used them operationally until about five years previously.

Two Heinkel 111s were brought to this country, but up to twenty were used for the shots taken in Spain. The Spanish Air Force still used them operationally at that time.

It had been hoped that the Stuka in the Henlow museum would be made airworthy and in fact the engine was started. But in spite of only fairly minor work being required on it, the money was not forthcoming and the project was dropped. However, there was a 'Stuka-shaped' ex-Percival Proctor which appeared in the film.

It is worth noting that all the Me 109s, the two He 111s, one Spitfire 9 and the Stuka/Proctor were bought by the film company for the film. The other aircraft were either hired to the company by private owners and the Royal Air Force or, as in the case of the Hawker Siddeley Hurricane and the Rolls Royce Spitfire 14, loaned by the company.

Other aircraft involved were two static Hurricanes, several static and several taxyable Spitfires and a large number of full size static fibreglass models of Hurricanes, Spitfires, Me109s and Stukas for shots of dispersal scenes. They also used half-scale free fall models for shots of crashes and quarter-scale radio controlled models of various types for other flying sequences. In addition to these aircraft models were a large number of models of Chain Home radar masts, a French chateau, the London skyline and other topical items.

Originally there were ten pilots seconded from the RAF, the Commanding Officer, Wing Commander George Elliott, four Squadron Leaders and five Flight Lieutenants, all from Flying Training Command. However, one member left early on in the detachment, so for the most part we were nine pilots strong.

The RAF Memorial Flight aircraft were always flown by Coltishall pilots and in addition there was one civilian pilot employed by the film company, Vivian Bellamy. He was extremely useful to have, having been a test pilot at one time and knowing the Spitfire very well. He also knew all the "ins and outs" of civilian flying and the Board of Trade rules and how to interpret them.

The Me109s and He111s were flown, in the main, by Spanish pilots, with some help in Spain from four members of the Texan organisation known as the "Confederate Air Force". One American, Connie Edwards, remained and flew the Me109 throughout the filming in England. We got on well with the Spaniards and found them to be generally very able pilots. They were led by the Chief Test Pilot of the España Aircraft works at Seville, Commandante Santa Cruz, an excellent man in all respects.

Four of the Spanish pilots and the American checked out in Spitfires and six of us in the Me109.

The Spitfires and Hurricanes were all initially serviced, and refurbished where necessary, by a firm called Simpson Aviation Services, of Elstree. They continued to do second line servicing of the British aircraft throughout the film and, in fact, were still involved with servicing the aircraft before they were returned to their various owners.

First line servicing of the British aircraft was done by RAF personnel, all of whom volunteered for the job. This not only included the flying aircraft but also the static and taxiing ones. As might have been expected, there was a very large percentage of senior NCOs in their number. They all worked very hard and produced excellent results from old and, in some cases, very tired aircraft.

The Spaniards had their own servicing team led by an engineer officer of the Spanish Air Force. They initially carried out both first and second line servicing, but as time got more and more protracted so they gradually left and eventually much of the Spanish first and second line servicing was done by the RAF and Simpson Aviation groundcrew.

The fact that, once in good flying condition, the aircraft continued to fly with relatively little unserviceability was a great tribute to all the ground crews involved, especially those loaned by the RAF.

I reported to RAF Debden on 28th April and met five other pilots who had already been there a week and the other four who were reporting at the same time as myself. We went to Pinewood Studios the next day and learned something of the background to the film, what we were expected to do, the aircraft we were to fly and so on. Flying started on 30th April at Debden.

At this stage we had one dual Mk8 Spitfire and two Mk9 Spitfires. Conversion consisted of 40 minutes in the front seat of the dual aircraft, with a pilot who had converted the day before in the back and consisted of general handling and three or four circuits. Then followed a couple of solo details in Mk 9s, then formation, attacks and tail chasing. We continued to make the odd trip in dual aircraft when the Mk9s were not available or full. The weather was very dull during this period and I did not seem to fly much above 700 feet for the first half dozen sorties.

Only two pilots were cleared to fly the Hawker Siddeley Hurricane, of whom I volunteered to be one. I collected it from Henlow in early May, having had a briefing at Dunsfold on how it worked. So then we had three Spitfires and one Hurricane.

We left Debden and operated from North Weald for about a week in May, until the Spitfires arrived at Duxford. At North Weald a lot of ground shots were done, with us taxying past as background action with real actors doing the running to and climbing into the static aircraft in the foreground. A little flying in support of this was involved, but not much.

Finally, we got to Duxford at the end of May and started doing upper air work. However, we had to move back to Debden in early June while they did a large amount of ground shooting on various sites built at Duxford and some Hurricane flying took place at Duxford, from a grass strip, at this time. However, the main flying, for large formation shots, was done from Debden during this period.

Back to Duxford in late June, and six Spitfires went off to Hawkinge for the week. The Hurricanes and I stayed at Duxford.

During this build-up period, further refurbished Spitfires appeared from Henlow, most of which initially had overheating problems. However, once sorted out they kept remarkably serviceable. Also at this time the Coltishall aircraft came on to the scene and so did the Canadian Hurricane.

Generally speaking, from then on we were at Duxford until the aircraft went to Sywell for filming of grass take-offs and landings in late September and got bogged down for a week. We all moved to Bovingdon at the end of September.

In the meantime, after a fortnight of extremely bad weather at Duxford, in early August the Spitfires, three Me109s and the camera B25 went for ten days to Montpellier in the south of France to film formation shots in good weather. They did a large amount of flying there, most pilots getting 25 to 30 hours during the period in transit and filming. Those, like the Hurricane pilots, who stayed at home hoping to achieve something with the Hurricanes, ended up doing endless taxying at Duxford on non-airworthy Spitfires amid exploding holes in the ground. Exciting in a way, but not exactly like the south of France by Spitfire!

Once at Bovingdon, everything got slower and slower and more and more half-hearted and the dread day came, on Friday 11th October, when all but one of us were told we were not required back on Monday. Typically, it was a wet, miserable day, so we could not even make an excuse to have a last ride in a Spitfire.

The flying was very varied and in some instances very exacting. It ranged from special take off and landing shots which had to be positioned in a certain way, formation take- offs and landings in similar conditions, individual and formation manoeuvres with the helicopter camera aircraft, to large formation mix-ups to simulate dog fights behind the B25 camera aircraft.

All flying exercises were preceded by a briefing in some detail of what the airborne director and cameraman wanted and this did not always match up with what was physically possible. Even when this was pointed out, the film makers, who after all controlled the money, tended initially to ride rough shod over our suggestions and we would have to go ahead and try what they wanted. After several wasted sorties with perhaps 28 aircraft airborne for an hour and a half they did start to see reason and our suggestions were sought more readily. This, the very bad weather, the language difficulty with the Spanish pilots and some rather poor communications equipment, all added up to a large number of wasted sorties and frustrations all round.

The method of trying to stage a dog fight provides an excellent case in point. The idea was to lead the formation in the B25 using the tail camera position. Follow that, maybe, by the two He111s in loose formation, and on perch positions on either side to have a mixed bag of Spitfires, Hurricanes and Me109s, say a dozen on each side. Over and above this was usually a Spitfire and an Me109 on a separate perch, whose job it was to provide foreground action close to the B25 using the various smoke devices with which they were fitted. Several aircraft in the main formation, both the He111s and even the B25, were also fitted with smoke. On the command "Action!" the two large formations would converge behind the He111s, within camera view of the B25, fan out into individual aircraft, weaving and tailchasing, and smoking where they could. And the two individualists would make a close pass on the B25, one on the other's tail. In amongst all this, one Heinkel would normally smoke and fall out of the formation. As can be imagined, it now and again got quite exciting in the middle of this lot and it was very frustrating when one saw the rushes to see how unexciting it often looked on the screen.

Add to all this, a film director in the B25 who was impatient for everyone to re-form formation as quickly as possible for it all to happen again, the B25 pilot knowing that he was going outside his designated area and wanting to turn round, a cameraman interested in which way the sun was, He111s which could only go at 160 knots or less, having to re-form formation, Spanish pilots who were initially not too happy with speaking English or with navigating over a foreign country and who did not like their Me109s for manoeuvring at much below 170 knots, and pretty poor communications and it is not surprising that people tended to get a little despondent now and again.

However, one or two shots which they did take of such formations were spectacular, and could be used with different cuts and different emphasis, time and again in the film.

In addition to the large formation filming, individual formations of Spitfires, Hurricanes and Me109s were filmed making attacks on their opposite numbers, from both the B25 and the helicopter and some of these looked very good indeed.

The two-seat Spitfires were used in large formations in the background where they would not be noticed, as were the Mk 14 and Mk 19 Spitfires with their rather different nose and tail shapes. The two-seaters also used to carry cameramen, who took film of formations from within, and one of them was converted to be flown from the back cockpit with a camera/mirror combination which provided film through the gunsight. Some good film was obtained in this way and I was lucky enough to do some of this flying, chasing a smoking Me109 and attacking He111s; so can claim to be director and cameraman of two or three sequences. It remained to be seen whether they used them in the film.

Another interesting camera mount was built into the wing of a Mk9 Spitfire in which the camera watches the pilot as he flies the aircraft and searches the sky. Me 109s appear in the background and flash past, the aircraft smokes and the pilot opens the hood and starts to undo the straps. Not unnaturally, it is not carried to the logical conclusion, the final part being from a mock-up at the studio.

The poor weather was the biggest bugbear of the whole film. We were not permitted to fly in Instrument Meteorological Conditions by the Board of Trade and not many of us wanted to do so, with some of the older and more unreliable instruments. For historical accuracy all filming had to be done in sunlight, if possible, with white fluffy cumulus cloud about. There was very little of either that summer and we waited endlessly at all the places we operated from, in varying degrees of comfort, for a miracle to happen, and it seldom did. Even on perfectly flyable days by any other standard we often could not fly because either the weather or light was not just right. This, and the fact that continuation training was practically non-existent because of the cost to the company were among the biggest morale drainers of the detachment.

To say that I was delighted and thankful for having been given the opportunity to fly Spitfires and Hurricanes, is a thorough understatement. I cannot remember, in 3,000 hours of flying, enjoying any type of aircraft as much as the Spitfire, very closely followed by the Hurricane.

I was thankful that there was a dual Spitfire available for the familiarisation sortie, because it was rather a surprise to have all the noise, rather rough sounding noise, after a Jet Provost or a Chipmunk, not to be able to see well for landing, and to find such sensitive elevators. However, after forty minutes I was very happy to go off, in poorish weather, in the Mk 9, which I enjoyed very much. But the aircraft I liked best of all is a Mk5 now belonging to the Shuttleworth Trust, which is a delight to fly, being lighter than the Mk9 and better harmonised on the controls. I cannot imagine a nicer pure flying aeroplane.

The Hurricane I flew from scratch and found very comfortable, but not as clean cut on the controls as the Spitfire. However, it had several good points, being very nice for general handling, more easily flown adequately by inexperienced pilots and, of course, having a wide undercarriage, is easier to control on the runway after landing. A bit lacking in performance compared with the Mk9 Spitfire, but nearly as good as a Mk5 – another delightful aircraft to fly.

I was also lucky enough to fly the Me109 for one sortie. I would have liked a couple more, to enable me to assess it better, but it again seemed a very pleasant aircraft once one got used to the unusual sports-car type seating position, non-adjustable rudder pedals, seat which had to be adjusted before flight, and the coffin-lid type canopy, which once shut can hardly be opened from inside. It does tend to swing about rather, particularly on take off, because of the narrow track undercarriage, which is a long way in front of the centre of gravity. I am told that this led to a large number of accidents during the war, and it certainly led to one at Duxford in which the aircraft swung on landing and was written off. The pilot, a Spaniard, was unhurt. In the air it handled very well in the rolling plane, not as well as the Spitfire in the pitching plane, and tended to slip and skid without the pilot noticing it. This was largely because there was no adjustable rudder trim on the aircraft. Those with a little more experience in the type liked it very much.

Although the part of the film we were mainly concerned with was purely flying the aircraft, we did have some opportunity of seeing something of the filming on the ground, particularly during shots of the various airfield locations at North Weald and Duxford. Here, as spectators, one got the idea of the tremendous amount of organising which falls on the location manager, who has to organise all the props, extras, actors, directors, cameras, cameramen, make-up men, hairdressers, carpenters and labourers into the right places at the right time, also house and feed them, and attend to complaints from local farmers about people on their land, and local school teachers about aircraft endlessly low flying over the school. Also, we saw the mixture of organisation and artistic ability required of the assistant director, who, with his various assistants, sets the whole scene up for the director proper. This really becomes harassing when aircraft are to be taxied as background to actors playing some scene, with mock bombs blowing up not far away, and the one-off shot of the Duxford hangar blowing up and burning down, also not far away. Add to this the vagaries of wind direction, blowing smoke over the cameras, and the sun only shining fitfully, and life for everyone became rather hectic, and at times a certain tartness between directors and others tended to creep in.

However, once we realised their problems and once they realised we were not prepared to attempt the impossible, or even the imprudent, at their whim and fancy, we did get along very well, and found it was a pleasure to work under conditions so different from the normal Service ones, and with people with such a different outlook.

I must finally mention the meticulous attention to detail in camouflage and markings of all the aircraft, and the enormous expense incurred in obtaining or making up authentic period MT and other vehicles, the provision of authentic uniforms, including flying helmets and flying kit generally, and the creation of airfield dispersals with fibreglass buildings, turf covered plywood dispersal pens, and the full sized fibreglass models, and, in one case, facade of the French chateau I mentioned earlier; all this only on the airfield dispersals. Far more was done in the studios and in Spain before we joined the film, and one can see that all this, with the immense cost of buying and operating the large numbers of aircraft involved, adds up to an extremely expensive film.

I flew 49 hours on Spitfires, 32 on Hurricanes, and half an hour on the Me109, over a period of nearly six months. Those lucky enough to go to France achieved about 28 hours more than I did. This flying in itself was great fun, and ample recompense for long hours of sitting around waiting for things to happen. But add to it the chance to see a film of this size being made, to meet the people making it, including the Spanish pilots, with whom we got on very well, and to serve as member of a 13 UE Spitfire/Hurricane Squadron of tremendous spirit, in 1968, and one can appreciate what a marvellous, rewarding and unforgettable experience it was.   [D.H.M.]

SPITFIRE DELIVERY

In November 1968, after all the flying sequences for the Battle of Britain film had been completed, I was given the "onerous" task of delivering Spitfire IIA P7350 from Bovingdon to the Battle of Britain Memorial Flight, then at Coltishall, the Lightning OCU. It was then, and probably still is, the oldest airworthy Spitfire, having taken part in the real Battle of Britain. For a long while it was kept as an exhibit at the RAF Museum Colerne, before being restored to flying condition for the film, and was then donated to the BBMF together, later, with Hawkers' "Last of the Many" Hurricane, which was also used in the film.

At the time I was a squadron commander, back at the College after all those years, and the CFI, Johnny Parker (also ex 54, and later tragically killed with his wife as passengers in a Citation which went into the sea near Stornoway) suggested that I should take the pretty route, and stop for lunch at Cranwell so the budding Phantom and Harrier pilots could have a look at a real aeroplane. Since a "suggestion" from the boss could be considered an order, and since it was fun, this I did. Neither of us had thought to put either 11 Group (I think) whose aeroplane it was, or Coltishall in the picture; mainly, I think because we knew jolly well they would have said no. So they both became a little concerned when their new toy didn't turn up on time!

After lunch I set off again in company with the escorting Jet Provost, which had to do all the radio clearances, because the Spit only had VHF, and the RAF bases UHF, and we duly arrived at Colt in amongst all the normal Lightning traffic. On the JP's call, I was given a green light from the runway caravan, and did the customary run in and break for landing. Downwind on a curved circuit, undercarriage down, start curved finals to keep the threshhold in sight past the nose, ease on a trickle of power round finals; no power, only a large three bladed propeller gradually coming to a halt! Luckily I was doing a tight circuit and was able to delay flap selection, and easily made the runway.

The Lightnings in the circuit, using more fuel for one circuit than I had used for the whole flight, must have been fairly concerned to see their only runway blocked by a stationary Spitfire, with the pilot frantically trying to push it to the nearest exit point. Fortunately, the runway controller had seen what had happened and I was soon joined by Wing Commander George Black (later AV-M retd), Colt's OC Flying, and between us we were able to push P7350 off the runway before any of the Lightnings got too low on fuel.

I seem to remember that some carburettor problem was put down as the cause of my embarrassment. That was my last ever flight in a Spit, and one I will always remember!   [D.H.M.]

HAIRY MOMENTS AT NIGHT

No 46 Night/All Weather Squadron at RAF Waterbeach was equipped with Gloster Javelins when I joined the squadron in late 1959. In addition to the High Level Interception role (HLPIs), the squadron had a secondary role, that of intercepting any low level airborne threat. To train for this we practised low level interceptions (LLPIs). Whilst we were very familiar with HLPIs, to carry out interceptions at 500 feet was quite a different matter. We practised these in pairs over the North Sea, each acting in turn as target and attacking aircraft. Since the fuel consumption of the jet engine is much higher at low level we conserved our fuel by switching off one of our engines when acting as the target aircraft. When you became the attacking aircraft you relit the other engine. LLPIs and night relights were quite "hairy".

During one particular HLPI sortie, the GCI controller called me on the R/T and directed me to intercept an unidentified aircraft flying inbound to the UK over the North Sea. On our way to intercept this "target" we were advised that it was well below, so I started what turned out to be a long descent from 40,000 feet. When within range of our radar, my Nav/Rad picked up the target and directed me in the normal way in a curve of pursuit.

I remember him passing me lots of "speed backs" – for me to reduce speed by 0.5 mach each time – and from my initial closing speed of some 400 knots I found myself flying alongside the aircraft at 3,000 feet and at 150 knots, not far off my stalling speed! I was able to identify the aircraft as a Varsity trainer, which had, it turned out, failed to put in a flight plan. Rather a disappointment to me, as I was getting quite excited at the thought of shooting down a Russian intruder!   [A.D.R.D.]

VISITS TO THE OLD NORTHWEST FRONTIER

In 1961 No 73 Squadron, based in Cyprus, was ordered on a full squadron detachment to the Pakistan Air Force Base at Peshawar on the Northwest Frontier. This was part of that year's first "Exercise Shabaz"(No. IV). The squadron deployed via Meherabad, Teheran, on 10th April, to remain until 16th. The leg to Teheran was initially north to avoid Syria and Iraq, over the lakes and great mountains of eastern Turkey, close to Mt. Ararat of Noah's Ark fame and the Soviet border. The Russians appeared to behave mischievously occasionally, transmitting on duplicate beacon frequencies apparently to lure an unsuspecting *CENTO* aircraft over the border where it would be shot down. This may have caused, or stemmed from, the shooting down of a USAF aircraft in the area some years earlier.

The flight to Teheran took about two and a half hours and for the final half hour was over the Iranian Elburz mountains, some of which rise to 16,000 feet and at this time of year were startling in their snowy whiteness. To the north, only a few miles away, was the coast and inland sea home of the best sturgeon in the world. During the descent and approach to Meherabad, the blue Caspian disappeared, the great sugarloaf shape of snow-covered Demavend (18,000 ft) was briefly proud on the eastern horizon, then the sand coloured roofs, tiles and minarets of Teheran became gold in the late afternoon sunlight as line up was made for the runway. To a new arrival it must always look fabulous.

Iranian representatives of British Airways acted as agents for the Iranian Air Force to handle aircraft refuelling and, when required, RAF personnel accommodation. This was still the time of rule by the Shah, before Islamic fundamentalism had taken over and risen to its current heights. There were fine hotels for all ranks, restaurants, bars and nightclubs, an excellent taxi service and visitors' facilities, all with an agreeably romantic Oriental flavour. The flight from Teheran to Peshawar was completed in one leg, made longer because of the need to ease south to avoid overflight of Afghanistan. The route went southeast over Khorasan and the great salt desert of north central Iran, remote, sparsely populated, and with few roads. Entering Pakistan near Zahedan and after 30 minutes easterly flight along the Afghan border, the route could at last swing northeast on a direct line along the North West Frontier Province to Peshawar. This used to be the tooth-cutting training ground of the British Army in India for a century and carried ringing names like Kohat, Quetta, Fort Sandeman, Rasmak and the Khyber Pass. The great craggy mountains of this area are not unduly high but even from transit height of 30,000 feet looked dark and forbidding; not a good place for a forced landing from any point of view.

The airfield at Peshawar had originally been built by the RAF, laid out in just the way which would be familiar to the present visitors. The messes had good facilities, including tennis courts, and the rooms were shaded but airy with well maintained fans. Officer crew were awarded a batman. The CO's batman, from a village seven miles away from which he walked daily, was a tribesman called Gulbha Khan, twice the age of the average squadron officer and plainly delighted to serve the 'Raj' again. The airfield was equipped with US manufactured F-86s having a ground attack role on the frontier as well as air defence. Their young pilots were of high calibre, well trained and disciplined, with whom the squadron exercised safely and profitably. Their ground radars were somewhat sparse so sometimes the Canberra escaped detection even at high level. In fact, most of the exercise 'raids' were at height in order to give existing radar and fighter squadrons a set piece scramble and interception situation against approaches from the east and south (i.e. from India!) as well as from the north. Attacks from the north were of course restricted in length due to the Afghan and Kashmiri borders but some crews enjoyed the magnificent views of distant Nanga Parbat, 26,000 feet of formidable snow peak.

It was normal squadron practise on these detachments to offer the host officers and their wives a party in their mess based on the supply of drinks brought from Cyprus on the aircraft. These were welcome as price and availability problems made such occasions rare for the PAF. They were quite jolly although the Pakistani wives tended to stay in a shy but colourful group to one side. On this occasion the squadron was immediately bearded by the local American CIA staff who wanted to know if the squadron aircraft had been modified for nuclear weapons yet? One officer said "Not yet", another said "Of course", and the CO said "Need to know, old boy"

The PAF hosts were happy to provide a bus, for a day's break, to take personnel on an outing up to the historic Khyber Pass, to the Landi Khotal village where tribal craftsman were making by hand perfect replicas of Lee Enfield, Browning and Webley guns. Middle aged locals, perceiving that the visitors were Christians, often spat in contempt, no doubt mentally continuing hill engagements with the British, pre-1947 . A demonstration of one weapon's capability was provided by Colin Hughes, for whom guns were a hobby. He loaded and fired a small Beretta type automatic before buying it. Nobody in the village took any notice of the shot which was no doubt commonplace. All the men went openly armed, many with handguns. None of the few Pathan women seen were veiled and they were beautiful but clearly well protected.

Continuing the journey to a high point looking down to the Afghan frontier post, a great white cloud-like strip high in the far distance towards Kabul was identified as the snows of the Hindu Kush. A long straight road stretched across the plain as far as the eye could see, groups of tribesmen were walking on it in each direction, at their typically long, striding pace, apparently tireless. They are said to be able to do the same uphill, for hours. On the way back through tribal territory there was a group of a dozen tribesmen engaged in discussion under a tree. The bus driver said that it was a bargaining contest between two families, a member of one having shot and killed a member of the other. The aggrieved family claimed either a death or other adequate compensation.

The squadron suffered no ill effects from eating the local food, although another squadron on a visit later that year had severe dysentery problems. The messes tried to tone down their standard cuisines to British tolerances but not very effectively. Perhaps it was expecting too much from unconscious thought habits in the kitchens. Even the fried eggs at breakfast were curried, or seemed to be. While everybody enjoyed the detachment, everybody was glad when it ended and return flights were made to Akrotiri via Karachi (Mauripur) on 16 April.

In November 1961, Shabaz V required 73 Squadron to go again to Pakistan, this time to operate from the PAF base at Mauripur, near Karachi, which had resident PAF B-57 squadrons. The detachment was broadly successful but there was less evidence of a PAF welcome and eagerness to help as compared with Peshawar. This may have been due to a misunderstanding by the Pakistani station commander of the role of a Royal Air Force exchange officer who happened to be on base for weapon training duties with the PAF. He certainly did not have the power nor the time to handle a large detachment and he had the squadron's sympathy. Things were sorted out at various levels and no loss of sorties or effectiveness resulted. Personnel were accommodated in good hotels in Karachi, not in the PAF messes, so automatically and regrettably they were more remote from the PAF throughout.

In November 1962 the squadron went to Peshawar again for Exercise Shabaz VII, happily accommodated as before in the PAF messes. On this occasion and following the excellent advice of the adjutant, the CO made polite overtures to the British Assistant High Commissioner who was located in Peshawar. He and his wife made squadron officers feel very much at home and gave them a rare insight into the activities and interests of the Foreign and Commonwealth Office.. Perhaps needless to say, the northwest frontier was as ever a place of unrest and intrigue. The Pakistan government had inherited all the Raj's problems and already were, like the British, tending to foster peace and stability by paying the tribes money. One or two tribesmen, like Baljar Ghul, remained implacable and seemed to attract frequent attention from the PAF. Afghanistan swarmed with Russian agents who no doubt would not have found it difficult to enter Pakistan at the time with the annual migrations of the Powindahs, a travelling pastoral people who had traded for centuries in spices, carpets, camels and gold. In addition, there were the barely concealed U2 aircraft operated by the American CIA whose grey suited 'heavies' were equally visible. It all made ordinary squadron training for actual war seem a much more straightforward process. Until, that is, a group of officers was sitting at the mess bar one day – the bar attendant was a magnificent figure, tall, grey-bearded, richly turbanned and cummerbunded. He looked with piercing eyes at the CO for a moment and said, "You know, sir, war is a very bad business".

The CO who was in a light, end-of-day mood, agreed that indeed it was, especially if one was careless enough to lose it. The magnificent figure looked at him steadily again for a moment, then said "I don't think it matters who wins, sir, (Pause) I was at both battles of Ypres. We won. I lost all my friends. War, sir, is a bad business." Nobody argued further.

For most visiting British in the 1960s, Peshawar was still a place of echoes, struck from boyhood memories of Kipling and Boys' Own Paper. The Peshawar Vale Hunt Club was still there, its long row of Masters of Hunt portraits intact, blue-eyed, fair-haired, straight from the shires of England. It would be ungracious to miss unduly such fair complexions in the faces of the last three Masters. However, the club and its furnishings had seen better days and the nearby British graveyard was a testimony to neglect. Inscriptions were remarkable for the relative youth of the interred who had met their deaths for flag and country in action, through sickness and, for women, in childbirth.   [C.H.F.]

MUD, GLORIOUS MUD

An odd, little-known corner of the Air Force, set up during the war, was the Airfield Construction Branch. They were still operating at the end of the Fifties, when I was posted to their depot at Wellesbourne Mountford as station adjutant.

There were a number of mobile construction squadrons scattered round the world doing various jobs on airfields. As adjutant back at base, I did not see much of these operational units, except for correspondence and signals passing across my desk to the CO and occasional individuals in transit to and fro. (I soon learned that a lot of the paperwork concerned MT accidents, for the squadron low loaders were always squashing Minis or removing traffic islands!).

The depot was responsible for storing and servicing masses of earth-moving plant. Tech Wing hangars were full, not of aeroplanes like a normal RAF station, but of scrapers, graders, bulldozers and other great crawling monsters. I believe that most of them had been purchased by the government for the ill-fated African Ground Nuts Scheme after the war. Since the Airfield Construction Branch, as far as I could judge, did nothing the Royal Engineers could not have done as well, if not better, I think it was kept going for political reasons, so that the Government could claim that the money spent on these machines had not been wasted after all, because the RAF had an important use for them.

The other activity at the depot was the training of the machine operators. There was a satellite area a couple of miles away where these guys did their circuits and bumps. I didn't manage to wangle any hours on bulldozers, but I did visit this training ground. A lot of the syllabus evidently consisted of pushing masses of earth into big heaps, then levelling it again. Given that this disrupted the natural drainage of the land, and that it rains quite a lot in England, the result was mud, mud, glorious mud, from one end to the other, several feet deep in places. It was quite easy to lose Wellington boots, and if you lost your balance trying to extract a leg from the suction, several people with ropes would have been needed to save you. The place gave a good idea of what conditions at Passchendaele must have been like.

The personnel were not quite like the rest of the RAF. The station commander was a nice chap who, I think, was a civil engineer by upbringing. He had a steel model bulldozer on his mantelpiece instead of a model aeroplane. Apart from the usual complement of admin staff, most of the officers were civil engineers, quantity surveyors, plant engineers, clerks of works and the like, with little in common with the rest of the RAF. Some of them had presumably got where they were by virtue of their academic qualifications, rather than by conventional Service careers. I was on the telephone one day when, out of the corner of my eye, I noticed a young person enter the office in pilot officer's uniform and stand politely to attention. I nodded at him to relax, and concluded my telephone conversation. Then I turned towards him to ask what he wanted, and saw that he was not a pilot officer after all. He was a wing commander. Probably had a first class degree in soil science or something similar.

The other ranks were just like the sort you get on any building site. A lot of my time as adjutant was spent dealing with complaints about fights outside pubs in Stratford-on-Avon, or with shopkeepers whose bills had not been paid. It was not just the junior ORs who were a bit rough either. We had to court martial the CMC of the Sergeants' Mess, who had gone to bed drunk and set himself on fire with a cigarette end. Another time, a hapless youth was Orderly Officer. Standing Orders required the OO to ensure that the Sergeants' Mess bar was closed at 23.00 hrs. I should have briefed the little lad that this meant, in practice, ringing the Orderly Sergeant and checking that it was. Instead, he steamed straight into the Mess in person, and ordered all the old hairies to shut their bar. Next thing, he was through the front door and into the ornamental pond outside.

A few quiet words were had next day with all concerned.

For some of the incorrigible troublemakers, fortunately, a lot of trouble was saved in courts martial and admin procedure by the co-operation of the medical staff, who would interview them and get them discharged within about a fortnight as unfit to serve on psychiatric grounds. I didn't argue.

It was at Wellesbourne that one of those slightly surrealistic incidents occurred which enliven boring jobs from time to time. It was during a practice parade for the AOC's Inspection. The entire station was duly formed up in flights and squadrons, and handed over to the station commander. He put us through all the drill with no problems. When the parade was finished, though, instead of handing over to me as parade adjutant to dismiss them, he decided to carry on and do the wet weather rehearsal as well, without any previous briefing,

So what did he do but order the parade to left turn, and march off in column of route to the hangar. It should, of course, have been a right turn. The result was the entire parade marching off in a sort of mirror image of what it should have been, with all the right markers at the back of their flights, all the flights and squadrons in reverse order, and their officers at the wrong ends.

The Station Warrant Officer and I exchanged one glance, and both of us abandoned our places and pelted over to the hangar. We were still trying to work out how to get the parade sorted into its correct formation (right wheel each flight twice, then right turn them? But the squadrons would still have been in reverse order.....), when it was too late. There came the ominous tramp of hundreds of heavy boots. No.3 Flight of No.3 Squadron loomed into the hangar, backwards, so to speak, followed by No.2 Flight, then No.1 and so on, with No.1 Flight of No.1 Squadron, who should have been leading, somewhere in the far distance. Also, of course, back to front.

There is something about the disciplined tramp of columns of marching men which strikes deep into the human psyche. The barbarians must have felt this when the armoured Roman Legions advanced towards them. It is something to do with the menacing rhythm of the boots, the discipline and drill, file after file coming towards you, all welded into an inexorable and relentless force. I had never realised this before, but now I stood awestruck in the path of these tramping men, like a rabbit in car headlights.

Desperately the SWO and I tried to stand our ground, shouting unheeded orders and waving our arms. We might as well have been in some railway roundhouse, trying to stop enormous locomotives with our bare hands as they rumbled menacingly in one after another. It was to no avail – we were caught up into the milling confusion, as those at the back cried "forward", and those at the front cried "back", and yet more squadrons crashed into those we had managed to halt.

Eventually, the only answer to dismiss everybody, shoo them from the hangar, and make them fall in, all over again, on their right markers outside. The station commander meanwhile was helplessly watching in the background, wondering what he had done, and what was going on.

All he had done was simply to get one single word wrong – "left" instead of "right"!! [R.H.R.]

EXERCISE SUNFLOWER 1 – A JOURNEY ROUND THE WORLD IN 31 DAYS.

Introduction

Until 1964 my experience and knowledge of Bomber Command had been gleaned from class-room studies, very short-term visits, books and pamphlets, and the anecdotal wisdom of some who had served in that great Command. My flying background was almost exclusively fighters (Vampire, Venom, Meteor and Hunter) although ETPS and tours of duty in the Experimental Flying Department, Farnborough and at the Aircraft and Armament Experimental Establishment, Boscombe Down gave me the opportunities to fly a wide range of multi-engined aircraft, piston and jet, including all three types of V-bombers. It came as a great surprise, therefore, in 1963 at the end of the Staff College course, to be posted to High Wycombe as Personal Staff Officer to the C-in-C Bomber Command! I was even further amazed, indeed shocked and a little apprehensive, at the end of the Joint Services Staff College course in early 1966, to learn that I was appointed to command No 9 Squadron, equipped with Vulcans at RAF Cottesmore , a station in No 1 Group. During an introductory lunch (accompanied by my new Station Commander) with the AOC 1 Group, the Senior Air Staff Officer and Group Captain Operations I was left in no doubt that I was expected to embrace wholehearted the "bomber culture" and the discipline demanded in the UK's Deterrent Force! I was told to put aside all thoughts of those balmy days flying fighters and the pleasures and excitement in the "civil environment" of test flying! Clearly, I had much to learn!

During my first year with "Nine" I was aware of the Far East crisis known as "Confrontation" and the UK's commitment to support Singapore against a threat from Indonesia. At that time reinforcement of the Far East was a responsibility of the Victor Force at Scampton acting in a deterrent role. But I soon learnt that changes were in the wind and that it was planned that the Vulcan Force would assume the Far East reinforcement task; No 9 Squadron was to be the first Vulcan Squadron to undertake the role.

The rotation of Victor Squadrons during the crisis was via the well-worn East route through the eastern Mediterranean, Middle East, Gulf and Indian Ocean areas and was known as Moonflower. However, political changes in the countries over which Moonflower flights were conducted were increasingly leading to refusals by the governments to allow these flights to take place as and when the UK wished. The alternative route was west- about across North America and this was the route to be undertaken by "Nine" late in 1967; reinforcement west-about would be known as 'Sunflower '.

The Concept and Plan

The Concept was not particularly complex. Eight Vulcans would deploy from Cottesmore to Tengah, Singapore, west-about, supported by an appropriate level of engineers and technicians, plus spares, to sustain the Force for an estimated period of concentrated flying of four weeks. Dedicated aircraft from Transport Command were tasked to deploy the ground element in step with and along the same route as the Vulcans. The plan included an air defence exercise based at Darwin with the Royal Australian Air Force and a similar exercise from Tengah organised by the Far East Air Force. At the end of the planned detachment two or three days were set aside for preparing the Force for its return to Cottesmore; not retracing the route across the Pacific and North America but continuing westwards in four easy "hops".

The deployment plan details were contained in the Sunflower Operation Order. When it was confirmed in early 1967 that I would be the detachment commander, I more or less sat back and prepared to enjoy, in anticipation, the prospect of an interesting "adventure" later in the year. How wrong I was! With some seven or eight months to go, a signal from High Wycombe tasked me to draft the Operation Order and gave me a month's deadline for a submission to Command for their approval. There was some relief in that I was assured that the annexes for the specialist details covering the engineering (personnel and spares) requirements, air transport support, communications plan and en route domestic arrangements would not be my responsibility. I was further relieved to learn that there would be an officer and NCO established at each staging post to liaise with the USAF staff to smooth our passage to Singapore. My responsibilities concerned those aspects relating to the flights, the aircrew and the knitting together of the whole. The pressure was certainly on and a "no-notice" nuclear generation exercise (Exercise 'Micky Finn') for the whole of V-Force was not helpful!

The route plan envisaged eight Vulcans departing Cottesmore on 8th November 1967 and staging through Goose Bay (night stop), Offutt and McClellan (nightstop), Hickam (two nights and rest day), Wake Island and Andersen (night stop) then into Tengah. The Air Defence Exercise at Darwin required five days and the remaining time at Tengah involved the Singapore Air Defence Exercise, live bombing and local familiarisation. The planned route home involved staging through Gan (night stop), Muharraq (night stop), Akrotiri and into Cottesmore. A "piece of cake" one would have thought, but the fickle finger of fate intervened!

A Political Decision Puts Sunflower 1 in Jeopardy

In the autumn of 1967 Harold Wilson and George Brown, aided and abetted by the Treasury and the Foreign Office, decided to accelerate the programme for withdrawal from Aden. This was to be implemented in November and December during the period of the Sunflower 1 deployment, and as rapidly as possible. The consequence for "Nine" was the loss of all of the air transport support that we expected for Sunflower; these aircraft being required for the evacuation of Aden and, therefore, not available to carry the engineering support necessary to activate the Sunflower deployment route. Worse still was the fact that there would be no servicing support for Vulcans at Darwin. Sunflower, therefore, was cancelled. Bearing in mind the Squadron's expectations of a "once in a lifetime" experience, the cancellation was a very great disappointment.

However, I was not prepared to give up easily. Having been PSO to 'Digger' Kyle, the C-in-C, I knew he would be seriously troubled, because of his strong Australian roots, in cancelling the Darwin AD exercise. He was a very approachable senior officer, always open to any new practicable ideas. I decided, therefore, to write to him direct proposing that consideration should be given to deploying the Squadron as "Lone Rangers" through the Sunflower route ("Lone Rangers" were training flights to overseas bases as singletons, in which the aircrew and two crew-chiefs were capable of dealing with all but the most serious of unserviceabilities, for example an engine change). I also believed that if a sizeable servicing group could be sent direct to Tengah, say by civil air or with Transport Command's routine scheduled flight to the Far East, it would be possible to carry out a Sunflower deployment and mount the support the Royal Australian Air Force expected at Darwin. There was, of course, an increased risk that the whole enterprise could fall apart. However, I emphasised that the Vulcan had an exceptionally good record for reliability and that, despite the risks, there was a very good chance that we could demonstrate the feasibility of a west-about Far East reinforcement and fulfill our commitment to the RAAF. He agreed and so Sunflower, albeit with some variations to the original plan, was reinstated.

The Revised Sunflower Exercise

The force was reduced to seven aircraft (later an eighth joined the squadron at Tengah) and each aircraft carried two crew-chiefs, providing a very wide spread of technical skills covering most minor unserviceabilities. In addition the bomb-bay panniers, which are enormous, were loaded with a comprehensive stock of spares including some of the heavier tools, trolleys and stands special to the Vulcan. The pannier in the lead Vulcan was filled mostly by various boxes of first class spirits drawn from bonded warehouses in Boston, Lincs and planned as gifts and hospitality en route!

Some adjustment to the timing spacing between aircraft was introduced in order to ease the task at each staging post, so that instead of a tight bomber stream we formed a looser formation. In the event our progress in the first three days was satisfactory enough to resume the original tighter formation and, indeed, to complete the final legs as pairs. The Americans on Wake and Guam were very impressed to see pairs of medium bombers approach and depart in "fighter"style.

While the Squadron deployed westwards a sizeable servicing and maintenance detachment was steadily built-up at Tengah, including our spare aircrews, using the routine Comet flights of Transport Command.

The Westabout Deployment

Day 1. On a cold, damp, grey 8th November 1967, "Nine" Squadron set off for Goose Bay, Newfoundland, Canada. As we climbed through the dense overcast and broke out into glorious sunshine and blue skies all the cares and hassle of the recent months were left behind us and minds became focussed on the task ahead and its potential for a fascinating and interesting adventure. The weather over the North Atlantic showed overcast virtually all the way and so it was at Goose where Precision Approach Radar was needed to land; flight time was 5hrs 10mins. Newfoundland was much as expected in winter, a bleak snow-covered landscape and very cold weather. The aircraft were taxied virtually right into the centrally heated hangars, rolling the last few yards with the engines shut down. By the time the internal post-flight checks were completed and the crew ready to disembark we had been towed well inside and the hangar doors were shut. A quick sprint between hanger and Mess was required to avoid eye-lashes and nostrils freezing up!

Day 2. After the routine pre-flight preparations, much as one would expect at an air base that was used almost exclusively by Bomber Command for low-level training, we were once more airborne in weather which resembled the conditions we had experienced on departure from Cottesmore. This day we had two stages; the first, an average 4hrs 20mins flight to Offutt which served HQSAC (HQ Strategic Air Command) at Omaha, Nebraska, and the second, to McClellan, near Sacramento, California. Soon after settling into the flight to Offutt we were warned of fog at Offutt and a diversion was a strong possibility. We had regular weather up-dates until the time for our descent for landing but fog still persisted at Offutt. After a discussion by radio with the Bomber Command liaison officer regarding the actual weather at Offutt, I decided to make one attempt and if it was feasible then we would all land at Offutt, if too foggy then we would divert. The conditions proved to be acceptable as the fog was beginning to thin; we all landed without too much stress and by the time the last plane was down the fog had lifted. The turnround was very fast and we were on our way again within the hour, heading for California.

The flight time to McClellan was three hours and we were glad to see a vast improvement in the weather as we crossed the line of the Sierra Nevada. Indeed, on disembarking it was a great pleasure to find conditions pleasantly warm. So, with spirits rising we saw the aircraft to bed and took our crew-bus down into Sacramento to our hotel accommodation. By general agreement our plan for the evening was a shower, a beer, a stroll along Sacramento's main thoroughfare and to enjoy a large steak. All the restaurants seemed to be of a common standard so it did not matter much where we ate. However, one restaurant was running an amateur topless competition so the choice fell to that one. After a few beers we settled down to enjoy the entertainment. Somehow the word got out that this crowd of English speakers were from the RAF en route to Singapore and as a result we received more attention than we needed, especially from the topless song & dance competitors. The girls were wasting their time, however, because as the evening wore on and jet-lag caught up with us (together with a very satisfying supper) most of us dropped off to sleep. The hotel bed was never more welcoming!

Day 3. McClellan Air Force Base was an enormous base with, seemingly, every type of USAF aircraft in the operational inventory parked there. Most aircraft tasked for operations over SE Asia from Pacific bases departed continental USA through McClellan. Consequently, the base had a major role for briefing crews thoroughly on the Pacific operational environment before flying out to the Pacific bases; great importance was given to the weather briefing because of the potential threat from hurricanes. It was mandatory for the Vulcan crews to follow the USAF regulations, particularly regarding the weather factors; later in the deployment we had first-hand experience of how the weather could affect operations.

With all the pre-flight preparations completed and no unserviceabilities to delay us "Nine" launched out over the Pacific heading for Hickam AFB on Oahu, one of the northern islands in the Hawaiian group. Hickam is a very interesting Base which supports Pearl Harbour and is an adjunct to Honolulu International Airport. Because of its strategic importance Hickam is a very busy airbase and its position on Honolulu creates a very complex Air Traffic Control situation if military/civil conflictions are to be avoided; the approach and landing was to prove to be an interesting and new experience to us all.

The flight of 4 hrs 45 mins was uneventful, pleasant and enjoyable; weather was excellent and the Pacific, stretched out all around, appeared from our cruise altitude to be calm. As we approached Oahu initial contact with Honolulu ATC provided permission to join the approach to Honolulu's main runway from the west over the sea; we were advised that civil and military traffic was very busy. How busy we were soon to learn!

As we settled into "finals" we realised that there was a second main runway in constant use which intersected our runway some two-thirds along from our threshold and at an angle of approx 70 degrees. The traffic on this other runway was a mix of civil and military, the latter being mostly fighters! Keeping a safe separation between the various aircraft must be a Honolulu controller's nightmare. Throughout the approach and after touch-down we were constantly asked to increase or decrease our ground speed in order to avoid arriving at the intersection at the same time as an aircraft on the other runway. Once on the runway the question was put to each Vulcan captain in a rather anxious tone. "Can you stop before the intersection?" Fortunately, all was well, the runway was long enough to allow the Vulcans to stop early enough without using the brake chute. A simple straightforward taxying round Honolulu Airport saw us safe and sound into Hickam. After the routine post-flight bedding down of aircraft and crews we enjoyed, over a very welcome beer, reflecting on a unique experience to us all.

Day 4. This was our planned "rest" day and what better place to enjoy the "perk"? There were, however, a few chores to be carried out concerning aircraft checks and flight planning for the morrow. Also, I was under orders to report to the Bomber Command Operations Centre by telephone on progress and problems (if any). I was in the fortunate position to be able to report that progress had been excellent, the arrangements en route had worked well, we carried no unserviceabilities and the prospect of completing the deployment on time was good. Satisfied that all the essential tasks were completed, we set off to enjoy our free time. Pearl Harbour was a must and what an impressive memorial that is – a never-to-be-forgotten reminder of that infamous attack on the USA. Acting on the advice of base staff we set off for a tourist's look around Honolulu. The recommended place for lunch was Fort Derussey (The US Army R&R camp) and we were encouraged to take swimming kit with us. Honolulu was like most wealthy tourist resorts; luxury dominated the city central area and wealth seemed to ooze from every nook and cranny. A very expensive place, but it had one surprise. Fort Derussey was situated right in the centre of Waikiki Beach, not set unobtrusively between or behind the more prominent buildings but openly occupying the prime position of this magnificent silver-sanded beach. On either side were areas of lovely colourful tropical gardens. The whole of this Army facility must have been the envy of the luxury hotels occupying the remaining areas along this outstandingly beautiful beach. A room overlooking the sea cost only $2.50 and our excellent lunch was less than $5.00. The rest of the day was spent on the beach soaking up the glorious sun-shine, enjoying a dip in the warm sea and lounging on the silver sand before returning to the reality of Hickam and Sunflower.

On return to Hickam I was greeted with a request to visit the Base Operations where there was a message for me. The message, in fact, was a general warning to all commanders who were planning to depart the following day for any of the western island bases, that a hurricane was developing to the north east of Australia and could threaten Wake and Guam, the next two staging posts for Sunflower. I 'phoned High Wycombe and reported this potential hiccup in our schedule. In 1966 a hurricane had devastated these bases with the loss of aircraft in the open and had also severely damaged radar heads and communications links. Now the authorities were being extra cautious and warning us that Wake and Guam might be closed until the threat had passed. It was possible, therefore, that we could be grounded for an undefined number of days. This was bad news, indeed, as regards to the Sunflower plan.

When I 'phoned Bomber Command to tell them the news, I detected a certain amount of scepticism at their end, over the fact that the possible delay gave us, possibly, additional spare time in the Hawaiian Islands. Their disbelief increased when I 'phoned next morning to inform them that the USAF had taken the decision to close Wake and Guam for 48 hours. Obviously, there was nothing I or they could do to change the situation as no alternative route to Singapore was available to us, so my advice to the crews was "Make the most of this opportunity and see as much of Oahu as you are able!" They did! My crew hired a car and took off on a sight-seeing tour of the island and spent one night at the Fort enjoying the warm, balmy airs and magical moonlight over Waikiki Beach. Next day we resumed the Sunflower route plan, albeit now two days behind schedule.

Day 7. The schedule for the day covered two stages; the first, to Wake Island for a refuelling stop and the second, to Guam for a night-stop. The pre-flight preparations were routine and no problems were raised about weather. The 4hrs 45mins flight was uneventful and the turn-round very quick. The Vulcans continued without serious problems so there was no delay in setting out on the second leg of the day's schedule. Wake was not busy, probably because activity had not yet picked up after the hurricane problem. The strip and its adjacent pre-fab buildings clearly indicated its flag stop capability and being situated on a featureless sandy atoll, we felt no sorrow in spending the minimum of time on the ground there.

The flight to Andersen AFB on Guam was short, three hours, and also uneventful. The weather was again excellent although some medium cloud developed over Guam which Air Traffic Control insisted required a Precision Approach Radar (PAR) approach. By this stage we were flying as three loose pairs and a singleton and because Andersen operated two parallel runways simultaneously we were "talked down" virtually as if we were a fighter squadron. This impressed the USAF staff who saw us in, especially when they realised the size of the Vulcan.

Andersen was a very busy operational base for mounting operations in SE Asia. It was set in very lush green tropical terrain and had a permanence about it, unlike Wake. I imagined that a full tour of duty by the permanent staff would be quite pleasant but there was nothing pleasant about the temporary accommodation provided for transient crews. Our rooms for the one night stop were in 2-storeyed steel pre-fabs; very austere, unadorned, unwelcoming and extremely noisy. Because of the round-the-clock air operations from Guam there was a constant coming and going which resulted in a level of noise from door-slamming which prevented sleep. We were not sorry to shake the dust of Andersen from our boots!

Day 8. Andersen to Tengah was the last stage of the reinforcement deployment, 5hrs 35mins making it the longest leg so far, and was uneventful. Despite the poor night's rest we demonstrated the operational, simultaneous engines-start feature of the Vulcan and a scramble take-off. The weather continued good although the monsoon season ensured that we had our fair share of instrument flying. We were fortunate to land early enough to miss the "duty" thunderstorm which usually hits the area in early afternoon. Tengah welcomed us like old friends and with relief that we had arrived intact without giving them any potential headaches prior to participating in the two Air Defence exercises. Equally, I was glad to see that a sizeable engineering detachment, including the reserve crew, had been assembled while we were in transit and to all intents and purposes we were at the full strength envisaged in the original Operation Order. The eighth, reserve, aircraft, making the full aircraft establishment, was not due at Tengah until we deployed to Darwin on the 22nd November.

The Tengah Experience

Accommodation at Tengah for the aircrews was in a self-contained, air-conditioned facility set apart from the main messing accommodation and used only by Bomber Command detachments. For obvious reasons this special arrangement was the envy of the permanent residents and gave rise to some initial bad feelings, which soon disappeared with sociable mixing. No flying from Tengah was planned at this point. Air tests, if required, would have been flown but in the event were not necessary. Our first day was a scheduled rest day and of the remaining time before departing for Darwin, two working days were spent in preparing the aircraft, and a weekend intervened. Aircrews were briefed on and familiarised with the Operation Order for Exercise "High Mars", the RAAF Air Defence Exercise in which we would act as aggressors.

'High Mars' called for only six aircraft and, therefore, in the interests of economy, HQFEAF decided that two Vulcans, i.e. the two not deploying to Darwin, would be sufficient to meet the requirements for testing the FEAF Air Defence, Early Warning and Command & Control procedures.

Exercise "High Mars"

Six Vulcans deployed to Darwin on time and we took stock of our surroundings. The first thing to strike us was the very strict and aggressive customs inspection. It was the first and only time that my suitcase had its lining ripped out to see whether I was smuggling any prohibited goods or material. Was this the way Aussies treated the Poms? Fortunately not; the intense customs search was the consequence of considerable dealings in copied wristwatches and drugs by RAAF personnel based at Butterworth, in West Malaysia. Our initial negative opinions of the Aussies were soon dispelled by a very warm welcome that evening by the Darwin Base staff and Mirage pilots with whom we would soon be in contest. It has to be said, however, that after a skinfull of Newcastle Ale and Melbourne Bitter, the Aussies become very brash and frank about the low regard they hold for Poms! By the end of the Exercise their regard for V-Force in both "social skills" and flying had soared. I fared better than most, probably because of my Scottish accent and my service with No77 Squadron RAAF during the Korean War.

High Mars lasted six days, in which time each crew flew two sorties, one at night and one in daylight, each sortie comprising a low-level attack against the airfield and a high-level attack against Darwin Harbour installations. The low-level attacks followed the standard Vulcan "lay-down" pattern and apparently caused the defences problems, and at high-level the Vulcan presented the Mirage fighters with considerable difficulties. We were equipped with pressure suits, which allowed us to exploit the Vulcan's exceptional high-level performance. After a low-level attack the aircraft weight was reducing rapidly and the climb out and cruise climb to set up the high-level attack ensured a very high altitude indeed. On my night sortie I registered a radar altitude above 60,000 feet. At that height the Vulcan still had some manoeuvrability which the Mirage could not match. Another problem for the fighters was the enormous cumulonimbus clouds which developed over the Timor Sea and drifted in towards Darwin. Any attempted penetration interception was fraught with a great risk of Mirage engine flame-outs; the Mirage re-light system seemed to be reliable and so there were no casualties but RAAF pride did take a number of knocks! These tropical CuNims were impressive if you were not required to penetrate them. Again, on my night attack we were required to navigate round one fierce thunderstorm in which the "pyrotechnics" display was magnificent; that cloud looked very much like a Chinese Lantern. The degree of turbulence was soon revealed when we passed under the "anvil" of the CuNim; we were registering 64,000 feet and the "anvil" cloud was still above us!

The last sortie was flown on 27th November and the following day we returned to Tengah to prepare for our return, continuing westabout, to Cottesmore. The reliability of the Vulcan and its systems was indeed excellent. We had demonstrated the feasibility of a Far East reinforcement with minimal support and completed the AD exercises commitment. Now, hopefully, back home for Christmas!

The Return Journey

The route home was expected to be straightforward; Tengah-Gan(in the Maldives)-Muharraq (Bahrain) –Akrotiri (Cyprus) -Cottesmore, and all eight aircraft behaving themselves marvellously. It was not to be! One aircraft was delayed at Tengah, first for a wheel change but then , more seriously, an engine change, resulting in a week's delay. The second had NavAttack system failure which delayed it at Gan (could there be a supernatural influence between the vast colonies of fruit bats resident on Gan and the No.9 Squadron badge which incorporates a bat – and even the Vulcan's delta shape?). At Gan a massive oil leak developed in my No.3 engine but I was in no mood to remain at Gan admiring the fruit bats. So after a careful discussion with my crew and the other captains I decided to do the final three stages on three engines. There were no apparent difficulties and so six Vulcans arrived safely at Cottesmore only two days later than had been planned earlier in 1967. The other two were home within a couple of weeks and the engineering detachment was home for Christmas, by courtesy of Transport Command's Comet fleet.   [A.McN.C.]

BOB AND EVA

At the beginning of December 1969 a signal arrived at Sharjah requesting a refuelling stop for a USAF C141 carrying Bob Hope and his troupe on his annual visit to entertain the American forces in Viet Nam Agreement was signalled without delay but then nothing was heard in confirmation or giving a date until late one evening, as I was getting into bed, the Duty Operations officer telephoned me to say that the C141 had made contact, with an ETA of 30 minutes from then! I put on my uniform and spoke to Ian Tapster (53 Entry Digby), the OC Admin Wing and PMC, who rushed into the mess to get the bar cleared up and arrange for some refreshments.

I went to the Ops Room and decided to meet the aircraft at the end of the runway and guide it through the barbed wire and so to a dispersal. This was conveyed to the USAF captain and I entered through the crew door on the port side behind the flight deck. After introducing ourselves and exchanging greetings the next thing the captain said was "Say, do you know a guy named Barry Mills?" I admitted I did and to my relief, instead of a remark such as "He owes me a hundred bucks", the captain said " Ah, Barry. Great guy, great guy!" and it appeared that our Barry had been on exchange with the same C141 squadron. Next, the captain pointed back to the navigator's table and said to me "And that's Mr Hope, over there."

So I shook hands with Bob Hope and when we stopped in the dispersal area he and I disembarked by the crew door and walked round the nose to the passenger exit on the starboard side at the rear. Word had spread quickly through the station and a crowd had assembled to watch, as it was thought, Bob Hope and his supporters leave the aircraft by the usual door. Bob was amused to stand behind all those looking ahead to see him. His entertainment company included "The Gold Diggers of 1969", Connie Francis and Miss World 1969, as well as his supporters, make up team and his "ad lib men". As we watched all these people leaving the aircraft I wondered which of all the lovely ladies was Miss World who, in 1969, was Eva Rueber-Staier of Austria.

I drove Bob Hope to the mess in my Landrover while the others were taken there in the Air Movements buses. Another crowd was waiting at the mess and Bob was less than amused to see a sign saying "Welcome Bing!" It seems that this was not an entirely original idea.

In the mess everyone settled down in the bar and ante-room for coffee and some drinks and plenty of talk. Bob Hope told a few jokes and we all got on very well. I mentioned his "ad lib men" and these were an absolutely essential part of his act. Their task was to stand out of sight in the wings of the stage and, at appropriate moments, hold up placards with some prompt words for Bob to see. Presumably they took the trouble to find out some information about personalities at the places they performed so that Mr Hope could bring in topical references to eg the base commander and thereby get a laugh. He also had a stooge or two and his son was with him, purely for the ride, I feel.

During this happy interlude I walked around trying to work out which of the ladies was Miss World, because they all looked eligible. Having been introduced, and Ian Tapster having got in on the act, we found her to be a very intelligent and pleasant young woman – certainly no bimbo. She, like the others, really had no idea where they were, but when we explained that she was in one of the Trucial States on the shores of the Persian Gulf she expressed the wish to see a camel! Ian volunteered his OC Admin Wing Ford Zephyr as preferable to my OC Flying Wing Landrover so we went out in that even though by then it was well after midnight. There were no camels within the compound fence and little to be seen anyway at that time of night but, as luck would have it, just outside camp, by the old Sharjah Fort (occupied by International Aeradio Limited) there was a solitary camel eating a cardboard carton – as they do if they can find one – it seems they find the taste of the glue appealing – so Ian stopped the car, Eva jumped out and with a very small camera took a flash photograph. It is doubtful whether the flash even reached the camel but she was happy. Next day Ian had a card typed "Eva Rueber-Staier, Miss World 1969, Sat Here" and taped it to the dashboard of the car.

Presumably the crew of the C141 knew where they were because they had the relevant charts and en route documents but, as I have said, none of the troupe knew where they were and that is a fact. I think they had come from Germany and were going to overfly India to go direct to Saigon. We did our best to explain where we were and why, and Dai Rees, OC Engineering Wing, produced a map on which the singer, Connie Francis, wrote "You are a wonderful person. Love and Peace, Connie Francis".

Apart from an incident when a pilot from 8 Squadron saw one of the hangers-on pick up and pocket the camera he had just put down on a table, all passed off well and we chaps on 13 month unaccompanied tours enjoyed a little diversion completely out of the ordinary. As a souvenir, Bob Hope gave me a cigarette lighter with, in relief, his cartoon silhouette showing his famous "ski jump" nose.   [F.D.H.]

YOU ARE NOT MAD – YET

Your squadron is on detachment to RAF Idris (near Tripoli, Libya, in the days before Gaddafi). You have to return to the UK for a couple of days.

An OCU Hastings is staging through, and the captain agrees to take you as supernumerary crew.

At the appointed departure time you clamber aboard. Right up at the front, by the cockpit bulkhead, beyond all the rows of backward-facing seats, is a Morris Minor, one of the "woody" station wagons. How and why it got there you cannot think, but no one else seems to be taking any notice of it, so you settle down and get your book out.

As the Hastings lines up for take-off, you glance forward, and see a flight lieutenant open the driver's door of the Minor and get in behind the wheel. Every time you look again, he is still sitting there, apparently driving the car, all the way to England. You look at the others but they are not batting an eyelid.

Can they not see him? Is he really there? Is the car really there? Are you the only one who sees it? Have you started to hallucinate? Dare you ask anyone? Maybe they will radio ahead, and have men in white coats waiting for you when you land. Maybe they have a strait-jacket in a locker in the aircraft – you are not sure what powers a Transport Command captain has to arrest and subdue passengers who go mad en route…

Finally, just as you are about to disembark, curiosity can be contained no longer. The crew explain. The car belongs to a corporal posted back to the UK. He and it are being flown back to the OCU as an indulgence. The corporal and his mates had to unlock and remove all the passenger seats so as to get the car right forward over the Centre of Gravity, then replace them for the flight.

As for the flight lieutenant driving the car, he is a navigation instructor with a pile of exam papers to mark. So he has been sitting in the car with the doors shut because it was the quietest place in the aircraft, where he could concentrate and not be interrupted.

So you are not mad after all. Well, not yet. It was a close-run thing though. [R.H.R.]

KEBABS AND TACEVALS

Once they were past the age of 50, I was surprised at how many of my Service friends became obsessed with their 'last postings'. Sitting at a Flight Safety desk at HQ 11 Group at the age of 52, I was far too busy with the accidents and incidents that always caught us unawares to have given much thought to where my own choice would take me. I was, therefore, unprepared when my personnel officer from Gloucester rang me one morning and asked me quite bluntly where I wanted to go.

"How about another flying tour?"

I knew the answer to that already but one can dream, can't one?

Unsuppressed giggles came down the phone.

"You have a house in Alconbury, haven't you? How about Brampton?"

I did have 'a hedge against inflation' in Alconbury but I had never yet lived in our house there. None of the available jobs in Brampton appealed to me at all. They all sounded very dull and I did not want a 'leafy lane' backwater.

"What else is on offer?" I asked and the answers I got justified my worst fears about my prospects.

"Anything overseas, diplomatic, liaison, anything?"

There was a short pause while screens were scrolled down or pages were turned.

"The only possible time fit is a NATO post in Turkey. It requires strike experience but I can massage you through. The present incumbent isn't even fast-jet. But are you sure you want to be in the back of beyond for a last tour? It is accompanied, but the support is minimal as the main force is Turkish and American."

I was given a week to decide but I knew the answer already. When I told my long-suffering wife that we were probably on our way to Izmir in a few months, her unexpected response was "I have just bought a book on 'Teach Yourself Turkish' and it will be much easier to pick up the language in a country where it is spoken".

So it was that I bought myself a suitably tough estate car (tales of atrocious road conditions in Turkey) to drive out there and arranged to do the required NATO preparatory courses on the journey – they being conveniently held at Oberammergau. My embarkation leave would cover a leisurely drive through Germany, Austria, Italy, Greece and into Turkey with a day or two to spare, I hoped.

Things did not work out quite as I had planned because, in the two weeks it took me to get from Oberammergau to Izmir, my predecessor's posting had been brought forward and I arrived at an empty apartment with a message pinned to the door saying that he was leaving later that day and would try and make time for a few minutes handover before catching his flight home. We did get a short time together in which I was told that on my desk there was a written brief I could refer to if I got stuck. I was shown how the water and the electricity worked in our apartment, told what action to take in the event of an earthquake, and shown the best kebab houses in the district – a vital bit of knowledge because the cost of eating out, the weather, the choice of food and the ambiance of the seafront establishments made home cooking an unnecessary chore.

The post itself had not turned out as planned. No strike tactical evaluation (taceval) based on a 'strike' capability had yet taken place in

Turkey, mostly because the Turks had no desire to be evaluated and found wanting, and they had consequently put every possible hindrance in the way of such an exercise. Both my predecessors had spent four years, back to back, between them trying to evaluate a strike squadron but without success. Instead, the strike evaluation officer was expected to help with the evaluation of radar and missile sites – in a ground defence, medical, security, etc, role. (The Turks had enough experts in the radar field to be able to conduct a meaningful evaluation but had none in the strike role and had to depend on un-malleable foreigners to give them their all-important ratings).

I made a silent resolution that I was not going to be fobbed off and that somehow I would plan, conduct and operate the evaluation of a Turkish strike squadron before my tour was over. It took me a further 12 months and a great deal of persistence but I did succeed, not just once but twice. It helped that I was experienced enough to have met all the excuses and prevarications before, and that I was beyond the expectation of further promotion and so could safely risk antagonising anyone up to and including our two commanding generals. Most importantly, I resolved to learn the language and not be dependent on the translators who accompanied non-Turks wherever they worked.

My main stories do not cover the strike evaluations (because I do not know whether that area is still covered by the official Secrets Act), but are confined to my early learning curve as a ground defence evaluator and my progress in that role. Four days after my arrival I joined a team despatched to evaluate a small radar station in the mountainous centre of the country. I had to use a plan devised by someone else without any idea of what to expect. A Turkish officer or NCO accompanied me like a shadow wherever I went. An exercise air raid would start; I would say to a group of soldiers guarding a perimeter "Two of your companions have been killed by shrapnel and three are badly wounded. What do you do?"

The translation always seemed more wordy and more full of discussions than seemed necessary. I began to suspect that my question was not being properly translated and that the answers also owed something to the expertise of the minders. One of my tasks was to check the aircraft recognition skills of the Anti-Aircraft gunners. Using flash card pictures on their own was not satisfactory because of the interruptions of the minders, so I had to devise flash cards for the answers as well and manipulate them so that only the gunners could see the aircraft picture and the choice of answers. Scores went down dramatically and I was not popular with the site we were evaluating or with my colleagues on the team. I had limited success in persuading them that it was better to get things sorted out in an evaluation than have to wait for a real conflict. This early experience did point out to me that a reasonable knowledge of the Turkish language was essential if one was to be effective.

The work plan I had inherited was not a heavy one and was based on several premises; no two emergencies can take place together, no emergencies take place during meal times, that an officer is always right in front of an NCO, an NCO is always right in front of an enlisted man, and that face-saving is more important than efficiency at every level. It was a very relaxed few days. Work always started after breakfast and stopped in time for a leisurely evening meal. Foolishly I made a rod for my own back by making my future scripts more demanding and more crowded and by including exercise night attacks from marauding forces at 3 am, as it meant evaluating officers having to be in place an hour earlier.

Our next evaluation was of a ground to air missile complex that guarded Istanbul. Again I was working off someone else's script and at a most placid pace but this time I did not complain and used the opportunity it gave me to see the city in an official capacity, glad of our shadows who took us everywhere and got us into places that were generally closed to the public. Turks are hospitable people and they were particularly keen that we should see their commercial capital at its best and remember it with pleasure. All our hosts went out of their way to make this possible. Meanwhile I was biding my time and working extra hard to get to grips with the spoken and written language, to learn some idioms and even to attempt some feeble jokes that did not always translate. I even went to the expense of attending a language course, supplemented it with hiring a private tutor and concentrated on military terminology and scenarios.

Six months down the line we evaluated a radar unit in the hills surrounding Ankara. I was still tasked with ground defence but this time the exercise script was my own work; I was in charge of the team and I rarely needed the help of an interpreter. It was here that I discovered the lengths to which the Turks would go to cover up their inadequacies. I was checking a machinegun post and had just tested the aircraft recognition skills of the gunners, their ability to cope with a ground based threat, and their basic first-aid skills. On a whim I decided to ask the NCO in charge to have the gun stripped down. He seemed delighted to do this and the team did the task very quickly. As I prepared to move on to the next gun post I observed that there was not the same urgency in putting the gun together again but put that down to the crew being more relaxed now.

The next site was further down a wooded, twisted path. I got the gun crew to go through much the same exercise as I had at the first post and thought I recognised one of the soldiers. (Did all Turkish soldiers in identical uniforms and with close cropped hair look alike?). At the end of the exercise with gun number 2, I pretended I was on my way to gun position number 3 but turned back and asked the crew to reassemble the gun that they had just successfully taken apart. They were unable to do so because there was no bolt available and my enquiries about where it gone was answered with downcast eyes and without words. The soldier who had looked familiar was no longer present. I ordered a member of my team to remain with the crew and see they stayed put while I returned to gun number 1 rather than on to gun number 3.

"Your perimeter is threatened by a group of guerrillas," I announced. "Prepare that gun for action."

Consternation!

It became obvious that there was no bolt available. Eventually I discovered that the six machine gun posts had only two serviceable bolts between them and that they were passed quickly from one to the other. The wooded, twisting connecting paths delayed inspecting officers just long enough to allow a soldier to slip directly through the trees taking the shared bolt from one unit to the next. Before reporting my findings to the Taceval Chief, I decided to have words with the Site Commander. He was out of his office but I decided to wait for him and made his PA give me the unit's combat order book to examine. It was 'Secret' but I was cleared to have such material. The orders were in Turkish and I suspected the loyal PA smiled inwardly as he handed the foreigner what most non-Turks would find to be gibberish. By sheer good fortune, on page 3, I noticed a spelling error, unimportant but noticeable (the omission of a cedilla which altered the meaning of this particular word).

It was obvious that the Commander had not expected anyone waiting for him and he was even more taken aback when the reason for my visit (shared machine gun bolts) became known. His initial reaction was to find implausible excuses, followed by bluster. The latter reaction made me irritated.

I reached for his order book and said very coldly, in Turkish, "and you cannot even get your own spelling correct." My thumb was on the offending word. The Commander looked carefully and the man so deflated before me that I felt sorry for him and decided that there was nothing to be lost by allowing him to save face, a wise move as it happened.

"Perhaps the orders were printed before you were in command and no one has checked them since."

No answer, but a slight inclination of the head indicated that we both knew, and accepted, what games were being played. My own stature shot up and word quickly spread that one of the RAF officers spoke and read Turkish. There were disadvantages because they gave me credit for a much greater facility with the language than I actually had, and there were times when some help with translation, or use of simpler words would have been useful.

Loss of face is an important factor in the makeup of the Turkish psyche (military or civilian) and the more experienced senior officers would anticipate and circumvent this in clever ways. The strike base that I eventually evaluated was commanded by a full general. I, a mere squadron leader, was in command of the whole evaluation even though there were many officers up to the rank of full colonel in my team of US, Turkish, Italian, German and British personnel. It was going to be difficult for the General to accept my daily orders and even more difficult to accept any criticism at the daily debriefing. He solved it by making me a full colonel for the duration of the evaluation and though I wore my squadron leader rank badges and received no extra pay, I was treated as a colonel and addressed as such by all my colleagues and by those on the receiving end of the evaluation. That general referred to me as a squadron leader in third party dealings but always addressed me as 'Colonel' whenever and wherever we met thereafter. And on those occasions he always brought the fiery 'raki' so beloved by the Turks. [C.G.D.J.]

ENTENTE CORDIALE

Exactly 10 years after my tour at HQ Allied Air Forces Central Europe in Fontainebleau in 1963, I had a second posting to France, this time as the RAF liaison officer at the French Air Force Strike Command HQ to the north of Paris. As a French speaker I was there primarily to liaise with the French on behalf of HQ Strike Command on all matters relating to RAF flights across and into France – including formations to Cyprus, Squadron Exchanges and general translation duties.

I made many friends there, and the occasion arose when one was being dined out on his retirement and I was invited. It proved to be a typical long French lunch lasting some five hours, with drinks flowing freely. How I made the 18 mile drive back to my flat in Paris (in my allocated service car) I do not know. I just remember finding a parking space not far from my flat and then I passed out. I came to with a knocking on the window (now 10 pm) and saw the faces of two French gendarmes. Apparently an old woman passing the car had seen my prostrate body slumped across the front seat and had sent for the police. I was in uniform, luckily, and had my French HQ badge on, but still I was afraid of being got for drunken driving. In fact, the two policemen kindly asked me where I lived, helped (carried) me across the square and delivered me to my flat. "He is yours, Madame?" said one to my wife, who was relieved to see me home.

However, my reception was not quite the "Entente Cordiale" as shown by the French police. In retrospect, I was lucky on two counts – there was no breathalyser in those days, and being in uniform saved my bacon. I went back to the car the next morning to give it a special clean before returning to work. [A.D.R.D.]

OLD COMRADES!

In the late fifties, my squadron was detached to Cyprus for several months. The EOKA bombing campaign was in full swing at the time. Every morning first thing, each crew had to search their Canberra for EOKA bombs. We were given to understand that we were looking for something like a lump of cheese with a biro stuck in it.

On the day in question, my navigator and I searched our aircraft and signed it off as clear. It did not fly during that morning, but the groundcrew did engine runs. At lunchtime, everyone packed up for an afternoon siesta before returning for night flying, leaving only a number of groundcrew armed with rifles to guard the dispersal.

About three pm, as we were dozing in our rooms, there was an enormous bang. My aircraft had blown up. The commotion can be imagined. A bomb had been put into the tailpipe of the port engine, blowing it open like a joke cigar. Since the engine had been run during the morning, whoever was responsible must evidently have hidden somewhere before dawn, probably under the latrines, for hours in the stinking heat. Then, after midday when everyone except the guards had departed, he must have sneaked across to the aircraft with the bomb, and escaped through the wire without being spotted.

I reckoned he deserved a medal, because he wouldn't have known that our groundcrew couldn't have hit a barn door at ten paces. In fact, even if their guns had been loaded, I doubt if they would have opened fire anyway, since they had never aimed to kill anyone in their lives before.

Needless to say, in a typical example of shutting the barn door after the horse had bolted, all the scrub for hundreds of yards was bulldozed, and masses more barbed wire put up. The aircraft was actually repaired in about a fortnight, I believe – mainly an engine change and new tailcone. The rear spar had not been damaged. Inside the wheel bay would have been a better place for the bomb, if the guy had only known.

Anyway, some thirty years later, I was on holiday in Paphos. Chatting to the hotel receptionist, who was Greek but had been brought up in Bradford, I mentioned this tale of long ago. "Wait a minute," she said "I know someone who could tell you more about it." She rang a number, said something in Greek, then handed the phone to me. I found myself speaking to a Cypriot who used to work at RAF Akrotiri. After some tactful sparring to find out who each other was, he invited my wife and me to his house for an evening get-together.

It was a pleasant occasion. Over fruit and drinks, our wives exchanged the usual chat about families – Aphrodite's baby had been taken to Great Ormond Street Children's Hospital, arranged by the RAF, for a serious operation, for which they were very grateful (I also learnt that her uncle had been killed in a shoot-out with the British Army).

When we got round to the subject of the bomb, our new friend said: "We know who did it. There were two of them. They live in Limassol and take part in a parade every National Day. There is an Old Comrades' Club in Limassol. If you like, I could take you there to meet them….."

At this point, I was hit by a sudden and very severe attack of caution. I politely declined his kind offer.

Afterwards I checked with the British Consulate in Nicosia, and with the station commander at Akrotiri. Both were interested in the story, but very thankful that I had not accepted the invitation. Goodness knows what propaganda might have been made of it in the tricky politics of Cyprus.

I wonder if the IRA have an Old Comrades Club?   [R.H.R.]

OTHER PLACES – OTHER WAYS

On leaving Bracknell at the end of 1961 I was posted to the Air Ministry, in the department known as AI(F), which was short for Air Intelligence (Foreign) and described as "Liaison with the Foreign Office". During my tour the service ministries were reorganised under the new Ministry of Defence and the job became DI(AI)14. I spent three years in that sphere and as my very first staff appointment it was something of an eye-opener in many ways. My boss was a Wing Commander who also had responsibilities for a Squadron Leader in another department and we were in contact with our opposite numbers in the Navy and Army. Most of our contact, though, was with civilian officers and staff. As to staff, I had my own secretary, as did everyone else; our secretaries were bright young ladies of the right sort selected on personal recommendation. In a later incarnation in a higher rank I had to learn to put up with having typing done in a typing pool if I could find anyone who was not already fully engaged in typing for somebody more senior, or even waiting while work was sent off to some typing service at the other end of the UK. There was none of that nonsense in our department.

As you might expect in the 1960s, most of the Foreign Office officers had been to the right schools and universities and a few were keen to let this be known to we lesser mortals. Having said that, in the main they were quite normal and at that time a good proportion had served in the armed forces during the war. There was no doubt that most were highly intellectual and the civilian officer I shared a room with at one time spent the first part of each day working on the Times crossword. After struggling for half an hour or so he would telephone one of his friends who, he said, completed the puzzle while shaving. The conversation would go something like : "Oh, Charles. I wonder, what did you get for 19 across?" "What! Daffodil? Good Lord, how could I have missed that." Then he would get down to the work of the day. That particular officer was a Japanese speaker – that is to say a speaker of Japanese – and he had ended the war in the RAF as a Flying Officer interpreter in Saigon working with the Japanese forces who had been allowed to retain their arms to assist in the administration and security of South East Asia. He had many stories to tell of those days.

A feature of life with the FO was that Christian names were used throughout. I assume that the chaps right at the top might be addressed as "Sir" or "Minister" but otherwise it would be "James", "Charles" "Neil" – or whatever other name they might have. This took a little getting used to.

The FO did not communicate by signals as did the armed services but by "telegrams" (a rose by any other name, you may think). I read many of these day by day and it was amusing, and sometimes disturbing, to read the account by a member of one of our embassies of an event that was also reported in the press. Occasionally the similarities were not all that easy to detect and I recall a report on an aircraft crash which was totally at odds with what was in the newspapers and purported to be the official report. Of course, it was the official report as released to the press, but it was not the actual official official report as kept within the ministries – if you see what I mean. If this appears to smack of "Sir Humphrey" then – you may think that, but I couldn't possibly comment.

After an event such as the above, one might see in an outgoing telegram some praise for the official overseas, usually in words such "You spoke well.....". No doubt similar accolades still emanate from the offices of what is now known as "spin".

Another little quirk was, it seemed to me, to avoid the point from time to time. Writing a memo containing a suggestion beginning "Might there not be some merit in........." left the door open to disclaiming any responsibility if the suggestion proved to be a dud. One can imagine the writer later saying "Oh, don't blame me, old chap. I merely suggested that there might be merit in looking into it". Memos also contained the occasional literary, historical or classical reference. I recall receiving a memo which said "As Lord Melbourne said to his Cabinet in 18–, it matters not so much what we say as that we all say the same thing." My reply pointed out that it was not my function to "say the same thing" but to put the actual facts of the matter at issue. Then one would see something like "I agree with your analysis and, *mutatis mutandis*, we could proceed on that basis". Of course, "the appropriate changes being made" could mean that the original analysis was of little use as it stood – but one would not care to be so coarse as to put it as directly as that!

My second staff appointment was also away from the RAF. This time I was sent to the Army so I was beginning to wonder what I had said and to whom, or whether I should perhaps change to Lifebuoy soap. This posting followed the end of my tour as OC No 103 Squadron operating Whirlwind helicopters in the Far East. The post was new and I believe that when it was created my name was suggested by Colonel Charles Carroll, by then at HQ Army Strategic Command, whom I had known when he was commanding the 1st/7th Gurkha Rifles in Borneo.

The job was not a mere attachment but a full blown secondment as a General Staff Officer Grade 2 (GSO2) in the G Training department of what was then HQ Army Strategic Command at Wilton, near Salisbury. Indeed, my boss, not Charles Carroll but one Colonel John R...... (Colonel, General Staff, Training, or Col GS Trg), was quick to point out to me on my arrival that it was a good thing I had been to Staff College because otherwise I ought not to be a GSO2 and on the General Staff as opposed to what might be termed the supporting staffs. Staff Officers who had not got the *psc* qualification were given jobs with titles beginning "SO", that is, without the prized "G" and, eg, a Captain might be 'SO3 Movements'. I had not realised that there was a hierarchy of this sort and this explained why Army officers were so keen to get a *psc* as opposed to RAF officers who were often desperate to avoid being sent to the staff college. Came the day that I was posted, Colonel John was quite upset to find that my successor was not a *psc* and he was not happy when I explained to him that in the RAF we did not much care about such niceties!

At Wilton I shared a room with a major in the US Army (Keith) and a British major (Roddy). Our job was to organise army exercises overseas and support for exercises in the UK. Keith was a Ranger and a Viet Nam veteran; he was responsible for everything east of the UK and I had everything to the west. Luckily, our exercises never extended so far round the world that our areas overlapped! Roddy was mainly responsible for policy and for things happening at home. I also had the task of arranging air support for army exercises in the UK and a few other odds and ends such as Battlefield Tours and the budget for civil flights for senior officers to visit exercises overseas. This led to a number of cajoling telephone calls but only one free lunch.

One thing I learnt very quickly was that Lieutenant Colonels commanding battalions or regiments had almost unlimited power. We might detail a unit for an exercise and issue the appropriate order only to find that the CO of the unit concerned might then simply ring up and say he was not going to do it because it clashed with, for the sake of an example, "Banglapore Day" which his regiment had celebrated since 1789!" Such a message would usually be to the Colonel who, to my surprise, would say "Oh, of course. Quite clearly we can't disturb your arrangements. I wonder why my staff didn't think of that. Sorry."

Colonel R..... was a man for whom I had a lot of respect but he did tend to listen to such complaints as I have described or complaints about, say, winter equipment or aircraft timings or baggage allowance. One day, braving the displeasure of Pirate, his killer bull terrier in permanent occupation of an armchair in his office, I taxed the Colonel with this and suggested that he should get our side of the story rather than simply take the complaint at face value.

As I said, I had a lot of respect for him. He had won a MC in Burma and one day told me how his company was under attack from Japanese and a Jap officer was hurtling toward him brandishing his Samurai sword in a most threatening manner. John fired at the Jap with his .38 revolver and missed, he fired again and hit him in the foot, fired again and missed, fired again and hit, fired again and finally brought the Japanese officer to the ground. He said he then threw away his .38 and got himself a .45 Colt automatic!

Another thing I had to learn was the order of precedence of all units in the British Army. This was necessary for the distribution of documents. Woe betide he who put the Pay Corps before the Artillery on the distribution list of an operation order or any other document! At this distance in time I am not sure whether the Artillery comes before the Cavalry or vice versa, but I know that the Household Cavalry have precedence over the other cavalry regiments, the Guards are first among the infantry, the Greenjackets are well up in the pecking order of infantry and that what was then the RASC and the RAOC (now the Royal Logistic Corps) and new-fangled corps such as the Army Air Corps came well down the list. It was also necessary to learn the Army system of abbreviations, so I became familiar with Fd Btys, Armd Regts, Engrs, A Avn and so on. I still tend to think of accommodation as "accn" and transport as "tpt". It is all very useful when you get the hang of it.

My last appointment in the RAF was in the Ministry of Defence. This followed my tour in command of No 33 Squadron at Odiham when I introduced the Puma helicopter into squadron service. I joined the Operational Requirements Division as OR21, responsible for the RAF's operational requirements for helicopters and fixed wing transport aircraft. So, at last I was filling an RAF staff appointment. However, khaki was still at hand inasmuch as I shared an office with a Lieutenant Colonel and two Majors working on the Gazelle and Lynx helicopters. This was because the Army Air Corps operational requirements came under the RAF at that time, in 1973. This was patently wrong and the section moved to the Army department in 1974.

In the RAF we tended always to think of the brown jobs as a bit lacking in the brain department and much more rigid and hidebound than our own young service. It became clear to me from my experience that this was very far from the truth. Yes, they had their own little peculiarities but also some great strengths. As I have said, the CO of a battalion carried much more influence than an RAF squadron commander or, indeed, Station Commander. In staff work, in our division of the MOD we were constantly writing papers and memos which would be altered by the next up, re-typed, altered by the next up the chain and so on. The Army practice was that if, say, a Major wrote a paper that essentially met with his colonel's approval, then that colonel would merely add his comments, in manuscript, and pass it up the chain. How, I wished that the RAF could have been that flexible during my time in OR.

Doing staff work with the Foreign Office and with the Army, coupled with my experience of working with the Army in Borneo, opened my eyes and, I think, broadened my mind. It is, of course, always unwise to generalise, and I saw only limited aspects of staff work in all three situations, but I have to say that working in the Air Force Department of the MOD helped me arrive at my decision to retire early from the RAF.

[F.D.H.]

6.   Civilian Life

Members of the entry found their way into a variety of employments and had many diverse experiences after leaving the Royal Air force. The scope of this book does not allow for full biographies of all of us but the following examples will serve to show just a little of the variety.

"WHAT DID YOU DO IN THE WAR, DAD?"

In 1969, I started working in the Computer Division of Shell-Mex & BP during my retirement leave. So, as I was still only thirty seven, I believed I was still a young man. When I arrived I realised that, among the staff of around one thousand, I was one of the oldest, which was quite a shock.

I joined a programming team and, apart from the leader, an ex-wartime naval officer, all the others were very bright young university graduates. Although very friendly, they viewed me with curiosity, amazement and incredulity. Often, during our coffee and tea breaks they would gather round me and ask" What did *you* do in the war, Dad?" They just could not believe that I joined the R.A.F. four years after the war had ended.

Finally, trying to put an end to all this, I said "Listen, during the war I was still in short trousers" (readers may remember that that was still the fashion then, unlike today). Whereupon one of the chaps was very quick to say "There you are! We have been right all the time – *you* were serving out East and wearing Khaki Drill!"

I couldn't win! [D.J.B.K.]

BUSH PILOT

My option time to leave the Service was approaching and it was time to take stock. I had spent my career flying fast jets but was approaching the age where I might be posted to heavy equipment or worse – to a desk. Neither prospect appealed. Furthermore, the fact that my erstwhile juniors first became my equals and then my superiors indicated that their Airships took the view that I was not built of the right timber for high rank. (They were wrong, of course; I would have made a splendid CAS!). I had enjoyed Air Force life but, considering these factors and with a somewhat heavy heart, I decided that the time had come to leave.

My last tour of duty was instructing at the Fighter OCU at Chivenor and, while there, some of my students were Saudis (who all seemed to be princes) in preparation for the Royal Saudi Air Force equipping with Hunters. Circumstances one day made it necessary for me to demonstrate to one of them (who subsequently became Chief of the Air Staff of the RSAF) an actual flame out landing at base in marginal weather using the "1 in 1" procedure. He seemed impressed, and perhaps this was a factor in my being offered a job as a civilian flying instructor at the new RSAF Fighter OCU at Dhahran. I would be flying Hunters, Lightnings and F86s. The pay was £10,000 pa tax free and all found. – rather good in 1968 – and a married quarter and tickets for my wife. It all sounded most attractive and we decided to accept.

I arrived in Dhahran and was shown the aircraft and facilities and allocated a comfortable bachelor officer's quarter.

"But where" I asked, "is the married quarter?"

I was assured that I would not get one and that none had been promised. I went up the chain of command and at each level was told not to expect one. I demanded to see the top man; they were very obliging and gave me a ticket on Saudi Arabian airlines to go to Riyadh to see the big boss – a recently retired Group Captain. I explained that if I did not get the promised quarter I would leave.

"Yes, old boy" he smiled, "and where would you get another job like this?"

"But you promised!"

"Yes, old boy, we thought that you might not come if we didn't. But now that you are here, you'll soon settle down!"

The only nice thing about that trip to Riyadh was that I had an evening with Paddy King who was instructing at the King Feisal Air Academy. An exit visa is required for each departure from Saudi Arabia, and it takes a few days to get. Back at Dhahran I asked the admin boss to start the procedures to get one. He smiled.

"Leaving us, eh? I bet you don't. And you'll soon settle down!"

But, perhaps to call what he took to be my bluff, he started the process. Before leaving the Service, I had met, through the auspices of the RAF Resettlement Branch, a Kenya farmer who had a Private Pilot's Licence and two aircraft and his own airstrip. He was thinking of starting an air charter business and was looking for an ex-Air Force pilot to help him set it up. He gave me a very nice lunch and we discussed possibilities, but neither of us made a commitment other than his assurance that I would receive a warm welcome if I ever went to Kenya.

I bought a one-way ticket from Dhahran to Nairobi and when my exit visa arrived arranged to leave the next day.

When I went to make my farewell, the local boss could hardly believe it and rapidly got on the phone to Riyadh. We were being herded from the terminal building across the tarmac to the Pakistani Airways 707 when the chief admin man rushed up to me.

"Don't go!" he cried, "The group captain says that if you stay he will provide a married quarter for you this week, whatever it takes!"

I considered the offer for a full second and then said: "Tell him he's too late".

The aircraft was loaded, the engines fired up, we taxied out and took off. Some hours later we landed in Nairobi, so starting for Sylvia and me a most agreeable part of our lives.

The immigration officer studied my passport and the stub of my one-way ticket.

"You cannot enter Kenya without a return ticket," he asserted.

"Why not?"

He thought for moment as if trying to recall something that he had once committed to memory.

"In case you become a burden on the state," he finally opined.

"But I will be more of a burden on the state if you keep me here than I would if you let me through to make my own arrangements." He considered this argument for a few moments and I could almost hear the cog-wheels grinding.

Then he pronounced: "You cannot enter Kenya without a return ticket."

"In that case, I will have to leave."

"Ndio, yes you will."

"So I shall need a ticket."

"Ndio, yes you will."

"So I must go through to an airline ticket office."

Once again he considered the logic of my remark for a few moments before finally deciding: "You cannot enter Kenya without a return ticket"

I wandered back along the hallway and noticed that luggage trolleys were being hand pushed through a swing door into a corridor that seemed to lead to the land side foyer. I went through, and sure enough soon found myself in the entrance hall. The nearest place outside East Africa was Addis Ababa, so it was to the Ethiopian Airline office that I went. They assured me that if I bought a ticket and did not use it, I could have my money back. I bought a one-way ticket to Addis, made my way back along the luggage corridor and presented myself and the ticket to the same immigration officer.

He stamped my passport giving me three months in Kenya, and he did not seem the slightest bit puzzled about anything. Entering Kenya legally now, the Ethiopians were as good as their word and gave me my money back.

I telephoned my farmer acquaintance and he said that he would be at the airport in thirty minutes to collect me. He was right on time. Then, instead of going out to the car park, as I expected, we went back to the air side, got into his Cherokee and flew to his farm at Narok. That was the first time that I flew over the beautiful Kenya countryside. I was to do it many more times, but never tired of it. At the farm I was given one of the guest cottages and two servants whose sole job was to look after me.

Next day he said that we would fly down to Kilifi on the coast to meet his sleeping business partner, who was taking a short break in his holiday cottage there. Tony invited me to fly the aircraft. It was the first time that I had flown a light aircraft off a grass strip 11,200 feet above sea level. But the take off went well – after all, I only had to open the throttle and be patient. He seemed impressed, however, and seemed equally impressed that I was aware of the fact that if you pull the stick back the trees get smaller. His admiration knew no bounds when I succeeded in finding the coast in a visibility of about 50 miles.

His partner was another most agreeable fellow and we got on well. I was given another guest cottage and a servant, met some very nice people and was introduced to water skiing. That evening I was invited to a dinner party at the Mnarani Club. The company was convivial, the dinner superb and the setting under the stars by the breakers and palm trees idyllic. After dinner I sent a telegram to Sylvia telling her to pack up and come on out.

The Company Operations Manual which I prepared was approved by the East African DCA; my East African commercial licence had been issued; the desk I built in reception seemed suitable; the passenger waiting room which I painted looked welcoming; the uniform which I designed looked smart; the brand new Cessna 206 sat outside on the tarmac and the flight planning set-up which I organised was ready. We were in business and I was about to become a bush pilot.

A flustered looking man arrived by taxi from Embakasi, the Nairobi international airport. He had missed the daily commercial flight to Mogadishu, the capital of Somalia, and wanted to charter us to take him there at once. My system worked well and I was able to quickly calculate the distance, time and price, which he immediately accepted. We were airborne in under ten minutes.

Wilson airport closed at 7pm and if I did not get back in time, I would have to land at Embakasi, which would have incurred navigation charges, landing fees, parking fees and the inconvenience of collecting the aircraft next morning. En route, I calculated that I could get back to Wilson if I could turn round in fifteen minutes. When I was within radio range, I called Mogadishu and asked them to have Shell standing by to refuel my aircraft, and I then dictated my return flight plan so that it would be already open when I arrived.

As I taxied in, I could see no sign of the Shell truck. And there was no one at all on the apron. I went up the stairs to the tower and angrily asked why the refuellers were not there.

"Their place is on the other side of the airfield."

"Well call them then!" I demanded impatiently.

"The telephone does not work."

"Well run across there then!"

"It's too hot!"

I exploded again, then asked if the flight plan had been put in.

"No."

"Who was on the radio to me?"

A nondescript scruff admitted that it was he.

"Why didn't you write down what I dictated to you?"

"I cannot write," the wretch replied.

I was in the midst of my next castigation when a smart man in a suit, complete with collar and tie, came into the tower.

At last, I thought, the airport manager has condescended to show up. I told him that this was the most inefficient airfield I had ever been to. (I had just left the Air Force, and up till then it was true). I went on that it should be shut down, the staff fired and the manager hanged.

"What is the problem, Sir?" he asked in perfect English.

I told him. He quickly dispatched a man on a bicycle to Shell, and got his own secretary to take down the flight plan.

"I hope that solves your problems, Sir." he politely remarked.

"It does, but you and this place are still a shambles and should be bulldozed into the sea," I crossly replied.

He did not appear to take offence and left the tower.

"Do you know who that was?" asked nondescript scruff.

"I don't know his name, but I presume he is the manager."

"No, Bwana, that was the Prime Minister."

I expressed disbelief and was invited to look out of the window. There was my erstwhile "manager" with a visiting Head of State inspecting a Guard of Honour.

"He is a good man," opined the nondescript scruff.

"Yes," I replied, "and he knows his place, too."

I was booked to fly a party from Nairobi to Kisumu on Lake Victoria. I was to use an aircraft which was on lease to us. The boss mentioned that the battery would have to be replaced soon, but that it would last out for this trip. We were night stopping in Kisumu and I hoped that the battery would last the night. I had already adopted the bush pilots' trick of leaving the aircraft beacon switched on. If the battery switch were also inadvertently left on, the beacon would be flashing and so draw attention to the fact.

Next morning we went back to the airfield. When I attempted to start, the battery was quite flat. The engine was too big to be prop swung single-handed and a two-man start requires expertise which was not available. Fortunately, I had thought to bring jump leads and so I looked around for a vehicle with a battery. There were none. I tried to telephone a garage but the telephones did not work. Then I found a local who 'agreed' to lend me his bicycle. I peddled into town to find a car or truck, but there were none in sight and the only garage was firmly shut. Then I spotted the Fire Station.

"Does the fire engine go?" I inquired.

"Ndio, Bwana, of course!"

"Then how about driving it to the airfield?"

"I would Bwana, but I cannot drive."

"Where is the driver?"

"There is no driver."

"There is now." I replied, "Get me the keys!"

I drove to the airport with the borrowed bike on the back, and parked the fire engine inches from the aircraft. Brakes on and chocks in, wires hooked up, and the aircraft started up at once. I cautiously drove the fire truck away, inches from the now turning propeller.

I could not leave an aircraft with the engine running, so had to abandon the fire engine.

"But how will we get the fire engine back to the station?" asked the flustered fireman.

"You must learn to drive it", I replied.

"I have tried many times, Bwana, but cannot do it," he responded, miserably.

"Then it does not really matter where the truck is, does it?"

He could just see the logic of this, but still looked unhappy, so I undertook that if ever I went that way again, and did not have an aircraft to look after, I would take the truck back to the station. This generous undertaking appeared to satisfy him. When I switched off on the apron at Wilson, my boss happened to be there.

"How did it go?" he asked.

"Never mind the details." I answered, "But you don't owe me a beer, you owe me a crate!"

Prince Philip was coming to Kenya to kill birds; he was going to stay at Eliye Springs, a remote, flyblown, and very basic fishing camp on the shores of Lake Rudolf. For the occasion it was transformed into a comfortable lodge. This required air transport and we got the job of providing it. I flew up several times taking knives and forks and other aids to gracious living. One of these was a gigantic mosquito net, made to order, which would form a sort of inner skin of the dining marquee. When it was ready, we got it into the aircraft somehow and I flew it up and helped them erect it.

The day before his arrival, I had my aircraft all ready to go with an external pannier under the fuselage. I got permission for the ice cream man to drive onto the tarmac, where we rapidly loaded the cool boxes into the pannier and I took off immediately and climbed to the cool air at 15,000 feet. (That's right. If you live at five thousand feet for a few weeks, you can fly at 15,000 without oxygen). At Eliye, they were waiting for me, and the boxes were rapidly placed in the gas driven refrigerators. The ice cream was in good shape.

There were few ladies in the area, but another of my duties was to fly them all (married or single) away for the duration of the visit. It was not satisfactory to do this before the arrival; it had to be done the day before so that they were not present on the same date. The lengths they have to go to avoid gossip! After the visit, I went again to bring back some the equipment that had been on loan. I asked Tony ——, the manager, how it had all gone.

"Very well indeed."

"How did he like the ice cream?"

"He politely declined it."

"Was the giant mosquito net satisfactory?"

"He took one look, said he hated mosquito nets, and asked to have his meals outside."

I was somewhat deflated by this news, but there was a consolation. I subsequently operated there several times, but was never bitten by a mosquito, and never ran short of ice cream.

I was taking an American Senator and his family on a three-day trip round the game parks. On the first evening I was having a quiet after duty beer when Arthur P——came into the bar. "Ah there you are! I've been looking for you."

Arthur was known to some as the 'flying greengrocer'. He had a farm on the slopes of Mount Kilimanjaro where he cultivated, among other things, high quality fruit and vegetables which he flew himself in his own aircraft from his own airstrip round the game lodges where it commanded high prices.

His aircraft had become unserviceable and it was important that he get back to his farm in the morning and he wanted me to take him. I explained that both my aircraft and I were under charter, but if the Senator approved I would oblige him. The Senator and his family were following the usual routine of having an early morning game run (the best time to view the animals), followed by a leisurely breakfast, pack up, and ready to fly on to the next game lodge at mid-morning. Just then the Senator came into the bar, heard about the problem, and generously agreed that, provided I was back by ten, he would have no objections. I resolved to be back by nine, which required us to get airborne at sun up.

This we did, and as usual there was some ground mist to contend with. We had to get over the saddle between Mount Kilimanjaro and Mount Meru, and as we climbed higher, the mist thickened, aggravated by the first heat from the sun. Soon we had the "wheels in the weeds", as the saying went.

Arthur remarked that had he been flying, he would have turned back by now. I assured him that he would have been quite right to do so, and explained that the Queen had spent a great deal of money and effort teaching me to do this and that he should not attempt it until he had much more experience. We landed at his farm and he said that he had had no idea that it was possible to fly, let alone cross the mountains, in such conditions.

For a moment, I was an Air Force flying instructor again. "Don't even think of trying this yourself, Arthur. You need much more experience, you must work up to it gradually, and you must have an instrument rating in case you can't get through and have to pull up into cloud." He seemed convinced by my remarks, and we briefly discussed the possibility of my giving him some instruction in instrument flying when he was next at Wilson.

A few weeks later I was having a post-flight beer in the Aero Club when I heard that Arthur had been killed in a flying accident. No one was sure, but it appeared that he had hit the ground in bad weather. I mentally reviewed our last conversation, and felt sure that I had been sufficiently emphatic to make my point. Nevertheless, I did sometimes wonder if…

The crooner Bing Crosby was a keen hunter and the walls of his trophy room at home were covered with the heads of animals that he had shot. (How gross!). He employed Terry M——, generally considered the best white hunter in the business. As the walls filled up, Bing wanted ever rarer animals. Terry was the only hunter who could be sure to find them. Bing was coming out on a hunting safari and wanted a lesser-spotted kudu and a reticulated oryx (or whatever). Terry decided to use us to fly his clients.

Using his profound knowledge of the bush, Terry would set out with his team, which was rather like an army move in brigade strength. He would locate the required animal, then, with his own equipment would construct an airstrip on the spot. This was all complete by the time Bing arrived from the USA. Terry then spoke to me by radio, giving the map reference of the strip. It was my job to fly Bing and his friends to the map reference and hope that neither I nor Terry had made a mistake. We had not and there, as advertised, was the new strip carved out of the bush.

The camp was unbelievably luxurious. The bathrooms had full running water services, and of course, hot and cold running water. The tents were air-conditioned, the bar provided every drink I had ever heard of (and some I hadn't) and a comprehensive wine list and plenty of ice. There was a well-stocked library. The dining room had immaculate white linen and the best cutlery, glassware and so on, and behind every diner stood a waiter clad in spotless white uniform complete with red fez. The menu was five star.

Bing got his kudu, and it was then my job to fly him and his party to the Mount Kenya Safari Club, a splendid hotel near Nanyuki in the foothills of Mount Kenya. They would stay there while Terry moved his whole outfit across country to the place where he had located the oryx. Then we did the same again. With oryx bagged, my last job was fly them to Embakasi to catch the flight home.

If a British civil servant ever reads this, he will perhaps fall off his stool at the thought of airstrips being built without the benefit of any planning permission. He need not worry, – within weeks they go back to bush.

Bing was very easy to get along with, and he soon had us on first name terms. In an idle off duty moment I once suggested to him that we sing a duet. His normal smile temporarily departed, and he said: "Brian, if you knew how many times people have suggested that to me, you wouldn't have said that." A second later his smile returned, he slapped me on the shoulder and added: "But of course, you didn't know!"

He was a gentleman, and it was a pleasure to know him.

Once a year, the Aero Club of East Africa held a "Flying Safari" a sort of airborne treasure hunt, with the clues being thrust through the window immediately before take off. It was a week-end event with a night stop at some agreeable hostelry at the coast. I entered as pilot with Jock Hay as navigator. Jock was an East African Airways navigator, but was ex-Air Force and known to several of our entry. Our aircraft was a borrowed Rheims Rocket – a souped up Cessna 172.

We were doing well. Each turning point seemed to be the right one and indicated, together with the written clue, the next one. About an hour out of Malindi, our destination for the night, it was clear that the fuel consumption was in excess of the book (and experience) figures. We would however still make Malindi but with much less spare than planned. There was nowhere to refuel nearer than Malindi anyway, so there was little choice but to continue as planned. We did not know it at the time, but a fuel line had cracked and fuel was steadily leaking away.

Half an hour to go and the fuel situation was worse – it began to be doubtful that we would make it. Fuel gauges in light aircraft are notoriously unreliable and it was normal practice to work on time and consumption. That does not work with this sort of malfunction.

I eased up to three thousand feet to give myself more time to set up a forced landing if the engine failed. Fail it did, about thirty miles from Malindi. We were over the Gedi Forest – trees in every direction as far as the eye could see, with the one road clearly beyond gliding distance. I set up the pattern and made a Mayday call to Malindi tower, explaining our problem and position.

The controller must have been a new boy, because he replied: "What is your ETA Malindi?"

"It depends," I replied, "On how quickly you get the crash wagons going."

Fortunately one of the other competitors had seen us and undertook to take care of the radio so that I could concentrate on the landing. On the way down, I remarked to Jock: "I have just said a prayer."

"Really?" he replied, "What did you pray for?"

"I asked the Almighty," I answered, "To ensure that if one of us was going to be hurt it was you and not me."

There was a pause for a few moments before Jock replied that he had just put in a counter-prayer.

I did not recall that RAF manuals mentioned much about landing in trees. But the subject was sometimes discussed among bush pilots and crop sprayers. The general consensus was that the best way was to be as slow as possible, nose high, and just before impact drop one wing so that it would hit first and absorb much of the surplus energy. I tried it and it worked – we were both unhurt and suspended in the tree tops, and the aircraft was surprisingly little damaged. I broke off the compass and we climbed down. Jock, navigator to his finger tips, brought his maps and set a compass course through the woods to the road where we were met by the Safari organisers. The following year he flew with another pilot on the Safari, and as they attempted to cross the saddle of the Aberdares mountain range they found that the ground was rising faster than they were. They did a passable landing at full power just before the crest. I don't think that Jock entered the Safari again.

Good old Jock – if you read this, my warmest regards.

I enjoyed bush flying immensely for over a year. No one cared how you did the job as long as it was accomplished. There were few navigation aids and the maps were a little suspect and navigation was always a challenge (no GPS in those days!). It was mostly map on knee stuff, similar in some respects to Air Force flying. The snags were the poor pay, the minimal time off, and not much chance of any vacation. I was discussing these snags with my neighbour who was a captain in East African Airways.

He remarked that had I been with them, I would now be on six weeks leave, have money in my pocket, and free tickets to anywhere I wanted to go. I expressed interest.

"Let's go!" he said, and we drove then and there to Embakasi, where he introduced me to the Chief Pilot.

I was offered a job at once, gave in my notice at Wilson, and embarked on another happy and rewarding career as an airline pilot. But that is another story.   [B.M.]

GAUDEAMUS IGITUR

The distant crack of leather on willow, the claps and cries of "Well played, Sir" have finished and stumps have been drawn. Now the evening sun is gilding the ivy-clad walls of the chapel as choir practice begins. The sixth form tutorial is over, and our teacher relaxes in the deep armchair by his study fire. Time for a glass of sherry before reading what those little monkeys in the Third Form have made of their essays. It's been a good day. A teacher's life is busy, but rewarding…

If only…!

After leaving the Service at my thirty eight/sixteen point, I got myself a university degree and then, in a fit of idealism, went in for school teaching.

The idealism soon wore off. In about three weeks.

We were warned during my teaching diploma course about "reality shock" when we actually started in the classroom. My first experience of this was when I was sent to do teaching practice in a school in Cowdenbeath. School dinners were pretty awful, so I usually went down to a Chinese restaurant in the High Street. Returning on a pleasant sunny day, I was addressed by one of the teenage pupils sitting with several others on the wall outside the school. He was dressed like his companions in the unofficial school uniform of blue denim, with knobbly boots, tartan scarf, shaven head and an earring. We exchanged the time of day. Entering the men's staffroom, I mentioned to someone that I had just had a pleasant chat with Angus McC…

The effect was electric. Horrified faces appeared from behind newspapers. Fags fell from open mouths. Tea was spilt. There was dead silence for a few seconds, then someone said, "For God's sake, man, ye didna let him know where ye live, did ye?"

For most of my years in teaching, I seemed to get more than my fair share of roughies and toughies that no one else could handle. To be more exact, that no one else could handle either. I remember one class where they not only wore ear and nose rings, but had little razor blades hanging from the rings. One of my ex-pupils knifed someone in a pub and got sentenced for murder.

But to be fair, it was often the roughies who gave you Christmas cards. It did a little to rekindle the idealism. For a moment, anyway.

Some of the girls could be quite nice when they liked. One day, Wilma F…. would tell me a joke, for my delight. She hadn't got very far when I realised the subject was something which, if it had come up in court, would probably have been written down in Latin and given to the bench on a slip of paper. She continued unabashed, holding my attention with her big brown eyes. A barrack room full of Royal Marines would have been reduced to shocked silence. I don't know to this day if she understood the joke. Anyway, I thanked her politely when it was finished and changed the subject.

She used to work in Woolworths after she left school, and I always got a beaming smile from her at the check out.

Various other anecdotes come to mind from those long years of grind. We ought, perhaps, to draw a veil over the field week in Scarborough. Or the head of the music department who went mad… What about the time I saved a young teacher's career though?

At Dunfermline High, Dave T… and I shared 3H for a double period on a Friday afternoon. (Any teacher will instantly know what that would be like!) One of us worked the slide projector and tried to engage the attention of the class in some undemanding topic, while the other patrolled at the back with a tawse.

At the time, there was one of those families that all teachers have met, which had a child in every year through the school. No sooner did one leave from the top than a young sibling arrived at the bottom to keep the progression going. In 3H there was a female representative of this particular clan. At fourteen, she was becoming nubile, and very aware of it. She was wearing a very tight jersey. I suddenly realised David was speaking to her.

"Janette, you've no got your school uniform on."

"Ay, ah hae so!"

"But you've no. That jersey's no school uniform."

"Ay, but ah hae ma uniform on underneath. You can tak a look for yoursel'!"

David was just about to have a look down inside the front of her jersey when I grabbed his collar and hauled him back. One could imagine the local press. *"Teacher suspended for lecherous behaviour. Outraged parents demand compensation. "Our daughter's life has been ruined for ever". Join your paper's campaign to stamp out this evil. Is there a secret teacher living next to you? Name and shame, we say! The public has a right to know!"* Etc etc.

To be serious, teachers walk a veritable tightrope these days, and are ever more in danger of appearing in court, their only defence being that they acted as a reasonable parent would have done in whatever circumstances. I recall a first aid course, when it was emphasized that you must never give a child an aspirin or other medicine, never put sticking plaster on a child, never pick a child up to comfort it, never *ever* take a child home in your own car. Always call an ambulance, even for the slightest scratch. When I read of cases of teachers blamed for children being drowned or other such accidents on fieldwork expeditions, I think to myself that there, but for the Grace of God, could have gone me. Take your eyes off them for a moment and children can be relied on do something or other stupid.

For example, there was the time I was asked to help Mrs H with her class of fourteen year olds, whom she was taking to the seashore for practical geography. The law required a minimum of two staff for the numbers concerned. Anyway, no sooner had our hired coach parked in a lay-by above the beach than Mrs H was away, followed by a crocodile of her pupils. By the time I had chivvied the last two girls off the coach, the rest had all disappeared. These girls, needless to say, were wearing totally unsuitable high-heeled shoes, despite being told not to time and again beforehand. They teetered through the trees till they came to where the zigzag path started down the fairly steep descent to the beach, perhaps a hundred feet below. They flatly refused to go a step further.

I could hardly leave them on their own in the coach with the driver – he was not legally qualified to be in charge of them. Besides, what if he interfered with them, or more likely, they accused the poor chap of doing so? On the other hand, I could see Mrs H far away out of earshot (no mobile phones in those days), busy handing out worksheets while hordes of children were swarming out of control over the rocks in all directions, playing chicken with the breakers or throwing sand at each other. So what to do?

What I did was to bully the two girls into going down the path, despite their squeals of protest. And what happened? One of them lost her footing and went base-over-apex down the slope, until brought to rest by some gorse bushes. All was well that ended well, thank goodness.

There, but for the Grace of God…

At that time, discipline was maintained by the tawse, or belt. The most sought after were the Lochgelly Specials, well known throughout Scotland. They were made in the town of that name by Mr. Dick, a saddler. I needed one, and since I was working only about half an hour away, decided to call at the shop rather than order one by post. Young David, mentioned above, asked if I could get one for him too.

So I drove over after school, covered in sweat and chalk dust, with aching feet and my ears still ringing from day-long exposure to one thousand eight hundred children.

Mr. Dick's shop turned out to be a very upmarket sort of place, with a window full of saddles and expensive-looking leather things. Inside, it was fitted with thick pile carpet and glass counters. A distinguished silver-haired elderly gentleman was serving one of those county-type women in twin set and pearls. When she finally left, I furtively told him what I wanted, like somebody asking for "something for the weekend".

"Certainly, Sir", said Mr. Dick, for it was none other than he. "Follow me." He opened a side door in the shop, and there was a veritable Aladdin's cave full of tawses. They were hanging all round the walls, two-tails, three-tails, black, all shades of tan, ivory ones even. Mr. Dick extolled their qualities. Ladies preferred the lightweight ones, while most gentlemen chose the medium. Heavy ones were a little more expensive because you couldn't get the right hides these days. As for the two or three tails, his clients found both equally effective and it was a matter of personal preference.

A final touch to this surreal situation was a display of miniature tawses. That's right, miniatures! I could not conceive who would use them, but Mr. Dick explained that some teachers, upon retirement, would buy one and hang it by their fireplace for old times' sake. No, honestly!

Nowadays corporal punishment is, of course, unlawful. Teachers have to rely on that innate courtesy and respect for their elders which typifies today's teenagers…

In my last couple of years as a teacher, I was elected the Hon. Sec. of the local branch of our professional association (or trade union, to be more accurate!). This was quite good fun, with regular trips to

Edinburgh for conferences and so on. It was also a challenge to deal with the surprising variety of problems that affected colleagues in their work, and try to sort them out amicably with their head teachers or the education authority. (One case was that of a Rural Studies teacher who threw a flower pot at an extremely aggravating pupil. He was immediately sacked, of course, and it was all in vain anyway. He hit the wrong pupil, not the one we would all have cheerfully murdered ourselves.)

The job entailed a week's training course at the Scottish TUC College in Kilmarnock, on employment law, grievance procedure, sickness, retirement entitlements and that sort of thing. The college warden had flown Spitfires during the war, so we had flying experience in common. The college, by the way, was a country house that had been beautifully fitted out by union craftsmen themselves. If the bosses could have conferences in fine buildings with gardens and golf courses, why should the workers not have a nice place as well? And why not, indeed?

In the college library were shelves of earnest books on such worthy topics as the struggle of the handkerchief-makers of Bootle in 1867, or the minutes of the international Socialist conference on something or other in 1890. In amongst them, I found one morocco-bound volume which turned out to be a text book on sexual deviances, fully illustrated. How it got there, goodness knows. Perhaps someone presented it as a practical joke, and it was assumed to be another earnest, boring book like all the rest. Presumably nobody had ever bothered to look at it before I did, or it would have been removed! There was also a complete set of the writings of Karl Marx. I was disappointed to find they had not been autographed by the author, though.

Whether or not my union activities had anything to do with it, I was offered redundancy, and left teaching with a sense of freedom, to the envy of all my erstwhile colleagues. Later, I returned to the RAF as a Retired Officer, on the staff of HQ Air Cadets. This did much to lift my spirits. The keenness and intelligence of the cadets helped to restore my faith in the youth of the nation. But my time at HQAC belongs to another story.   [R.H.R.]

BRUSHES WITH THE LAW

By the time I arrived at Odiham in 1971 I had had four moves in three years and a few short courses thrown in. Thinking it was time to settle down, I began to consider life outside the service so one day I sat down with a pen and a blank sheet of paper and wrote down what I saw as the pros and cons of various possibilities for a second career. I thought that the life of a solicitor in a provincial town might suit me so I approached the Law Society to find out what would be required, and in due course enrolled as a student. At the same time I started on a correspondence course run by the College of Law. At the end of my tour as OC 33 Squadron I was posted to the Ministry of Defence. I began to go to evening classes at the Central London Polytechnic and in the summer of 1974 sat and passed three of the five subjects of the Law Society's Part I Qualifying Examination and passed the other two the following year. I continued to study for the seven subjects of Part II and began to look for a place as an articled clerk. Before going to Sharjah I had bought a house in Salisbury to house my family during my unaccompanied tour so I looked there and was eventually lucky enough to be offered articles of clerkship. Not having been selected for redundancy, I applied for Premature Voluntary Retirement only to be told that as there was a redundancy scheme in progress only two in my rank and branch were to be allowed PVR and the two had already been selected. I appealed on the ground that it was most unlikely that another opportunity for articles would come my way and so I was allowed to go in 1975, with a deduction of 10% from my pension entitlement.

That decided, I signed up for a course at the City of London Polytechnic, limiting my sights to only four subjects of Part II and passed all four in February 1976. Then I began work as an articled clerk with Messrs Trethowans, in Salisbury. At first I was placed under Bill Sellwood, who had been what was previously known as a Managing Clerk but had been recently been renamed "Legal Executive". His speciality was conveyancing and probate and so I was set to drafting contracts and conveyances and wills and helping generally. The work was varied and I found it fascinating, with some very complicated transactions involving "settled land" and many other aspects outside the run of the mill sales and purchases of houses. I saw a different aspect of people in general, particularly in relation to wills and probate.

I saw members of families at odds over who should have Mum's fridge and I wish I had ten pounds for every time I have heard words such as "Grandad always told me that it would be mine when he died" – "it" being anything from a complete farm, to a house, a picture or some mundane piece of furniture or household equipment. It was often useless to tell people that the value of what they hoped to obtain was much less than the cost of achieving it. That brings me to the second stock phrase "It's not the money, it's the principle" and, again, if only I had ten pounds for each time I have heard a client use that expression! The third stock phrase was "I don't care what it costs" – but this usually came from clients depending on legal aid. As an aside, when asked to pay the contribution calculated on an assessment of their means, they would then often argue about the unfairness of it all.

On the subject of the strangeness of people I recall, early in my time as an articled clerk in 1976, a married couple having over £20,000 in a current account. It had not occurred to them to place all this money on deposit to earn interest! They were both teachers and thus presumed to be intelligent.

After almost a year I was moved to the litigation department and received a grounding in criminal work, employment law, family matters and general litigation including personal injury, boundary disputes and so on. As a mere articled clerk I had no right of audience in the courts but occasionally attended with a barrister in the Crown and County Courts. However, I made my first appearance as an advocate before an Industrial Tribunal. I represented the employers in a case lasting two days. Among my souvenirs is the lump of coloured glass thrown at another member of staff and which constituted the last straw leading to the dismissal of the applicant. Strangely, she was successful. I was unhappy at the result but the employers did not appear unduly concerned. The case turned largely on whether the employers had followed the prescribed procedure of warnings.

A criminal case I remember well was that of a man in his seventies charged with a number of offences against small boys. When I had to conduct him to the magistrates' court to be committed for trial in the Crown Court he asked me about the procedure because he had never been to court before. This caused me to wonder how he had come to have served three years for a previous set of offences. In preparation for the trial I had to gather evidence in support and as he said that he attended services in the cathedral and paid covenanted offerings I wrote to the Dean for a character reference. The Dean confirmed that the man did indeed attend evensong frequently and that the verger was briefed to ensure he was kept as far as possible from the choirboys! The Dean nevertheless said that he would pray for our client.

When the day came for the client to be tried in Winchester I was asked to take him there in my car. He had been a mainstay of the local cycling club in his youth and arrived at the office on his racing bike – evidently confident that he would not go to prison. In the car he produced a plastic shopping bag full of photographs of himself as a Boy Scout and of youths and boys dressed in what I took to be ancient Greek costume and striking poses with spears and bows and arrows. I advised that this collection was unlikely to help his case. As we walked up the steps of the court the client suddenly said "Has anyone ever told you that you have nice hair?" With one mighty leap I moved about four feet sideways! The old man was convicted and sentenced to five years. He appealed against sentence and I attended the Court of Appeal in London when counsel argued that it was too long for an old man and that his tendencies must surely have diminished with age. The Lords Justice held that in view of his past record his age should not be taken into account and young boys must be protected. This brings to mind the man of eighty sentenced to 25 years, "But I shan't live that long!" protested the man. "Never mind" said the judge, "Just try to do as much as you can!"

On the family side, I was required to draw up divorce petitions and documents relating to the custody of children and, of course, the financial and property side of marriage breakdown. It was then that I became familiar with another stock phrase "I want to take him for every penny he's got".

Once I was given a thick file to sort out for a case which had been running on and off for years. Things had come to a head because the ex-husband had come to England demanding to see his child. The mother objected. She was British, had married a Christian man from the Middle East and had divorced him outside the United Kingdom. First I had to get an authorised translation of the decree of divorce and orders relating to the child. But I also had to find out what to do. Nobody in the office had a clue and so I telephoned the Chief Clerk of the Family Division Registry, put my cards on the table, and admitted that we did not know how to move on this. Of course, the man was only too pleased to be able to display his knowledge and, as it were, show these country hicks a thing or two, and he put me on the right track. For this enterprise I received a rocket from the elderly senior Legal Executive who was the fount of all knowledge in the firm. He told me how wrong I had been to ask advice from the court staff, because we were supposed to know the answers. This caused me to reply that he did not know the answer and neither did the solicitor whose file it was and that as they gave it to me to sort out then that is what I had done and that the court official had been most friendly and glad to be of service.

As well as sitting behind counsel, I attended before what was then known as the Registrar of the County Court (now known as District Judges) very frequently, sometimes for a full hearing of a case for maintenance or custody and access, and sometimes merely applying for "directions", namely an order requiring certain things to be done, such as filing documents, so as to get a matter moving towards a hearing.

During this time I had continued to study and passed the last three examinations to qualify as a solicitor. After the due time elapsed I obtained the required certificate from the partner to whom I was articled and applied to be admitted to the roll of solicitors. On paying the fee I was admitted, and received my certificate dated 1st September 1978 and signed by Lord Denning, the Master of the Rolls.

Mention of Lord Denning reminds me of a famous case, "Lloyds Bank v. Bundy", in which my then firm had acted for Mr Bundy. Nowadays when anyone is asked to agree to their house being security for a loan to another person it has to be certified that they have had independent advice from a solicitor. Mr Bundy had agreed that his house could be security for a loan to his son and when things went wrong the bank tried to gain possession of the house. The case came before Lord Denning, whose judgment begins "Broadchalke is one of the prettiest villages in Wiltshire and there lives old Mr Bundy as his father and grandfather did before him..." No guesses for who won! Denning said the bank ought to have made sure that Mr Bundy had been made aware of the implications of the transaction. Another Denning judgment begins "It was bluebell time in Kent...." and it quickly becomes clear who is going to win that case. Lord Denning was often criticised as making his own laws but he tended to be on the side of the little man and did his best to make the law fit the outcome he saw as fair.

My contract required me to remain with the firm for 12 months after admission and I began to appear in the magistrates' court and the County Court. My first defended case was before the magistrates in Tisbury, a small town or large village west of Salisbury. It was a case of criminal damage in the toilets of the village hall. The prosecutor was a police inspector who knew his magistrates, knew his Tisbury and knew his job. Things were not going at all well but my client was not the brightest and was becoming confused when cross-examined by the inspector; in fact he was so confused that he was admitting everything put to him. I intervened and, pointing this out, suggested that my client was clearly of limited intelligence and did not even understand what he was being asked. To my surprise, he was acquitted. The police inspector believed it was an open and shut case and felt hard done by. He was not amused.

After a few months I began to look for another job and in answer to my request to be released from my obligation to stay with the firm the partners said I could go when I found something. I found a place with a small firm in Winchester.

At Winchester I was again employed largely in the same sort of litigation but also did a small amount of conveyancing. I tried to avoid the latter as I disliked all the problems on completion day with clients saying they were "waiting outside the new house, where were the keys and just because the bank had not transferred the money was no reason to keep them hanging about."

I appeared regularly in the magistrates' court in Winchester and on one occasion was actually reported in the Daily Telegraph. My client was a woman charged with the theft of traffic cones and the flashing lamps placed on them at some road works. I explained to the court that she was pregnant and one of the peculiarities of her pregnancy was that she had developed a longing for prawns, which she would take from the fridge and eat in the middle of the night. Also, she was fascinated by the flashing lights on the traffic cones and over a period of time had gradually accumulated a set in her house as she found them comforting when she was lying awake at night.

Another case I remember well involved a young man serving a sentence in Winchester Prison who was brought out to be sentenced for a breach of an earlier Probation Order. He was given an extra month to serve and the chairman of the magistrates, a lady, said to him "No doubt you thought the extra month was to run concurrently with your present sentence, but it is not. So go back to prison and tell all your friends!" This client, I recall, was most aggrieved that while he was in prison for theft some rotten thief had stolen garments from his wife's clothes line!

There were amusing incidents now and again such as when some clients who had helped themselves to lead from a church roof arrived in a scrap yard with it in the boot and a witness described the vehicle as having the back end scraping the ground and the front wheels hardly touching it. Another time the police, in a car, were after some lads escaping with a lawn mower they had stolen. On reaching a dead end in a road, the lads climbed over a wall, the police officers got out of the car to give chase but overlooked the fact that they were on a hill. In their excitement they omitted to apply the handbrake and the police car rolled back into some parked cars and caused a great deal of damage.

There was occasionally some amusement to be had in the County Court as well. Once I sat in court waiting for my case to come on and listened to a case between two families of gypsies disputing over a small piece of land. There was evidence about Romany customs and lore and what constituted a binding contract between Romanies. A man with very long black greasy hair and a bright green suit was called to give evidence about these things and was described as being a member of "The Romany Council of Great Britain" (or something similar). Only one family had a solicitor, the other relying on a "Mackenzie Friend" (a person who could not address the court, not being qualified, but who could advise quietly). After a while the judge said to the solicitor that this had all become rather involved and he felt that some research was needed into the decisions in similar cases. He said he would adjourn for this purpose and asked the solicitor to look up the relevant cases and come back in the afternoon to continue. When I left the court about half an hour later I found a throng of people fighting in the street outside and recognized them from the courtroom. I had to go back in the afternoon and the Romany case was brought back on. The judge turned to the solicitor and asked for the case law only to be met with the response "I am pleased to tell your Honour that the case is withdrawn as the parties managed to settle it out of court during the adjournment!" I have sometimes wondered if the learned judge had guessed that this might happen.

While at Winchester I appeared in my first full County Court civil case, which was about a shoddy job done in repairing a car. To my horror, this was to be heard by a judge I will refer to as Collins, a very strict judge believed to dislike solicitors almost as much as he disliked the wrongdoers who appeared before him. Unfortunately, I was so lacking in experience and wit that I did not perceive that the judge was very much inclined to accept my clients' version of events and so when we were on the point of adjourning for lunch and I was asked if I intended to call any more witnesses it turned out to be wrong to say that I did. The judge retired in some dudgeon to his chambers and sent out a testy message to the effect that he was sorry that I saw the necessity to waste his time. Came the afternoon, I decided to take the broad hint. The judge found in favour of my clients and even awarded costs, that is, he ordered the other side to pay our costs. This was strange as my reading of the County Court Rules indicated that there were reasons why costs could not be awarded in this case. So I was surprised when the judge asked me if I intended to apply for costs. My opponent jumped up and objected but, with a broad smile, His Honour Judge Collins QC said "Oh no, Mr Murphy, Mr Hoskins must have his costs". Nevertheless, I walked out of court feeling about four inches tall.

The villains also were afraid of this judge. A young client came out of prison from a three-year sentence and came to me to help him gain access to his daughter, his wife having left him while he was in gaol. He was one of those who said he intended to have his day in court no matter how much it cost. When I calculated that he had to pay £3 for his initial legal aid he was indignant! In due course the case came up in the Southampton County Court and on checking the list I found that the judge was Collins. My client, I will call him Mr West, turned pale and said he would not go into the court room. "He gave me three years and said that if he ever saw me again he would give me five" said Mr West. "Nonsense" said I, "this is a civil case and anyway he won't remember you", "Oh yes he will", said West but eventually he agreed to enter the court. As we took our seats the judge looked over, "Good morning, Mr

Hoskins" he said "I see you've got young Mr West with you". West would not accept that the judge knew his name only because it was, obviously, on the court list and, quite candidly, I was not entirely convinced myself. This judge had been in the area for many years and knew what was what and who was who.

As it happened, West did go back to prison very shortly afterwards. He had been making a sandwich late one evening and so, of course, it was only by pure chance that he had a carving knife in his hand when he went to remonstrate with two people creating a disturbance outside his front door and became involved in a fight..........

This judge could deal with cases very quickly; he was not disposed to tolerate lengthy proceedings. Once I went before Judge Collins with a lady wanting an injunction against her violent husband. We were on the point of taking our seats when the judge said "Your client wants an injunction Mr Hoskins, but she is not going to get one!" I tried to say that, with respect, his Honour had not yet heard the evidence.

"I've read the affidavits and she is not getting an injunction. She has had one before and she took him back. Nobody plays ducks and drakes with my court. Application refused. Good morning."

On that occasion I did not even get the chance to sit down!

Then there was the time when, with counsel, we were opposing an application by a prisoner in Wormwood Scrubs for an order requiring his wife, who was intent on divorce, to bring their son to visit him. At the end of the man's case, the judge turned to our side and said "I don't need to trouble you. It is quite clear to me that prison is an unpleasant place and this lady should not be compelled to take her small child there to visit his father. Application dismissed!"

But this judge could be so pleasant when he felt like it. A very new solicitor in his first case in the county court, and thus his first time dressed in gown, wing collar and bands, was understandably very nervous and had some difficulty with his costume. At the end of the case the judge asked him to come up to the bench and whispered to him "Next time, I suggest you put on the collar with the wings at the top!"

It was with some trepidation, that one day I asked to see the judge in his chambers on a personal matter. I wanted to ask him if he would let me name him as a referee on an application I wished to make for a certain appointment. The judge was all charm, and in the course of conversation told me that he had been in the RAF during the war. He could be a hard man and tolerated no nonsense but I grew to like him as well as respect him. He was robust, fearless and definitely not politically correct.

Applications for injunctions for domestic violence figured frequently in my work. Some were relatively trivial and one detected an attitude in some women of "I have told you my problem, let me know when you've sorted it out!" One such was the young woman for whom I prepared her affidavit of evidence and by the time she came back to take the oath I had already fixed an appointment before a judge for the Friday following and told her to meet me at court at 10 o'clock. "Oh? Why should I go? I've told you all about it; you go and see to it." "But the judge will want to see you and ask some questions. You have to be there or you won't get the injunction". "No, I'm not going. I've got to go to the social for my money." So she did not appear and, to my surprise, the judge granted the injunction as the husband didn't appear either to defend himself.

In another case the applicant had been very badly beaten. She was wearing sunglasses and when I asked the reason she raised them and I was shocked to see that the whites of her eyes were bright red. The medical evidence was that she had been within seconds of death by strangulation. We went in to see the judge. The husband did not turn up. The judge said he had read the affidavits so I asked him to make the order. "You're not getting one!" was his response. "But, your Honour, look at the injuries she has received!" "I said you're not getting an injunction! I have a letter from the husband. He is sufficiently remorseful". So that was that. The lady took her husband back – as so many of them did.

After about fifteen months in Winchester I had the chance to return to Salisbury to another firm, with the probability of a partnership. I took it and by the end of 1980 I was a partner in the firm of Lemon Winwood and Trethewy. There was still a Trethewy but Mr Winwood had retired and Mr Lemon had died almost twenty years before. One day an old man came in on business and was shown to my room. As he left he turned to me and said, with some feeling, "I saw Mr Lemon himself when I came in last time!"

There were many sad cases, particularly in family matters. One very nice man was devastated when his wife left him and petitioned for divorce. He simply would not accept it, scrawled all over the court papers and pestered his wife so much that she was granted an injunction. He assaulted his wife and threatened to kill the man with whom she was associating. He was charged and while awaiting trial he was remanded in custody and went on hunger strike. At the end of his trial, when he was lucky enough to be treated sympathetically and given a suspended sentence, his ex-wife left the court quickly but my client decided to follow as he wanted to speak to her. This was in breach of the injunction and in breach of what had just been decreed in the Crown Court. He would not listen to reason and suddenly rushed out of the Guildhall into Salisbury market square. I ran after him and our barrister ran after me, still in his wig and gown, and a policeman ran behind him! Thus we dodged through the market stalls, but the client got away in the crowd.

Other mishaps followed and one day as he sat opposite me in the office he said he wanted to end it all and started to cram Anadin tablets into his mouth. I called one of my partners who rang for an ambulance. We got the man to the door but the ambulance men said they could not take him unless he wanted to go. They said they could not compel him to get in the ambulance, but I had no such inhibitions and pushed him in. He was saved, but his ex-wife died shortly afterwards, and he gave up his job so that he could visit her grave for hours every day. This did not go on for long as after a few months he also died, as literally as it can be, of a broken heart.

Some criminal clients were amazingly loyal and I acted for almost every member of one family – Dad for a GBH, Mum for shoplifting, one of the daughters for shoplifting and two sons for a variety of crimes, including burglary, theft, taking vehicles without consent, and assaults of various grades of seriousness. One of the sons in particular came back time and time again over the years and had received sentences across the whole spectrum: fines, supervision, probation, community service, youth custody and prison. He could not read or write, despite the efforts of the prison system, but when he was free to do so he worked as a labourer. He was not the sort of person one would choose as a friend but in many ways he was almost likeable. He did not often plead guilty but if the evidence against him was clear then he would. He never complained about his sentences and used to say "If you can't do the time, don't do the crime". This was sometimes seen scrawled on cell walls at the court – together with other impolite inscriptions dedicated to the police!

On one occasion this young man was charged with six others of taking cars and committing a number of related offences. He pleaded guilty and we sat in the court waiting while the solicitor acting for all the others droned on and on, telling the magistrates all about their underprivileged backgrounds, broken homes and so on. The magistrates were bored, I was bored and so was my client. I had warned him that with his record the magistrates might decide that their powers were insufficient and send him to the Crown Court for sentence but, obviously, I said I would see what I could do. I felt a tap on my shoulder and turned to my client in the row behind "Tell 'em I want to go to prison", he whispered, and we discussed that point. When it came to my turn I simply told the magistrates that my client was remorseful, he accepted that he had done wrong, accepted that he was facing the strong probability of a prison sentence and even felt that such would be appropriate. They gave him six months and he was delighted, knowing that if he had been sent to the Crown Court a judge might well have given him more.

That family came to me so often that I suppose I must have done a reasonable job so far as they were concerned. At Christmas the Mum would bring me a bottle of sherry – causing the cynical retired police inspector employed by us to say "I wonder which off-licence was done last night?"

Most petty criminals know how to work the system to their advantage but are not very bright in their day-to-day activities – that is why they get caught, of course. One regular of mine, another likeable young man, was seen leaving a building he had burgled and ran off, pursued by two policemen. He jumped into a stream and hid under a bridge. However, it was January and very cold. The wily coppers had seen him but stood on the bridge chatting. After a few minutes out came a wet and shivering burglar – "OK. It's a fair cop". Another time some residents heard a continuing loud noise in the middle of the night and called the police who found our lad sitting outside the supermarket with a hammer and chisel trying to make a hole in the wall. In May of one year he was charged with several offences and I made a successful application for bail. Before his case came up he was charged with more offences and again I persuaded the magistrates to grant bail. This went on and on and I could not understand why bail was granted, but my client instructed me to apply so I did. His case was finally disposed of the following February when he pleaded guilty and was sentenced for about twenty offences, mostly committed while on bail.

The things that can influence a court are quite interesting. Once I represented a plausible and good looking young black man who had come down from London and used stolen cheques and credit cards to obtain goods from several shops. I applied for bail and was successful even though he had been released from prison only a few weeks earlier. He did not have enough money to get back to London so I lent him five or ten pounds. When he came back to court several weeks later he pleaded guilty and looked certain to go back to gaol. I told the court of his ambitions to be a dress designer (true) and that he had a promise of a course of training. I also told them of the loan and that he had paid it back without my having to ask him for the cash. He was given a non-custodial sentence and some days later the lady magistrate in the chair on that day told me that what had swung the balance was the repayment of the loan! Weeks later I received a holiday picture post card from him expressing his thanks. I've often wondered whether he succeeded in going straight – and designing dresses.

"How can you defend someone you know to be guilty?" is a question frequently asked. The answer is that the lawyers must not be judgmental and must keep their personal opinions to themselves, they do not know for certain whether a client is guilty unless the client makes an admission. Even then, he is entitled to require the prosecution to prove its case. Again, a crime is not committed unless it is shown that there was the required mental intent as well as the physical act. A good example is where my client, a soldier, fully admitted that he had hit another soldier with a baseball bat but he denied intending to commit grievous bodily harm. He was willing to plead guilty to a lesser charge but this was not accepted so the evidence had to be heard to decide on the intent factor. The General Court Martial gave him five years.

There were some notable cases such as a conspiracy to murder, and some serious GBH, fraud, robbery and so on, but mainly it was petty crime and quite a lot of motoring offences. At the time of the summer solstice in 1985 we became involved in defending a large number of people arrested after the Battle of the Beanfield when on their way to Stonehenge. The Stonehenge people came from all levels of society. One was a hospital doctor, others came down from good jobs in London just for the holiday. In the police station I assisted a well-spoken young man who had a degree in astro-physics and whose father was senior partner in a firm of surveyors. The youth was, though, unkempt, to say the least. As I sat opposite him at the interview table I watched, fascinated, as a bug crawled down out of his matted hair, walked across his forehead and back into his hair. In the Guildhall for court, I was descending the stairs when I came face to face with a rat sitting on the head of one of the accused. It ran down onto his shoulder and then back up onto his head. Some of the defendants were dressed as clowns and one of the young women in court that day was clothed only in a green velvet curtain.

Eventually I became tired of criminal defence work, with the same old faces, the same old offences and the same old excuses. One of my partners wanted more criminal work so I said he could have mine – but I would leave the duty solicitor panel. That had had its moments but some detainees were very fussy, considering that were not required to pay for a solicitor. One Saturday afternoon I was called out while working in the garden. I changed out of my boots into shoes and drove to the station. The arrested person, a woman, said "Are you sure you're a solicitor? Prove it! You don't look like one. You're not wearing a suit!" I replied "You don't get a suit on a Saturday afternoon".

Then one night I was in a police cell with a boy of 16 or 17, who refused to give his age, name or address, was spitting and swearing at two policemen and lashing out with feet and fists and it came to me that there must be better things to do with my time.

Before the formation of the Crown Prosecution Service the system in Salisbury was that a police inspector was responsible for prosecutions. He and a colleague appeared in court to prosecute on first appearances of defendants and on guilty pleas but prosecutions in defended cases were farmed out to three solicitors, including one of my partners. The preparation of cases for the Crown Court was also farmed out in this way. It worked splendidly, partly because the two inspectors made sure the PCs did their paperwork and got things ready for court in time. Now and again I would be asked to prosecute by the police or, later, the CPS and one incident sticks in the memory. It was not a usual court day but a man had been arrested and had to be taken before the magistrates. It would have been a long way for a CPS prosecutor to travel at short notice so I was asked to go over to the court. The man was duly placed in the dock and the court began to consider the question of bail. My instructions were not to oppose bail but merely set out the facts. The court required to hear evidence about the defendant who was subject to a Mental Health Act order and living in a hostel. In the course of the evidence the lady in charge of the hostel was asked to give her opinion and she, an Irishwoman as I recall, told the magistrates in a very forthright way "There's nothing wrong with him that a good kick up the backside wouldn't cure!" This caused the man, who was quite small and weedy, to wrench the rail from the front of the dock and hurl it onto the table in front of the court clerk and me. Several men sitting with the Irish lady then speedily jumped into the dock and held the man down. Bail was refused!

On the subject of the Irish, some Irish tinkers moved into a camp near Poole and three were arrested after they drove their van into the yard of a factory near Salisbury and loaded it with aluminium castings awaiting delivery. The men were in the scrap metal business, but this was not scrap. I was called to these men in the police station and it was difficult to follow what they were saying as they spoke exceedingly quickly in English, Irish and Romany, sliding from one language to another. The situation was even more complicated by the fact that they all gave several names. They explained that it was their custom to use the surnames of their father, mother or uncle and the choice seemed to vary from hour to hour. They could not read or write and could not even read road signs, they claimed, but set out every day looking for scrap to trade and finding their way home at night. In court the magistrates decided to require surety for bail and a woman appeared who was the aunt of one or more of them. "How is she to find £1,000?" I asked. "Will you speak to her and tell her to get the building society book from under the roof lining of the Transit van – the one with no wheels". Next day she turned up at court with £1,000 in notes. How did she withdraw money from her nephew's book? I didn't ask.

The time came when I was asked by the CPS to prosecute fairly regularly as their agent. Usually this would mean a half or full day prosecuting a large number of road traffic offences or else prosecuting defended cases while the CPS lawyers dealt with all the routine stuff such as remands, bail and putting the case after guilty pleas. Prosecuting was not too difficult when the papers had been well prepared but more often than not one did not see the file until the morning of the hearing or, if lucky, perhaps the evening before. Sometimes it was hard to understand the approach of some of one's fellow solicitors. One day in the magistrates' court a solicitor put his client in the witness box to give evidence in his defence on a charge of careless driving. In fascinated disbelief I heard the defendant begin "I always wanted a Porsche…" and then "Well, you know how it is when you're driving a Porsche. You just don't realise how fast you're going……."

I retired from partnership in 1992 but continued to work a little less than full time with my own firm and also assisted a sole practitioner in Amesbury. In that connection I began to appear at Courts Martial. I won several defended cases and also lost a few. My experience was that most cases in all courts end up with pleas of guilty and that where the case is fought it is more often won by the prosecution. Courts Martial are, as I believe is well known, far more fierce in punishment than Magistrates or Crown Courts. In one of my cases a junior NCO pleaded guilty to stealing a parcel containing a fairly expensive jacket while he was in charge of the regimental post room. In mitigation I referred to his previous good conduct and that to discharge him from the Army would mean the loss of pay and other benefits out of all proportion to the offence and said that magistrates would probably impose a non-custodial or suspended sentence. To no avail; he was given six months detention in the Military Corrective Training Centre and discharged. Not only is the MCTC regime much harder than in H M Prisons, but the loss to the soldier amounted to about £11,000.

I have mentioned the case of the soldier sentenced to five years. It was very serious, and the trial before a General Court Martial lasted five days, but in my opinion he would not have received more than two or three years in a civil court. He had been mentioned in despatches and all he wanted in life was to be a soldier like his father and his brothers. He was the sort of real fighting soldier that his mates would want with them in a tricky situation but, unfortunately, he did not always confine his fighting to that required of him by his country. He had been up and down in rank several times over the years and could have been a sergeant but for his propensity for trouble.

That case was my last Court Martial but I continued in the civil courts and at a desk for some months until retiring finally in 1996. I have mentioned a few of the highlights that occurred from time to time, but there was also a lot of boring hard work! [F.D.H.]

LAND'S END MEMORIES

One of the splendid people concerned with the making of the Battle of Britain film was Vivian Bellamy, a very well known ex-Fleet Air Arm pilot, who was one of the stalwarts of civil general aviation in the 50s and 60s. He had once owned one of the two-seat Spitfires used for conversion training for people like me, and subsequently in the crowd scenes where they wouldn't be noticed and for air to air shots with either a cameraman, or just a camera at times, in the front seat, while being flown from the rear seat – a long way back! He was also well known in the replica field, and for modifying things like Chipmunks to take a small turboprop engine. A strange looking gull wing Proctor, looking a bit Stuka-like, was one of his inventions for the film, and though it was never used, I did see it flying on the odd occasion.

He and I became good friends, and he was a fount of good advice for us novice Spitfire pilots. He had done the test flying of the various ex-Gate Guardians and Museum Pieces that had been resurrected for the film, which I am sure must have been quite exciting at times. I don't remember him flying Spits in any of the film sequences, though I seem to remember he flew one of the Spanish Hellls from time to time. Vivian died in 1998, and it was a short obituary to him in "Aeroplane Monthly" that brought him, and my time with him at Lands End Aerodrome, back to mind.

Among the things said about him and his flying career, was that the sequences taken through the gunsight by a camera mounted in the front seat of the two-seater in the Battle of Britain film were flown by him. I had been boasting to my children, grandchildren, and anyone else who would listen, that for those pictures I was director, cameraman, gaffer, best boy, script writer, and anything else needed to make a film, because I flew those sequences. I wrote to "the Aeroplane" pointing this out, and added my own bit of a tribute to Vivian. They didn't publish it, but I have kept it and refer to it now and again, because I remember him with great affection.

After departing Her Majesty's service, straight into the 1973 fuel crisis, I had done a couple of non-career type flying jobs, the second of which was as a member of the Rothmans Aerobatic Team, flying Pitts Specials, trying valiantly to hang on to the rest of the formation in the No 3 slot. About that time I became a grandfather for the first time, and at the end of an exciting year of unusual attitudes, in formation, I was pondering whether it was wise to press on for another, when the decision was made for me by the team inventor/leader/manager, and good mate, Manx Kelly (another who, alas, is no longer with us), who tactfully equated the team image with youthfulness, and, between the lines, suggested that grandfathers should find more peaceful pastures.

So, perusing the positions vacant column in "Flight", I came across "QFI/Air Taxi Pilot required at Lands End Aerodrome", and found that the boss down there was Vivian; he remembered me, I had enjoyed his company, so Lorraine and I went down to meet him, and over a couple of pints of Cornish ale, I was employed.

I became QFI on the Airtourer 150, a nice little aerobatic aeroplane, and 'round the lighthouse' pilot in what must have been one of the oldest Cessna 172s in the world, which could only just outrun Viv's mad Black Labrador, called, naturally, Blackie, and a sworn enemy of our dog. Blackie spent his time doing curves of pursuit on the take off run of the Cessna, to the delight of the grockles waiting their turn to see the lighthouse from the air. I was also the Air Taxi pilot on the Apache 235, another nice aeroplane, which was mostly employed on the Scillies run, typically three trips out in the morning, wait all day, three trips back in the late afternoon. I got to know the islands quite well.

There were a number of other aeroplanes there I was able to sample; the Isaacs Fury, a mini replica of the pre-war Hawker Fury, and a Stampe, much better for aeros than the Tiger Moth, in spite of looking much the same, stand out particularly. Vivian also had the nastiest aeroplane I have ever had anything to do with, a thing called a Volmer. If I remember, this had Aeronca Champ wings and tail surfaces mated with a home-built amphibian fuselage. With a neatly cowled Lycoming or Continental engine, this might have been quite a nice machine; but Vivian happened to have a rattly old Pobjoy radial lying around, and this was mounted as a pusher with a big four-bladed wooden propellor on a "Forth Bridge", (or I should now say "Sydney Harbour Bridge") type frame above the fuselage, so the whole contraption looked rather like a Walrus minus the top wing!

I think I did a couple of circuits in it and was delighted to put it on the ground again, whereupon I completely lost control taxying in a cross wind and left it in the middle of the airfield in disgust. I'm not sure if it ever landed on water, and seem to remember a brave Irishman buying it in the end.

While I was there Viv and his son Roderick were building a replica Fokker Triplane, which may still be in the airshow circuit, and the last time I went down there a full size Hawker Fury replica, complete with RR Kestrel engine was just about complete. I have a feeling that it went to Belgium. He also built a Fairey Flycatcher replica for his friend John Fairey. I would like to have had the opportunity to fly them, they were all works of art.

Great, if impoverished, days! I well remember Viv taking me off for advisory talks of the "I can only pay peanuts, and you are not a monkey" variety, and eventually I had to go off and find a proper job. The last time I saw my old friend was from the cockpit of a German-registered Canberra as we did a quiet and restrained flypast of Lands End Aerodrome to wave goodbye and say thanks for the hospitality shown us by Viv and friends when I took my German crew down there to say hello, during a navigation exercise to St Mawgan.   [D.H.M.]

HEART ATTACK – ME?

A heart attack means you get a terrible pain, clutch your chest, and fall to the ground writhing and groaning… Well, sometimes maybe, but it can be much less dramatic. In fact, some people apparently do not believe that they have had an attack at all, until a doctor tells them.

You may not have noticed earlier warning signs, or just dismissed them, like me, for example when walking the dog one day up a Lake District hill, or going out to get the paper one winter morning. It was a tight feeling in my chest coupled with a sort of raw feeling at the bottom of my throat, as though breathing harsh cold air.

I just put this down to my own fault for not taking enough exercise. The best way to get fit seemed obviously to press on and work through the breathlessness.

Wrong! It was angina, and you can't beat it by pushing on doggedly, and indeed it is dangerous to do so. Your heart is not getting enough blood supply. You must stop and rest. If it doesn't go away by itself in, say, ten minutes, you need a doctor.

My actual heart attack came on one night just as I was coming out of the bathroom on my way to bed. A sort of ache developed, quite localised, about the size of a hand. It was triangular, between the inner ends of my collarbones and the top of my breastbone. It was a bit like bronchitis, although it was strange that a chest infection should be so sudden. Anyway, bed seemed the best option. Gradually the ache spread down my arms and up the sides of my neck to my ears.

It wasn't that bad; just enough to make me thrash about and not get to sleep. Obvious remedies, like a cup of tea, hot water bottle on chest, pacing up and down and a little gentle swearing, did no good. Eventually I had to wake my wife up to ask where the coproximol was. She wanted to call the doctor. Although I had decided by this time that it probably was angina, which my mother used to get, I wouldn't let her telephone 999.

Wrong! I thought the pain would go away, not realising that if it had not already done so after ten minutes, it was hardly likely after two hours.

Looking back, there was a lot of denial going on. Who wants to leave the security of home, a nice warm bed and wife in the small hours of the morning, to be driven off in an ambulance with flashing light and siren, and then be hustled into a great neon-lit hospital with endless corridors and people in white coats waiting to operate on you! How much more comforting just to get into a corner and curl up!

Wrong again! The sooner a heart attack is treated, the less damage it does. Once my GP learned next morning what my symptoms were, I was in the cardiology department of the Sunderland Royal Hospital within the hour. Still pretending to myself that I would just be a day patient, I had not even taken my pyjamas with me (in the Services, you were supposed to take your 'small kit' whenever you reported sick, I remember!).

The National Health Service gets a lot of stick these days, but I could not fault the treatment and the care. In no time, there were ECG electrodes all over my chest, a little tap in my arm for drugs, blood was being taken for analysis and I was having to swallow all sorts of pills. Sure enough a heart attack was confirmed, and I got a stern telling off for not taking it seriously at the time, but waiting till next day.

The consultant asked if I had been a doctor myself, or had other medical training. I said no. "Right", he said "In future don't take it upon yourself to judge whether your chest pains are serious or not. Let us professionals decide that, not you!"

My only excuse was that the symptoms were not as bad as you might imagine, otherwise perhaps I would not have been able to kid myself so easily. Also, to be frank, we are always being told how overworked doctors are, so you are reluctant to call one out if it is not important.

My main memory of the night is indeed not so much real pain, as of just utter and total misery. (The nearest comparison was when I was put on a train as a small boy in September 1939 with gas mask, teddy bear and name label, to go to an unknown billet amongst complete strangers miles from home.)

Do not make the same mistake yourself. If you do get chest pains, or perhaps merely distress and shortness of breath, get medical attention, even if you are not sure what it might be. Even a mild attack can do damage that makes a further, perhaps fatal attack, more likely. Certainly, the medical profession takes chest pains seriously. Mention such symptoms at your medical centre, and you will likely find a path is cleared to the doctor's door like the parting of the Red Sea, straight past the queue of mere backaches, bad colds and in-growing toenails!

The aftermath was a week in hospital, followed by eight weekly physiotherapy sessions and a treadmill test. Five pills have to be taken daily forever (or at least until the day I die, whichever is sooner!). Damage to your heart muscle can be repaired with care and aerobic exercise. However, the angina, which caused it in the first place, by choking the blood supply, is always liable to come on again. This seems to be particularly when you are out in cold windy weather, so you have to be aware of the warning signs.

It is now nearly a year since it happened, and so perhaps this is an appropriate time once again to commend the NHS, and all the staff at Sunderland Royal Hospital. The young nurses were marvellous. For example, one old guy was away with the fairies, and in the small hours of the morning would tear off all his drips and electrodes, not to mention his pyjamas, and fall out of bed. The girls would all rush in, heave him back into bed again, and dress him, giving soothing little murmurs and calling him pet, flower and bonny lad all the while.

It was sobering to realise how much worse some elderly fellow patients are than yourself, with operation scars down their chests, or oxygen masks for their emphysema, or even cancer to add to their heart problems. There was a comradeship and sympathy towards each other in the ward that spoke much for the decency of these older folk and their wives. All had gone through so much in their lives already – unemployment, the war, years spent at sea or hewing coal deep underground, skimping and saving to bring up their families.

Still, you don't want to find yourself in a hospital ward if you can help it. Remember what the consultant said, and don't decide for yourself whether a chest pain means something serious or not. Get it checked. It may be nothing to do with your heart after all. A cousin got one recently, and sure enough, it wasn't a heart attack.

It was a pulmonary embolism… Just thought I'd tell you that to cheer you up. [*Name and address supplied!*[6]]

---

[6] The author wishes to remain anonymous because all of us face medical problems as we grow older. This account describes just one typical such experience. It was originally written as a tribute to the local hospital for their staff to read.

A MEDICAL ADMINISTRATOR

A second tour of duty at the Ministry of Defence endorsed my decision to retire and seek employment in civilian life. Interviews for various jobs ranged from Bursar at Dulwich College and at St Mary's Hospital Medical School to teaching French at my old school, heading a firm in Paris translating technical documents and working for Brittany Cruises, supervising the leasing of motor cruisers on the canals in southern Brittany. In all cases the circumstances and salary were unsatisfactory. I finally accepted the job of Administrative Services Secretary at the Royal Society of Medicine in Wimpole Street, London.

The RSM is a learned society which brings together all the different speciality groups of medicine and provides a national forum for discussion and debate. It is open to all registered medical, dental and veterinary practitioners and currently has some 20,000 members worldwide. There are 34 different speciality sections; each hold monthly meetings and there are many inter-disciplinary meetings and forums in the variety of meeting halls available. My own responsibilities included building services, overnight accommodation facilities and the in-house printing department. The meeting halls were used extensively by the in-house sections and also by outside organisations associated with medicine. The overnight bed and breakfast accommodation comprised some 40 bedrooms and were much in demand. The printing department provided all the Society's printing requirements, including the monthly RSM Journal and all programmes for meetings.

Although it was like a breath of fresh air to have the benefit of a PA and shorthand typist – luxuries denied me in the RAF – and the freedom of sending out letters and correspondence without clearance of a draft beforehand (memories of MOD), there were nevertheless many problems to deal with. These centred mainly on personnel – primarily in the catering department – but I also became involved in the planning and building programme for new Society premises. The adjacent site, vacated by the Post Office, was purchased by the Society and new premises were built over a four-year period. A further 18 months was devoted to refurbishing the existing building and the two complexes were linked together. These new and refurbished RSM premises comprised new kitchen and dining room, bar, meeting rooms, a conservatory, 45 en-suite bedrooms and an upgraded and modern library. The fact that the decision was made to continue operating during the building/refurbishment programme meant that I was inundated with problems. The main ones were complaints by doctors trying to hold meetings and forums while drilling was going on, snags with operation of the new lifts, false fire alarms entailing complete evacuation of the building, heating and air-conditioning problems and, not least, the re-housing of all departments while refurbishment was being carried out. However, the whole project was eventually completed and the Society's new premises came on line. All was ready for the official opening.

The new premises were officially opened by Her Majesty the Queen, accompanied by His Royal Highness the Prince Philip, Duke of Edinburgh, on 2nd July 1986. Past and present dignitaries were present, including the Lord Mayor of Westminster, the Society's President and many past Presidents. After the President's welcome to the Royal Party, HM the Queen unveiled a commemorative stone in the new Foundation foyer. The Royal Party then met guests in various areas of the complex, took tea in the new accommodation area and finally signed photographs and the Society's Roll of Fellows.

After the busy four years from 1982 to 1986 it was something of an anti-climax to find myself settled into a nice new and spacious office with only my routine day-to-day work to keep me busy. The opening of the new complex was as if a stage in my life had come to a close, which indeed it had, with all my energies having been devoted to that building programme and to the multitude of problems associated with it. In fact, snags and day to day problems continued to be highlighted long after the departure of the contractors. It became evident that I was becoming bored and fed up. So I tendered my resignation and took retirement (for the second time), this time to live in Cornwall, taking with me a set of crystal whisky glasses, engraved with the Society's crest, which were presented to me. [A.D.R.D.]

GLIDING ALONG TO RETIREMENT

Before retiring for good and all, I spent some enjoyable years as a Retired Officer on the Air Staff at HQ Air Cadets. My remit was to look after the many Air Cadet gliding schools. Over the corridor, Ricky Crowder looked after all the Chipmunk Air Experience Flights. He was another of half a dozen old Cranwellians in the HQ.

My work included tasking, manning, flight safety, the Flying Order Book and Air Staff Instructions, fuel allocation, annual conferences, medical queries, AOC's inspections, new equipment, training programmes and almost anything else that arose, including settling squabbles!

The Central Gliding School at Syerston was manned by full-time professional gliding instructors under the command of an RAF Wing Commander, and across the country there were another twenty eight volunteer gliding schools (abbreviated to VGS). These were run by a cadre of RAFVR(T) officers plus a lot of civilian gliding instructors. The total instructor strength was about five hundred. They operated mainly at weekends, except for week-long special courses during the school holidays.

These VGS were spread out across the whole UK, from Manston to Predannack, and from Swansea to Kinloss, plus one in Northern Ireland. It was a great job, because I used to get out of the office and visit them all. At each, there was a warm welcome from the enthusiastic part-timers, who were mostly in awe of a pilot from the "real" air force. Of course, you got some flying too.

We had a total of about 140 aircraft – quite an air force in its own right. About 70 of these were superb glass-fibre sailplanes, winch-launched, named "Vikings". They had a gliding angle of about 1 in 40, and given the right conditions, you could actually start a downwind leg at 1,000 feet and reach 1,200 feet opposite the caravan.

The others were so-called "self-launching gliders". These were actually little powered aeroplanes, but it was a bit of sophistry not to admit that, because sixteen year old cadets could be sent solo in "gliders" but not legally in powered aircraft. These motor gliders equipped VGS on airfields that were unsuitable for winch operation.

When I first started in the post, we had rather horrible things called "Ventures", which had a Volkswagen-derived engine, and were built out of plywood and fabric. They had a single main wheel and outriggers, which often snapped off. The side-by-side seats were upholstered in patterned fabric like a cheap German car, presumably chosen by the manufacturer's wife.

I never trusted the long, bendy wooden wings, although none broke off while I was there. The only thing to be said in favour of these machines was that you could get the controls horrendously crossed, and all they did was waffle about. I think their stalling speed was about 35 knots. The object was to train cadets to take-off and climb to circuit height, then switch the engine off and glide round the rest of the way to land.

Later, the fleet was re-equipped with very expensive modern fibre-glass motor gliders, known as Vigilants, with a proper undercarriage and a more potent engine of Porsche ancestry. Apart from their enormously long wings, these were configured not unlike some remote, skinny descendant of the Percival Prentice. Again, the idea was to switch the engine off once up to height, and glide about instead, which they did quite well, if you like that sort of thing.

Of course, few if any of the VGS staff had had any experience whatsoever in any of the Services. Most of them were keen, dedicated people, who worked hard and were good instructors within their limited role, but part of the fun of my job was rescuing some of them from the silly situations they got themselves into, and gently pointing out what they should have done, if they had had any Service Knowledge at all. Some of the VGS commanding officers were autocrats who thought that they owned their own little empires, and sometimes you had to be firm with them, and at other times you could only summon up a world-weary smile.

The standards we learnt at Cranwell had to be applied with tact. I caused an explosion at Salmesbury once, by telling them that it was conduct unbecoming officers and gentlemen not to pay their mess bills at the nearby Army mess. Another CO, at West Malling, when gently chided over the continual lateness of his flying statistics, is said to have torn my letter into pieces and jumped up and down on it.

Slightly less amusing was when a VR(T) Flight Lieutenant CO had a USAF Warthog infringe his circuit while gliding was going on. He took it upon himself to telephone the American Base Commander and harangue him about it. That had to be smoothed over.

Another time, I remember a telephone call from a chief instructor. They had a teenage girl on a course, but (I think I have the story right), her father had just killed her mother, and her brother was so upset that he had thrown himself in front of a train. Did I think it was all right to send her solo?

The flight safety side occupied a lot of time, for we had over 140 reportable incidents each year. Fortunately we never killed anyone, although there had been fatalities before my time. I think all our volunteers were well aware that they were looking after other people's children, but I kept a very unpleasant accident photo in my desk just in case some reckless fool needed reminding.

Before I go on to mention some of the dafter things I remember on the flying scene, it is worth telling about an interesting affair in HQ Air Cadets itself, where degrees of lunacy were not unknown. The most senior civil servant there, whose title I forget – something like Org 1 or Finance 1 – always seemed to have very liberal working hours, long lunches, afternoons playing golf and so on. Files used to disappear into his office and never come out again. Quite a pleasant laid-back bloke, in a slightly supercilious way, but he never actually did very much.

Then, one day, sinister-looking men came in trench coats, and were locked in his office with him. Files were impounded. Rumours began to spread. Then our friend was to be seen no more. His deputy had to move up to do his job. Within a fortnight, she had a nervous breakdown and went on extended sick leave. As a result, all the other fifty or so civil servants had to be moved up to the jobs of their superiors, till even the lad who made the tea in the registry was put on to filing letters instead. None of them, of course, were competent in the jobs they now had to do. Nobody knew where anything was, who had done what, and who was supposed to have done it in the first place.

Eventually, it transpired that our man had been running several bogus companies, and sending invoices on headed paper to the girls in the finance department. They did not know that these were rubbish, so they made out cheques in payment, which again someone signed without cross-checking. So, for example, Air Cadets were paying rent for a number of premises that they actually owned themselves.

I think he got two years in gaol, but it was pleaded in mitigation that our friend had repaid half the fiddled hundred and fifty grand. Meanwhile, chaos reigned back at base...

But to get back to flying, what about the case of...

1. The CO who wondered if the wind was too strong and gusty for cadets to fly. What more logical way of finding out than to send up a probationary cadet instructor to see how he would manage – and then as an afterthought, to offer me a passenger ride with him.

2. The aged instructor who actually ran out of fuel on take-off in a Venture, and blamed the previous pilot for using too much.

3. The probationary civilian instructor who thought he was undershooting. Panicking in case he stalled, he deliberately put the glider down short of the aerodrome in a little field full of thistles, where RAF Locking used to graze their goat. There was no room for the glider to stop, so he aimed for a gap in the far hedge. The fuselage might have got through, if not the wings. Unfortunately the gap was closed by a wire fence. When the horrified rescuers got there, they thought he had garrotted himself, because he was pinned in the cockpit by a wire across his throat. They had to send for wire-cutters to release him. He was all right, fortunately.

4. The time when the Viking that I was landing stopped almost immediately on touch-down, and I apologised to the CO in the back seat for landing with the brake on. "No, it's not you" he said, "We have sunk into the ground" – and we had! They liked to give launch instructions in Welsh at that VGS, by the way.

5. The time when a CO exceeded the flight envelope of a Viking while on SCT, and got wing flutter, which bent the aileron rods. At the subsequent inquiry, his second pilot was asked what airspeed had been reached. He didn't know: the vibration was too severe to read the ASI. Did he think the wings were coming off? Yes he did. Did he contemplate baling out? Yes. Why didn't he then? He didn't have a parachute.

6. The VGS which, before regular control caravans were issued, used a modified 2-wheeler touring caravan, with a cupola for the Duty Instructor. Flying was in full swing when I visited, but they had been too idle to put the corner jacks down. So every time anyone walked to the back of the caravan the whole thing tipped up and the DI had to shout for them to come forward again.

7. The young cadet being asked about a heavy landing – "I could tell it was going to be a crash, and it was. I thanked my instructor for the flight, and got out and went to the toilet –!"

8. The CO who resigned (to the great relief of all his staff, as we later found out) and then, after his successor was nominated, tried to change his mind and stay on. Too late for this, he left in such high dudgeon that he did not say goodbye to anyone and stuffed all the keys down the side of a crewroom chair.

9. The CO who was accosted, during gliding operations, by the managing director of Courtaulds complaining about aircraft noise, and who told the said managing director that he should have employed a better lawyer before buying a house right next to an airfield, and now **get off RAF property!** (that one got to the Commander in Chief at Support Command!).

One final incident, which might not have been so funny, occurred during an advanced ridge-soaring course for cadets. This young lad was flying along, minding his own business, when a civilian glider, whose pilot was not looking where he was going, came up behind and knocked the Viking's rudder off. Both pilots landed safely, and by all accounts the cadet's landing was much the better.

Anyway, having had a think about this, I telephoned MOD and spoke to a Mr. Fox, who was absolutely delighted. He said that he spent his whole life paying compensation to farmers whose cows had aborted, or to people whose greenhouses had been shattered, allegedly from low flying RAF aircraft. We got a cost breakdown from the engineers for the rudder repair, and Mr. Fox extracted £3,500 from the civilian's insurance company, with much glee. Indeed, one's day is not wasted if one can at least make somebody else happy!

There is much more, but perhaps better left unrecorded! Like the Giant Rat of Sumatra, they are stories for which the world is not yet prepared...   [R.H.R.]

DOWN TO EARTH

54 Entry's graduation took place long before the exploration of space began, but it had been spoken of and forecast as inevitable and, inspired by Dan Dare of "The Eagle" comic, our final revue included an item in which a group of "Space Cadets" were receiving the equivalent of a Night Flying Briefing. How could we have even dreamed that one of our number, Colin Foale, would become the father of Michael Foale, the first British-born astronaut? Now follows a chapter from Colin's book, "Waystation to the Stars", in which he describes his son's return after months in the space station 'Mir'.

The landing of Atlantis had been scheduled for shortly before midnight, UK time, on Saturday, 5 October. Saturday was already a significant date. I had been approached many weeks before by our celebrated local butcher, Peter Welton of Wallers in Cambridge, who had invited me to be the final judge and arbiter of the Cambridge and East Anglian Federation's first annual sausage-making competition. I have always liked sausages and I was flattered to be considered a potential connoisseur. Perhaps I am, but I had of course been asked because of my fleeting celebrity status, conferred on me by Michael. Mary was to judge the hams. She tasted ten hams and I tasted thirty-six sausages 'small pieces', all excellent, and eventually the results were pronounced, followed by prolonged applause for the winner.

At the end, I was asked to say a few words. The company present knew, of course, who I was. I said, 'You all know how the press and TV have concentrated only on the black side of Mir. Some quotations are Troubled Mir, Ageing Mir, Mishap-stricken Mir, Crisis-hit Mir. After two most pleasurable hours of your company here, a new, even blacker phrase comes to mind, depressingly true but not so far used by even the least responsible representative of the press – Sausageless Mir!' I had said the right thing.

After returning home and collecting our bags, we departed for London to watch the late-night landing of Atlantis in the studios of ITN. Our continued cooperation with various agents of the media was again to pay off, and this time ITN had invited us, with Susan, to London to watch the landing live at Cape Canaveral. We had gladly accepted, but the landing was delayed by twenty-four hours because of high crosswinds on the runway at Kennedy Space Center.

We are in the habit of welcoming any precautionary measure, whatever the inconvenience, and this has been a feature of both my RAF life and our family lives, particularly since we were with Michael at the time of the Challenger disaster eleven years ago. We had incidentally begun to receive many letters of relief and congratulation on Michael's imminent return, which pleased us, but also made me feel slightly uneasy. It is all to do with the superstitious side of being an RAF pilot (any military pilot will agree), and is concerned with avoiding the tempting of fate. Michael had shown this in his care not to rely too much on the planned Atlantis launch and docking dates. A letter which we received later from a very distinguished Air Vice-Marshal called Michael Lyne, who had known me since he was a squadron leader and I was a flight cadet at Cranwell, said it all, in a note to me: 'We know that a landing is not complete until your feet touch the ground at the bottom of the steps – and that a delayed landing is an additional hazard.' That was exactly what was in our minds. The shuttle's opportunities to attempt a safe landing had automatically been reduced by one. (We were saddened to hear of Michael Lyne's death after illness later that year.)

It was with more relief than we probably showed that, on the following night, we watched on the studio's enormous TV screen the great birdlike shape of Atlantis make its final steep turn in the early evening sky high over Florida. The winds had abated, the straight-in approach was steady and precise and, at the moment of flare as the nose was raised into the landing position, the fragile-looking wheels of the undercarriage assembly appeared and locked. A few seconds later there was the gentle kiss of each tyre, together, at 225 mph, touching on the Cape Canaveral tarmac. The wheels held, the braking parachute was deployed and the craft slowed to a stop. It was a moment of immense satisfaction for everybody. For us, the landing was indeed over in spite of not yet seeing Michael walk down the steps. In fact, like many spacemen who have been weightless for months, he felt nausea as the unaccustomed gravity of earth again took charge of his delicate balance mechanisms, unused for so long, and he needed several minutes to adjust before getting up.

Mary, Susan and I sat silently watching the now still Atlantis. He was back. Soon we would see him. But the transmission had ended. We had to wait until a later transmission before we saw him, rather gaunt and wearing a hat that was too big for him, but happy and surrounded by his family. The sight made all three of us very happy indeed.

He told us later that on rising from his prone position in Atlantis and reaching the door, he felt like a parody of Neil Armstrong arriving on the moon (a small step for man, a giant leap for mankind), except that for him the shuttle steps before him struck him as being the most enormous step he had ever had to make in his life.

He had been asked what he would like best to eat when reunited with his family. A cold beer, pizza and lasagne were, without hesitation, his express wish, and all were duly provided not long after he left the shuttle. That night he was accommodated, under medical supervision, in the Kennedy Space Center crew quarters, shared, after special arrangements had been made, by his very contented Rhonda, Jenna and Ian.

On the following day, barely fourteen hours since his landing, he 'phoned us at home in Cambridge. There was a peculiar thrill for us to know that we were now talking with him on earth. There was a strange new feeling throughout the call. We probably looked no different nor sounded different. Neither did he. But in our heads seemed to be the warm, deep calming music of knowing that he had returned to safety. There were no longer occasional brassy discords to be pushed aside, no shrillness of alarm notes to be ignored, like those old-fashioned radio atmospherics. Just serious, emotional music in majestic cadences, a mental weightlessness to be enjoyed in its flow. We all felt it, looked at each other and knew that the others did too.

Yes, he was quite well now, but he had felt nauseated on landing. Yes, he had eaten the food he had asked for. His balance was still shaky, and if he shut his eyes while standing, he would fall over. His medical checkout had been satisfactory and as expected, and the children had both been thoughtful and kind to him. He regretted speaking of his first Mir crew commander, Tsibliyev, during his post-landing TV interview, which we had watched, because of the strong emotional reaction he had felt on Tsibliyev's behalf. I had of course noticed his difficulty, and told him that his emotion had come across with sincerity and friendliness, and it was perfectly all right.

Vasily Tsibliyev was later asked by a British television company what his feelings were now for Michael. He said, 'If you are a drowning man and Michael comes and saves you, you will remember him for the rest of your life'.

Michael asked us to call him at home in Houston the next day. He said that President Clinton had sent him a warm congratulatory note, which he appreciated. It was good to dial the familiar Texas number, knowing that he would be there. On his first day at home, he told us that both Jenna and Ian had been nauseous in the night, so poor Rhonda had had no sleep. While still in Florida, he had had a brief noonday swim with Jenna and found his muscles were very stiff. For twenty-four hours he still had no balance if he shut his eyes, and his ankle ligaments were very weak. He was well protected from intrusion at home, and two police cars were permanently stationed outside. However, an overzealous builder had started to excavate the site next to his shoreline home in such a way as to threaten his house foundations. He felt that he had returned just in time.

I told him how pleased many people seemed to be over the way he had championed international cooperation in space. I had earlier written to the British government through our MP, Anne Campbell, about the need for more British government recognition of the existence, let alone importance, of space exploration and experience.

On 10 October I got a second friendly telephone call from the Russian ambassador, offering Michael his congratulations on his safe return and his excellent work on Mir. He understood that Michael was now enjoying terra firma with his family. He asked me to pass on to Michael and his family his congratulations, thanks and good wishes when I next spoke to him.

Over the next four weeks, Michael was encouraged to rehabilitate at his own pace. He was given two weeks of real leave, the first of which he spent quietly with his family in a secluded retreat in the Bahamas, which they could not really afford. Then followed nearly a week of media attention, when the scale of his impact on the world gradually sank in. Thankfully, NASA's plans for him made it possible for the whole family to come to England for Christmas at our home in Cambridge for two weeks, followed by a week for all of us to join his godfather up in Morayshire, beyond Inverness, for Hogmanay.

In the last week before their departure from Texas for London, arrangements had been made for Michael to attend meetings in New York with the editorial boards of several newspapers and broadcasting networks, to allow their members to ask penetrating questions. This formidable chore was to be softened. On 7 December, Jenna's birthday, Mary and I telephoned her home in the morning, Houston time, to sing Happy Birthday, which she gracefully acknowledged. Then Michael said that they had to hurry, because they would be leaving for Washington in two hours, not to attend any hearings, but to respond to an invitation for the whole family to meet President Clinton at the White House.

Michael had done more than just survive in space. He had brought honour both to England, the land of his birth and upbringing, and to America, the land of his mother and the space organization that fearlessly and imaginatively continues to explore space. From 25 June there had been few days when he was not deeply involved in recovering from a crisis or weathering the effects of inadequate power and life support. With his fresh crew, he rose to the occasion and carried out unique internal depressurized power repair work and, later, a lengthy and successful external examination of Spektr, during the EVA with his new commander.

Mir and its international programme had been preserved against considerable odds. The Americans were staying in the Mir game to field at least two more astronauts. The possibility of future, wider international space cooperation and how it could proceed had been reinforced by Michael's show of dogged but inventive determination. He had been heroic. Two Russian crews had found that he would never let the unexpected deflect his aim to achieve what he thought was right. The

Russians on the ground had been moved by his inspiration into a period of being more forthcoming with their space partner, and indeed the world. The Americans had been encouraged in their conviction that cooperation with Russia must continue, but perhaps in future they should expect answers to more questions. The world had been given a lesson in just how unexpected events in space could be, a timely reminder for the design of the International Space Station (ISS), and its construction and manning. [C.H.F.]

7. Final Thoughts

We introduce some thoughts of what might have happened if the Royal air force had not been created as a separate service and there had never been a Royal air force College at Cranwell...

WHAT IF...? A HISTORY THAT NEARLY WAS

Our College at Cranwell was very much Lord Trenchard's creation. As flight cadets there, we were very much his protegés, brought up under his shadow, his portrait in the hall a reminder of his brooding presence, even though he had retired long since. Maybe we took it all for granted, but what if...?

It is 1952. High above Lincolnshire soars a Focke-Wulf Super Kondor of Imperial Lufthansa on its way to India, the vapour trails of its four Rolls Royce Nenes painted pink by the setting sun. You have finished your checklist and set the Siemens automatic pilot, and now you can settle back in the second officer's seat and relax for a moment.

You glance across at your captain, puffing on his usual cigar. Not a bad chap, Wolfgang, for all his little Hitler Youth ways. But you wonder sometimes how it all might have been different.

Supposing back in 1940, when you were still at school, Britain had been defended by modern fighters able to meet the ME109 on equal terms. What if something like air traffic control radar had already been set up in those days, and we had been able to see German attacks coming? Could we have held out?

It would have taken an independent Royal Air Force to do it, of course, because neither the Royal Navy nor the Army really understood air power. What might such an RAF have been like? Perhaps there might have been a special blue uniform, and different rank titles. Officers might well have started their training as "flight cadets", not midshipmen. There might have been a new RAF College on the lines of Sandhurst or Dartmouth. That old abandoned naval aerodrome out there to starboard for example, near Sleaford, would have been just the place for it. .

Ah well, too late to rewrite history now. Back to work. You check the approach chart for the next stop – Berlin, capital of Europa.

Some of us may still have our Cranwell notebooks somewhere. If we dig them out, we will find that most of the stuff we were taught has stood the test of time quite well. The basics of aerodynamics, weapons, meteorology, engines and so forth are still much the same today. When we come to war studies, a lot here is also still applicable – the invasion of Sicily, the Battle of the Atlantic, Arnhem and so on. Modern historians have been able to add to the picture, of course. We didn't know about Enigma in those days, for example, nor about all those political controversies and clashes of mighty egos amongst our leaders.

The strategic bomber offensive featured particularly prominently in our course. We are all familiar with the story. Douhet, Mitchell, Balbo, Trenchard and their school were sure that air power offered a new way to win a war by passing right over the front lines and striking the enemy's heartland such devastating blows that the population would be totally demoralised. Their leaders would be forced to surrender. The appalling infantry casualties of the 1914-18 War would be avoided and the war finished in weeks not years. It was claimed that "the bomber would always get through", especially when armed with powered gun turrets.

It did not turn out quite like that. When war started in 1939, the stark lesson was soon learnt that our bombers could not get through; certainly not in daylight. Although they suffered fewer losses by night, it was a long time before they had the technical capability to find and hit their targets. Nevertheless, long-range bombing was the only way that Britain could hit back at Germany, and we are all familiar with the long years of struggle to make it effective

The national effort that went into the bomber offensive was staggering – immense industrial resources, of course, but more than that, the human courage and sacrifice. (At a time when the majority of people left school at fourteen, Bomber Command lost the equivalent of two or three thousand sixth forms from across the empire.)

After several years of war, Bomber Command was eventually able to inflict massive damage, but the fact remains that the bomber offensive failed to achieve the quick and decisive knock-out blows that its fervent advocates had promised. Yet this doctrine was the prime justification for having an independent Air Force in the first place.

Trenchard had to fight hard in the twenties to keep the RAF intact. What if he had failed, and it had been disbanded and divided once again into an RNAS and an RFC? What effect might that have had on history – and on us?

It is 1925. In the War Office and Admiralty there are several forceful and air-minded officers with personal experience of front line

air combat in the Great War. They argue the case for air power, but senior posts are filled by traditionalist generals and admirals.

The generals consider the re-established Royal Flying Corps as a tactical arm. They see the value of aircraft for reconnaissance, gun-spotting, attacks on targets on and behind the battlefield, supply dropping, casualty evacuation and communications. Of course, they understand the need for local air superiority if these tasks are to be carried out free from enemy interference. One junior colonel called Montgomery is suggesting trials with parachute or glider-borne troops, but has received little encouragement so far.

The RFC has been constituted a specialist Arm on its own, like the Royal Artillery or the Royal Engineers. Most of its officers, however, are on secondment from their historic regiments, to which they return between flying tours. In the mess they make much of their old traditions and celebrate Minden Day, drink the health of the King of Sweden, or eat their porridge standing up looking out of the window. In other words, flying may be their great passion, but the regiment rather than air power bulks large in their careers. Likewise RNAS officers are expected to be Navy first and airmen second, and they learn seamanship on the bridge of a warship before learning to fly.

There is, of course, no RAF College at Cranwell. Would-be aviators have to go through cadetships at Sandhurst, Woolwich or Dartmouth instead.

Now it is 1936. The international situation has made re-armament a priority, and the two services began to get large sums of money at last. What are they doing with it?

The Army have placed large orders for more artillery and Matilda tanks, but have also been thinking about what aircraft are needed. They have decided to buy more Fairey Battles, Bristol Blenheims and Westland Lysanders. Specifications are also being drawn up for a heavily armoured ground attack aircraft like the Stormovik. The opportunity is being taken to enhance troop transport capacity, and some more Bristol Bombays are on order. (With two bomb racks under the wings, these can be used as well for night bombing of ammunition dumps, railway junctions and other targets behind enemy lines – if they can find them, that is).

A Rhodesian farmer called Harris wrote to The Times a while ago, advocating trials of American dive-bombers, but no one took any notice. However Germany has taken up the idea with enthusiasm, so the War Office thinks it might be prudent to buy a few of the new Blackburn Skuas for the RFC just in case.

Meawhile two civilians, Mitchell and Camm, are trying to sell their private venture designs for futuristic high-speed monoplane fighters. The only staff officer listening to them is a Major Dowding, but he has little influence. Everyone else dismisses these proposed fighters as too expensive, too complicated to service and repair, too difficult to fly, and too fragile to operate from front line airfields. The Gloster Gladiator is being chosen instead; a simple and well-proven biplane design, cheap to produce, very manoeuvrable, easy to repair in the field, running on low octane fuel and well-liked by senior officers who earned their spurs dog- fighting in World War One.

Dowding is worried by the advanced specification of the Messerschmitt 109. He has secretly been talking to Churchill. Having seen the Italians winning both the Schneider Trophy and the air speed record (unopposed!), Churchill is urging the government to buy some Macchi fighters, but is being shouted down in the House of Commons.

The War Office believes the real answer to enemy bombers lies in large numbers of 3.7 inch anti-aircraft guns rather than fighters. Sound location is not proving very effective, it has to be admitted, but given enough rounds, some enemy aircraft should be hit sooner or later, even flying at 150 mph and five thousand feet. (Incidentally, someone who suggested that, with a modified mounting, this excellent gun could be used in an anti-tank role like the German 88 has been told to leave such matters to the experts.)

In the Navy, big gun battleship admirals still rule in the corridors of power. Aircraft carriers are tolerated but disliked. Naval airmen have to put up with some fairly dismal aircraft. This is due partly to financial stringency, but mostly to the small number of aircraft that can be taken to sea by carriers, and hence the Navy's desire to make each of them do as many different jobs as possible. In other words, naval aircraft tend to be jacks of all trades and masters of none.

Now re-armament has begun, the Navy is giving priority to its fleet. There are to be more King George V class battleships, more cruisers, destroyers and submarines. Older ships like HMS Hood are to be given badly needed refits. However, the critical importance of defending the sea lanes against U-boats and commerce raiders is well recognised and the RNAS is to get several new purpose-built carriers – sister ships to the Ark Royal. There will be more squadrons of Short Sunderland flying boats. The Americans are known to be producing a four-engined long-range land-plane for maritime patrol, the so-called B 17 Fortress, but the Admiralty prefers to stick to the proven flying boat concept.

As in World War One, the RNAS has a major role in the air defence of Great Britain. The problem here is the RNAS tradition of specifying multi-role aircraft. A naval fighter, in order to operate from a carrier, needs a low stalling speed, folding wings, a stronger undercarriage and airframe, a navigator, more fuel, and extra equipment like arrester hooks, flotation bags, bigger radio sets and so on, all of which mitigate against high performance. The designs of Mitchell and Camm are too specialised for the RNAS. Besides, it would be out of the question to buy such expensive machines for the sole purpose of intercepting raids on mainland Britain, when they could not be used on carriers as well. So the RNAS is being updated with the new Fairey Fulmar, to serve on land as well as sea. It carries no less than eight machine guns, although its speed and climb rate are mediocre.

There is some talk of a secret early warning radar chain and fighter control system being developed for the UK, which will be a massive project if it ever comes about. At the moment, it has not been decided who will pay for it and who will be in charge. Meanwhile, Fulmars with their good endurance will be ideal to carry out standing patrols, ready to dive on any enemy bombers they see and blow them out of the sky with their .303 machine guns.

The Messerscmitt 109, although winning impressive trophies in competitions, obviously has too short a range to escort bombers from Germany to Britain. The Fulmars' manoeuvrability will beat the clumsy Me 110 hands down. (No one in Europe could have imagined the Japanese Navy's Zero at that time!)

Now it is 1940, and the "Phoney War" period is over. Neither side actually wanted to fight – Hitler would have preferred a free hand to drive eastwards, if only the Allies had accepted peace feelers, and Chamberlain hoped that economic warfare would bring Germany to its senses. Then open warfare broke out, and the Norwegian Campaign was badly mishandled. Long-range heavy bombers and high-performance interceptors would have played no part, even if there had been any.

When the Germans invaded France, the British Expeditionary Force was able to hold out for a while, because it had comparatively large numbers of tanks, guns and tactical aircraft. Nonetheless, its slow and ill-armed Battles, Blenheims, Lysanders and Gladiators suffered devastating losses from German fighters and flak. The RFC virtually ceased to exist. Then the French collapsed and the BEF was cut off in Northern France. It has managed to hold a small enclave round Dunkirk, but without any air cover, it can neither fight back nor be evacuated to safety. Two hundred thousand troops are now Hitler's hostages.

So last month the Luftwaffe launched massive attacks from its new bases in France against Britain. Huge formations of Messerschmitt 109s escorted the Heinkels and Dorniers. Without early warning of attacks, or controllers to vector them, and manning hopelessly inferior aircraft, the RNAS aircrew sacrificed themselves in vain. It was all over in days.

A German invasion has not been necessary. Churchill has been thrown from office, and the peace party ("realists") have taken over. Hitler had always said he did not want to destroy Britain and her Empire, which he saw as a force for stability in the world. All he would have insisted on was recognition of German dominion on the Continent, and the return of the old German colonies. Well, now we shall see. The politicians meet in Versailles next month.

Turning back to real history, it can be seen that it was not the bomber offensive itself which saved Britain from defeat, ironically, for it could not, and did not, turn out to be the magic weapon prophesied. It was the very theory itself that did so, because it saved the RAF as an independent Service in the twenties.

Trenchard himself was so sure of the efficacy of the bomber that he considered it unnecessary to defend the home base because the bombing would win the war so rapidly. He considered fighters to be a diversion of resources – a flaw in the strategy – and did not want any in his air force. He grudgingly allowed a few in deference to the handful of air force men and politicians who had the wisdom and courage to argue the point. Fighter Command was not allowed to become an effective force (and then only just) until Trenchard ceased to be Chief of Air Staff

So the country was not saved in the Battle of Britain by something Trenchard planned for, but by something he planned *against*.

Meanwhile, we would still have been at school when all this was going on. What if the war actually had been lost?

Obviously there would have been no cadetships at the RAF College Cranwell. We would never have met at Sleaford railway station and become 54 Entry. We would not have all known each other, except by chance meeting, for we would have had to make what separate flying careers we could. That would not have been easy.

It is now 1952. *What are we doing? Well, one or two of us have got jobs with Imperial Lufthansa, flying to the Far East and India (still British, thanks to Hitler's loan of German troops). Our Focke-Wulf Super Kondors have been built under licence by Handley Page.*

Others are fighting with the British Volunteer Air Division, alongside the Luftwaffe in Russia, flying Merlin-engined FW 190s built under licence by Hawkers.

One or two are flying Cant trimotors on a high-speed torpedo-dropping course, run at Lee-on-Solent by Italian instructors (acknowledged world leaders in the technique.)

Not so happy the chap selected for an exchange posting with the Japanese Navy, flying Zeros from the old carrier Akagi. Not just the sharks – war with America is bound to break out soon. Japanese code-breakers have uncovered secret American plans for a surprise attack on their naval base at Truk.

Back home, some of us are employed in Air Sea Rescue, operating Westland-Flettner Wirbelwind helicopters.

A few more are crewing big Short Shetland flying boats, ranging far out into the Atlantic to intercept any American ships which do not have special licences to enter the 500 mile limit of European Territorial Waters.

Our selection boards were more rigorous than those at Ramridge House. Besides the usual medical board and initiative tests, we were interviewed by unsmiling men with rimless spectacles. We had to satisfy them about our racial make-up, the political record of our parents and relations, the friends we chose at school, what papers we read, what did we understand of Nazi ideology, what did we think of the Jews... and so on. We would like to think that many of us would have failed!

This alternative history could have happened. But it didn't. Let us then salute Lord Trenchard, whose determination and vision saved the Royal Air Force. His strategic vision proved to be out of reach but, nonetheless, without the Service whose foundation stones he laid, Britain could never have won the Second World War.   [**R.H.R.**]

But that was supposition. There <u>was</u> (and still is) a separate Royal Air Force and a Royal Air Force College at Cranwell – and this is how many of those privileged to have been Flight Cadets view it...

"WISH YOU WERE HERE!"

Burton Coggles, Stoke Rochford, Boothby Pagnell! How the names on the signposts thrill as I drive from Colsterworth along the top road, Ermine Street, to Cranwell once again! More signposts, Welby, Oasby, Aisby, then Ancaster, Barkston, Rauceby and Caythorpe and then into view comes the tower and cupola of the college!

At 10.00 am Brian 'phoned from Spain with greetings and good wishes for those attending the OCA weekend of 14/15 June 2003. At the time I was drying myself from my bath and getting my gear together to depart and, to be honest, asking myself whether I really fancied driving for over four hours on a hot day to go to a reunion when I was not even sure who would be there. The feeling of a lack of enthusiasm gradually wears off on the journey, and from Stamford things get better. I refuel at the Ram Jam (where else?) and then turn off to begin seeing that catalogue of evocative names. I admit to a lump coming into the throat at that moment and that I love, and have always loved, that last 15 miles on the way to Cranwell. On a lovely June day the greenery of the trees, hedges and fields is beyond compare. Byard's Leap, two more turnings and then past Daedalus House and into Cranwell Avenue. Name ticked off the list at the security checkpoint in Lighter than Air Road and then to the college to park the car behind the squash courts.

The combination for the lock on the door appears to be unnecessary as the doors were open all the time. At reception I pay my mess bill in advance, £21.50, and am given the key to Room C7. Yes. Thank you, I do know the way to C wing! The room belongs to Officer Cadet Rogers and is on the ground floor on the corner at the back, overlooking the area between C and D wings. The rooms have all been refurbished and are smart and comfortable. The doors have been replaced and the old enamelled number plates discarded – if I had known I would cheerfully have offered £10 for my old "C37" room number plate.

It is now getting on for 3.00 pm and I have yet to see anyone I know, but the names of Alastair Christie, David Keats and Bob Hutchinson are on the board. I mooch around the photographs, looking at ours as "Senior Term December 1951" and some of the sports photos; there I am next to Barry Mills in the swimming team, and there is Paddy King in the rowing eight. Also in the rowing photo is Malcolm Cowper in his colours blazer and with a grin as big as his cap! Then I wander towards the A and B end and on the way recall that the huge globe of the world was removed many years ago.

Outside in the bright sunshine they are playing croquet on the Orange – no more cricket on that ground. I note that the trees along the side of the path we traversed to and from Block 77, Daedalus House and Flights are now about 40 to 50 feet tall. I hear the sound of ball on racquet and a murmur of applause from the tennis courts and find a gate through the fence onto the main sports fields and thence to the Sultan Qaboos Pavilion by the No 1 cricket pitch and where tea will be served. Again there is not a soul I know personally although I recognise a few. I watch the cricket for a few minutes and see the Chief of the Air Staff, playing for the Old Cranwellians, hit the ball high into the air and get caught. On the way in he smiles and says "The highest of the day!" I decide to go back to the college (or College Hall as we really must get used to calling it).

Another mooch around and then, tea time approaching, a stroll back to the Pavilion. Good! They are setting out the plates of sandwiches and the elegant little fancy cakes, and the serving of tea begins early. A cup of tea and several sandwiches later and some of 53 Entry appear, Alan Merriman, Tabs Tabernacle and Ken Davies. At least there are now some chaps to talk to and then Keith Smith arrives and, first of 54, Bob Hutchinson. Sadly, he says that Phil Farmer-Wright has not been well. Alastair Christie arrives and then David Keats. Several more cups of tea and several more sandwiches later an old friend from apprentice days and an Associate Member, Bill Northmore appears, so now there are plenty of opportunities for conversation. Bill and I decide to go to look round the church as there has been a suggestion that our ex-apprentice association should place a commemorative stone outside it.

By then the bar is open so we enjoy a large cool shandy before changing. The bar waitress begins to mix lemonade and ginger beer when asked for a ginger beer shandy so we have to explain – I have met that problem before; they think that ginger beer is substituted for bitter beer! In the wings I find that the bathrooms and WCs have been refurbished with some lovely white and blue tiles and that there are separate facilities for males and females. My apprehension as to getting into my 1956 dinner suit after a lapse of two years is justified to a certain extent as to the trousers and yet when all is buttoned up the cummerbund goes on easily and I congratulate myself that it was easier than before! It must be all the swimming and walking I have been doing lately.

There is hardly time for another drink before the AGM and, thank heavens, the AGM is disposed of in about 25 minutes. There has been a "late millenium bug" problem with the computer system so our direct debit subscriptions were not collected last January, the bank cannot sort the problem out and the only solution is to collect double subscriptions next January. In the meantime, £8,000 has to be transferred from deposit to cover the income shortfall. The portrait fund is going to run out in a few years so water colours of distinguished Old Cranwellians will be commissioned instead of oil portraits of each Old Cranwellian CAS. The Guest of Honour this year is the present Chief of Air Staff, Sir Peter Squire, who retires in six weeks His oil painting is unveiled by our president, Sir Jock Kennedy – ought he not to be the subject of a portrait himself? The Commandant says that it is customary to make the Guest an honorary member and give him an OCA tie but Sir Peter is already a full member and has a tie so we won't give him one and he is not getting away from subscriptions. Laughter and applause. The dates for the next two OCA reunions will be the 19/20 June 2004 and 18/19 June 2005.

Early from the AGM and early into the front hall, but the drinks are not delayed. The usual hubbub of talk and the flowing of drink. Among us is another guest, the tall figure of the Rt Rev Tom Burns, RC Bishop to the Forces; he is clad in black with purple buttons, sash and skull cap. Fanfare! Into the dining hall to the sound of "The Roast Beef of Old England" (quick! before some moderniser abolishes it) and, Yes! We have a full band in the minstrels' gallery this year! Unlike previous years when we had to make do with a string quartet or similar, under the direction of a corporal, this year we have the complete band under a warrant officer. Could this be in any way connected to the fact that CAS is Guest of Honour?

The menu is a break from tradition. There is a delicious cream of mushroom soup in place of mock turtle and in place (no pun intended) of the poached salmon we have fillet of plaice stuffed with prawns. No duckling this year but breast of chicken stuffed with smoked duck and cranberry. No strawberries and cream but, instead, a wafer basket of Chantilly cream with pieces of strawberry, kiwi fruit and pineapple. To end, a Welsh rarebit on French bread. There is no sherry with the soup and the wine with the fish is a Chardonnay. A robust claret accompanies the main course and there is the usual port – but I see no Madeira this year. Mints in College Hall wrappers are served with coffee.

The band plays well, of course, but is somewhat loud for conversation across the table where we are – near the bottom. The Post Horn Galop is probably the most complicated in its variations that I have ever heard and the soloist no mere *virtuoso* but a veritable *virtuissimo*. The Lincolnshire Poacher is heard and then the national anthem after the loyal toast.

The commandant's speech is commendably short and little more than an introduction to the Guest of Honour. CAS speaks well and amusingly, mainly about his own experiences and his entry, 89, which is there in force to celebrate 40 years on. Of course, he touches on the state of the service today and its capability being greater than ever before. Our President, Sir Jock, says a very few words to round off – and so to the bar at just after midnight.

There seem to be fewer people in the bar than I have known but although I confine myself to one glass of tonic water I still do not leave until 2.00 am. It is significant at our ages that as well as "Do you remember old so-and-so or such and such?" the conversation includes a fair amount of discussion on the medical aspects of our lives. Bill abjures the bar as he has to leave well before breakfast, Alastair says he is leaving as soon as he can after breakfast, as is Bob, but David and I agree that we will go to church in answer to the Commandant's particular plea that Old Cranwellians should do so.

I awake early and feel much better than has been known in the past. At breakfast I sit with some of 53 entry, Ivor Simmons, Ken Davies, David Hobday, Tabs and Alan Merriman. Conversation is animated. All agree to go to church except one who declines on the grounds that he might be struck down for past sins!

After breakfast I pack and hand in my key to the hall porter – female. Anyway, it seems to be called "reception" nowadays.

By this time there are cadets to be seen in and around the building. They are wearing woolly pullies – can they be going on church parade? Surely not! We drift along the corridor towards C Squadron and saunter out through the doors we used to rush through to get on drill parades. No evocative click of heels on the steel gratings – no gratings. The College Warrant Officer, I assume of Jamaican roots, is an impressive man, very smart and with a good voice, shouting for the Parade Orderly. Cadets set out canvas chairs for spectators – including us. The parade marches on – and they are indeed wearing woollen pullovers and berets. But the flight commanders are in No1 dress with swords, and the colour party, a Flight Lieutenant Ensign and two Flight Sergeant Escorts, are also in No1 and armed. The band is on the College steps. The parade marches to church the long way round the Orange and we walk the short way. After a few minutes we are ushered inside. In all these years and many visits to Cranwell I had never previously entered this church. On this my first visit I am impressed by its simplicity and beauty. There is plenty of room for the band and the choir. We of the OCA are shepherded into reserved pews behind the Commandant's party and staff and a surprisingly large number of cadets fill the pews to the left. Mainly they look as we did except that there are females among them and some are evidently older than cadets were in our day.

The choir and clergy enter and include Bishop Burns and two OD chaplains as well as the C of E chaplain. After "All people that on earth do dwell" the trumpeters play a fanfare and I find I still do not take to fanfares – far too showy. The Colour is brought in at the slow march and laid on the altar. Then follows the national anthem, a welcome from the chaplain, and prayers. Another hymn, curiously, to the tune of the "Dambusters' March" and the lessons read by the Commandant and a Squadron Leader.

The padre introduces the RC Bishop to the Forces as having a naval background. The bishop then takes the pulpit to give the sermon. He speaks in a loud clear voice and begins with a humorous story to illustrate his first theme. "On his return from holiday a man sits at the back of his parish church and the priest is delivering a long sermon. Bored, the man finds he has an unused picture postcard in his pocket so he takes it out, writes something on it and passes it to the man in front with a whispered request to pass it on. It reaches the priest who reads on it the words "I am sitting at the back listening to your sermon. Wish you were here".

On the same topic the bishop refers to the spirit of camaraderie in the services and then draws a grimmer picture "Troops are landing on a hostile shore under heavy fire. Mike looks back and sees that his mate, Joe, has been hit and he asks if he can go back and bring him in. His officer says "No" but Mike goes anyway and brings Joe in. Unfortunately Mike is seriously wounded in the process and Joe has died. The officer says "I told you not to go, but you did, you are seriously hurt and Joe has died. Was it worth it?" "Oh, yes" says Mike, "as I crawled up to him Joe was still alive and he smiled and said "I knew you'd come for me". It was worth it for that. We were mates". Bishop repeats "Wish you were here". Bishop develops the theme philosophically and theologically and ends his sermon with "Wish you were here".

Hymn "How great thou art", prayers, "O God our help in ages past", final prayer and blessing and the colour is marched out.

Back on the Orange we see the parade march back and behind us are a hundred or so cadets, also spectators, also in berets and pullovers and in the charge of, evidently, a leading cadet in the shape of a female with a parachute instructor's brevet on her pullover. I have to admit that the parade is "up to standard". Perhaps the standard is just a tiny bit lower than our old standard, but I might be biased. The commandant is on the dais, the parade advances in review order; general salute. The commandant presents the annual "Jack Holt Memorial Pace Stick" to a Flight Sergeant. The colour is marched off and the band plays "The Point of War" and "The Lincolnshire Poacher". Strangely, the colour party does not go up the steps into the main entrance but disappears to the west. The parade marches past and off .

We go up the steps ourselves and join the throng for drinks. Just orange juice for most of us. I engage in conversation with the padre and one of the flight commanders. She explains to me that some of those on parade have been in the service only eleven weeks and have yet to be issued with No 1 uniforms, so for the sake of uniformity it was decided to have all the cadets in berets and pullovers as this was all they had in common.

During the morning Keith Smith and I talked over old times and old friends. We make our farewells and I drive away with a certain sadness.

This continues as I drive back along Ermine Street in glorious sunshine. I cannot think how many times I have passed along that road but calculate that I spent nine years and two months at Cranwell as apprentice, Flight Cadet and flying instructor. It was fashionable to decry Lincolnshire but it has many facets from fens to wolds and I am very fond of it, particularly when the sun is shining.

My feelings are mixed. I feel satisfaction at having coped successfully with the trials and tribulations of our eight terms and am thankful for all the fun that went with it. I feel gratitude for having spent those eight terms with such a great band of young men who have turned into a great band of old men. I feel thankful and privileged to have had these things and for having had the chance to associate with so many other men of stature and personality from other entries – perhaps it would be invidious to name names. The bond that was forged at Cranwell is greater than most other bonds. Nobody feels like this about their university. I understand that Sandhurst does not have an equivalent to the OCA.

I suppose that what I feel is a great sense of nostalgia. What is nostalgia? If it be a disease then it is incurable. If an addiction, then I shall need another fix next year.

"Wish you were here." [F.D.H.]

Appendix 1: No 54 Entry – Graduates

Bones	K.B	*Killed in Flying Accident 4.5.53*
Bragg	R.H.	
Christie	A.McN.	
Cooper	C.E.F.	
Cooper	D.A.	
Cowper	G.M.	*Killed in Flying Accident 28.5.52*
Dark	M.E.	*Graduation delayed to 55 Entry because of sports injury*
Dawes	A.D.R.	
De La Harpe	D.S.	*Killed in Flying Accident 11.9.52*
Dodson	A.P.J.	*Killed on Operations in Borneo*
Farmer-Wright	I.P.	*Transferred to Equipment Branch; graduated with 57 Entry*
Foale	C.H.	
Fox	R.W.	
Francis	L.R.	*Died 2002*
Glass	N.G.	
Hoskins	F.D.	
Hutchinson	R.S.	*Transferred to Equipment Branch; graduated with 57 Entry*
Innes-Smith	N.A.	
Jevons	P.J.	*Died 1991(?)*
Jonklaas	C.G.D.	*Died 2003*
Keats	D.J.B.	
King	R.P.J.	
Lund	F.R.	*From 53 entry*
Meadley	B.	
Mills	B.C.	*Died 19.11.97*
Mills	D.H.	
Nuthall	W.F.	*Killed on Operations in Cyprus, 10.2.58*
Parker	J.M.A.	*Killed as Passenger in Flying Accident*
Peters	E.A.	
Ridout	H.J.	
Robson	R.H.	
Thomas	A.R.	*From 53 Entry; Killed in Flying Accident 1952*
Weerasinghe	N.E,	*Injured in air accident. Retired. Died*
Wood	D.H.	

Appendix 2: Aircraft Types and Hours Flown by Members of 54 Entry

Members flew aircraft in many roles, including: Day Fighter, Night Fighter, All-Weather Fighter, Fighter/Ground Attack. Fighter Reconnaissance, Photographic Reconnaissance, Maritime Reconnaissance, Bomber, Transport, Flying Instructor, Test Pilot, Support Helicopter, Search and Rescue

MILITARY AIRCRAFT				
Piston & turbo prop		Jet	USAF	Helicopter
Single engine	Multi-engine			
Prentice	Varsity	Meteor	T33	Dragonfly
Harvard	Valletta	Vampire	T29	Whirlwind
Tiger Moth	Mosquito	Venom	B25	Sycamore
Chipmunk	Hornet	Hunter	F84	Belvedere
Proctor	Oxford	Swift	F101	Wessex
Provost	Anson	Sabre	C141	Puma
Pioneer	Lancaster	Javelin		Bell 47
Beaver	Lincoln	Gnat		Scout
Auster	Sunderland	Canberra		
Tempest	Shackleton	Valiant		
Hawker Hart	Hastings	Vulcan		
Hurricane	Argosy	Victor		
Spitfire	Devon	Comet		
Me 109	Heron	Avro 707		
	Beverley	Sperrin		
	Andover	Ashton		
	Britannia			
	Dakota			
	Bassett			
	Pembroke			

CIVILIAN AIRCRAFT		
Piston & turbo prop		Jet
Single engine	Multi-engine	
Boeing PT17	Viscount	HS125
Pitts Special	Islander	Boeing 737
Stampe	Trislander	Tristar
Piper Cherokee	DC3	VC10
Cessna (various marks)	Twin Otter	Super VC10
Dozens of other light aircraft!	Ford Tri-Motor	Dassault Falcon
	Aztec/Apache	Learjet

FLYING HOURS

The average flying hours of those surviving are in the region of 2,500 to 3,000 each in respect of military flying. Civil pilots amass many more but the type of flying is different. The vast majority of the military flying by members of 54 Entry was in the various fighter roles and as flying instructors. Very few of the sorties in those roles would have exceeded an hour and most would be between 40 and 50 minutes of intensive activity – as opposed to flying a route with the aid of an auto-pilot. Every 100 flying hours by an instructor would be likely to represent 130 sorties and probably 200 landings. Those who took up careers in civil aviation flew, additionally, between 6,500 and 10,500 hours. Brian Meadley has 132 types and marks in his log book and a total of 14,000 hours

Appendix C: Glossary of Terms & Abbreviations

AFB Air Force Base (USA).

AOC Air Officer Commanding (usually commanding a Group).

AOC-in-C Air Officer Commanding in Chief, or C-in-C. He commands a "Command" comprising several groups.

AFS Advanced Flying School; the next stage of training after the award of wings.

ASI Airspeed Indicator; displays the speed of the aircraft through the air, but **not** the "True airspeed" (TAS), which needs corrections for altitude and temperature.

ASI Air Staff Instructions - orders relating to the conduct of flying.

Asymmetric Flight – where the engine power on one side is greater than on the other, as when one engine fails on an aircraft having two or more engines.

ATC Air Traffic Control.

"Balbo" A colloquial expression for a large formation of aircraft. After General Balbo, an Italian who led large formations of aircraft on pioneering flights in the 1930s.

"Bingo" the word called by a pilot to indicate that his fuel has reduced to a minimum level stipulated by his formation leader.

Bombex A bombing exercise involving a number of aircraft.

C Class Driver A person qualifies to drive RAF vehicles but who was not specifically employed as a driver.

CENTO Central Treaty Organization.

CO Commanding Officer.

CFI Chief Flying Instructor.

Chief or Chiefie A Flight Sergeant groundcrew, presumably derived from the navy Chief Petty Officer.

Chimay the trophy awarded to the squadron achieving the best results in inter-squadron sports each term.

CMC Chairman of the Mess Committee (of the Sergeants' Mess).

CRDF Cathode Ray Direction Finder. The bearing of an aircraft from the station is determined by listening to a radio transmission and is displayed on a cathode ray tube.

CTFI Chief Test Flying Instructor (at ETPS).

DF Direction finder.

DF/GA Day fighter/ground attack.

DI Drill Instructor.

DI Direction Indicator based on a gyro.

DR Dead Reckoning, the procedure of navigation based on the use of time, speed, direction of flight and the speed and direction of the wind.

ETPS Empire Test Pilot School at Boscombe Down.

EVA Extra-Vehicular Activity, "space walk".

F252 RAF Form 252 is the charge sheet on which the name of the accused is written, together with the offence with which he is charged.

F700 RAF Form 700. An aircraft's record of servicing and modification, signed by the pilot as accepting before flight and to confirm any unserviceabilities after flight.

Ferris The Inter-Squadron Drill Competition held each term, and judged by officers and Drill Instructors from the Royal Military Academy Sandhurst, for the Ferris Cup.

"G" The force of gravity is "One G". In certain manoeuvres an aircraft and crew are subjected to many "G".

GCA Ground Controlled Approach. A radar system whereby a controller on the ground can give instructions to guide a pilot to land in conditions of low cloud and/or poor visibility.

GCI Ground Controlled Interception. Where, with the aid of radar, a controller on the ground can give instructions to guide one aircraft to intercept another.

GCT Ground Combat Training.

Gee H An electronic aid to navigation and bombing.

GNS Global Navigation System (also GPS).

Ground Loop An unwanted manoeuvre whereby an aircraft with a tail wheel undercarriage describes a circle on the ground. Usually caused by bad handling on landing and/or a brake failure.

GPMG General Purpose Machine Gun.

HE High Energy – referring to the igniters to start a jet engine.

HP High Pressure, referring to the fuel fed under high pressure from the fuel pumps to the jet engine.

IP Initial Point. The point on the ground from which to start the final approach to a target.

Knocker The Inter-Squadron physical training competition held each term for the Knocker Cup.

King's Squadron the squadron winning most points from the inter-squadron competitions for drill, PT and games was designated "The King's Squadron" and as such carried the King's Colour on parades and occupied the central table in the dining hall with the colour behind the head of the table and held in the claws of a large bronze eagle.

IF Instrument Flying. The process of flying an aircraft solely by reference to instruments in the cockpit.

Mach Run A flight at a speed high enough to feel the onset of compressibility on approaching the speed of sound (Mach 1).

Mag Drop Piston engines in aircraft have two magnetos to produce the sparks. Before take-off the pilot switches each one off in turn to check whether the engine RPM are affected. Any reduction in RPM is known as 'mag drop'. See 'Salt water mag drop'.

NDB Non-Directional Beacon, a radio aid from which aircraft fitted with the appropriate equipment can obtain bearings.

NCO Non-Commissioned Officer, SNCO a senior NCO, sergeant or above.

OCU Operational Conversion Unit; the final stage of training intended to prepare the pilot, and crew if appropriate, for joining an operational squadron.

OD All Christian religious denominations other than Church of England and Roman Catholic.

"Orange" The Orange; the circular expanse of grass in front of the College. At one time it included the cricket square.

PI Practice Interception, where defending fighters are guided by radar onto attacking aircraft. HLPIs at High Level, LLPIs at Low Level.

PJI Parachute Jump Instructor.

PNR Point of No Return. The point beyond which an aircraft has insufficient fuel to return to its starting point.

PMC President of the Mess Committee of the Officers' Mess.

psc a symbol against the name of an officer in the Air Force List denoting having passed through staff college.

PSO Personal Staff Officer.

PT Physical Training.

PTI Physical Training Instructor.

QFI Qualified Flying Instructor, graded B2, B1,A2 and A1. A2 and A1 carried the symbol "cfs" in the Air Force List.

QHI Qualified Helicopter Instructor, graded as for QFIs.

RAE Royal Aircraft Establishment – the experimental establishment at Farnborough.

R/P Rocket Projectile.

R/T Radio Telephony.

Rumble Seat An additional folding seat, as available next to the pilot in a Canberra. The name is thought to be a corruption of 'Rumbold', the manufacturer.

SASO Senior Air Staff Officer; the chief of staff of a Group or Command.

Salt Water Mag Drop (See Mag Drop) 'Salt water mag drop' is the sudden loss of power, or the onset of engine rough running imagined by many pilots to take place on crossing the coast for a long sea crossing, particularly in a single-engined aircraft. The same effect is sometimes experienced at night. Another effect sometimes felt at night by pupil pilots was that the controls became heavier on approaching to land, when receiving dual instruction. However, this effect was not imaginary but caused by the ill-disguised helping hand of an anxious intructor.

SBA Standard Beam Approach. A system of overlapping radio lobes, one transmitting the letter "A" in morse code and the other the letter "N". Where the lobes overlap a beam is created in which a steady note is heard and this beam is aligned with the runway.

SMG Sub-machine Gun.

"Snowdrops" RAF Police; from the distinguishing white covers on their caps.

SP Service Police –'snowdrops'.

SWO Station Warrant Officer, equivalent to a Regimental Sergeant Major.

Taceval Tactical Evaluation, the process of evaluating a unit's combat readiness.

Tawse An instrument consisting of a strip of thick leather split into two or three tails at one end and formerly used in Scotland to enforce discipline in schools.

TAF Tactical Air Force. The RAF in Germany in the 1950s was the 2nd Tactical Air Force (2TAF).

TI Target Indicator, a bomb which, when exploded, spread burning coloured materials to indicate a target.

"Uncle Oboe" U/O, Under Officer. The most senior Flight Cadet in each squadron.

V Force Bomber Command's force of V-Bombers, namely Valiants, Victors and Vulcans.

38/16 Point The first point where an officer could retire on pension, either on his 38th birthday or completing 16 years of commissioned service.

Junior Cadets in 1949 *(from left to right:)*
N.E. Weerasinghe, D.S. de la Harpe, A.P.J. Dodson, F.D. Hoskins, R.H. Robson, A.M. Christie.

NAAFI Break for Cadets Peters, Bones, Cowper, Dodson, Robson, Meadley and Morrice.

In the gymnasium (above) and Dinghy Drill (below).

Marshal of the Royal Air Force Lord Trenchard inspecting 'B' Squadron, July 1949.
Cadet B.C. Mills on the far right.

Her Royal Highness Princess Elizabeth inspecting 'C' Squadron, July 1951.
Flight Cadet F.D. Hoskins second from the right.

(above) Cadet M.E. Dark, 1949.

(right) Cadet R.H. Bragg, ready to fly, 1949.

Flight Cadet C.G.D. Jonklaas and Prentice, 1950.

Percival Prentices over the College, 1950.

North American Harvards.

54 Entry 'A' Squadron, 1950 *(from left to right)*.
back row: I.P. Farmer-Wright, D.S. de la Harpe, C.H. Foale, P.J. Jevons, R.S. Hutchinson, L.R. Francis.
Front row: A.P.J. Dodson, D.J.B. Keats, A.N. Christie, M.E. Dark, C.E.F. Cooper.

Parachute Course.

F.D. Hoskins and A.M. Christie in London, 1951.

C.H. Foale, M.E. Dark, G.A. Priechenfried,
A.P.J. Dodson, Lincoln Cathedral, 1951.

In Malta, 1951.

July 1951 with HRH Princess Elizabeth and the Commandant, Air Commodore L.F. Sinclair GC CB CBE DSO RAF.

December 1951, Visit to de Havillands at Hatfield.

54 entry as the Senior Term, December 1951.

Back row: B. Meadley, L.R. Francis, G.M. Cowper, A.D.R. Dawes, N.J. Glass, D.H. Mills, N.E. Weerasinghe, A.R. Thomas, C.G.D. Jonklaas, E.A. Peters.

Middle Row: R.H. Robson, D.A. Cooper, K.B. Bones, D.S. de la Harpe, N.A. Innes-Smith, R.W. Fox, D.J.B. Keats, C.E.F. Cooper, D.H. Wood, A.P.J. Dodson.

Front Row: F.R. Lund, R.H. Bragg, W.F. Nuthall, B.C. Mills, R.P.J. King, J.M.A. Parker, P.J. Jevons, F.D. Hoskins, A.M. Christie, C.H. Foale, H.J. Ridout.

54 Entry Graduation Parade, 12 December 1951.

'H' Flight, 12 December 1951.
Brand new Pilot Officers with brand new 'wings' standing behind their Instructors.
Back row (from left to right): B. Meadley, C.E.F. Cooper, N.J. Glass, C.H. Foale,
K.B. Bones, F.D. Hoskins, D.A. Cooper, E.A. Peters, C.G.D. Jonklaas.

Meteor T7.

Instructor's view of student in Meteor T 7. Instruments show both engines
at 11,400 rpm (cap on coaming owned by N.J. Glass).

Meteor T7s and F8s

Meteor NF 14s.

R.H. Robson's Meteor after sustaining damage from collision with towed target glider that disintegrated on its main spar being hit by 20mm rounds.

A.D.R. Dawes and C.G.D. Jonklaas, 92 Squadron Germany, 1952.

C.H. Foale and Vampire, Canal Zone, Egypt, 1953.

A.D.R. Dawes and Vampire, Germany 1952.

(top left) A.M. Christie with 77 Squadron RAAF in Korea, 1953.

(top right) F.D. Hoskins, Commander of Guard of Honour for Director of Operations, Malaya, 1954.

(left) R.P.J. King with his F101 Voodoo at Myrtle Bay AFB, 1956.

B. Meadley's Hunter FR10.

No 4 Squadron's Formation Team 'Four's Four', led by B Meadley .

Short Sunderland.

Damage to Sunderland RN302
'C' December 1953.

Hornets of 33 Squadron at Butterworth, 1954. Penang in the background.

Pre-flight check by F.D. Hoskins of a Hornet before a strike.

Vampire T11s over the Orange, 1956.

Javelins.

N.J. Glass with Chipmunk.

Canberra PR9.

A.M. Christie with Vulcans of No 9 Squadron.

A.M. Christie in distinguished company of Marshals of the Royal Air Force Elworthy, Harris ('Bomber') and Portal.

Whirlwind 10 of 103 Squadron with 105mm gun detachment, Sarawak, Borneo, 1965.

Pumas of 33 Squadron, Otterburn, 1972 .

R.H. Robson with CF 104.

F.D. Hoskins, Jebel Akhdar, Oman 1970.

R.H. Bragg MA.

R.H. Robson.

B. Meadley with RF84F.

1989 - Forty years on from starting *(from left to right)*: R.H. Bragg, R.H.Robson, R.P.J. King, D.H. Mills, N.A. Innes-Smith, P.J. Jevons *(behind)* N.J. Glass, D.H. Wood, R.S. Hutchinson, B. Meadley, E.A. Peters, F.D. Hoskins *(behind)*, I.P. Farmer-Wright, C.H. Foale, R.W. Fox, D.J.B. Keats.

2001 - Fifty years on from graduation *(from left to right)*: F.D. Hoskins, A.D.R. Dawes. E.A. Peters, A.M. Christie, R.W. Fox, B. Meadley, I.P. Farmer-Wright, D.J.B. Keats, N.A. Innes-Smith, C.G.D. Jonklaas, N.J. Glass. *Back Row:* D.A. Cooper, R.P.J. King. R.S. Hutchinson, C.H. Foale.

RAF College, Cranwell.

The Dining Hall.

Inside the Rotunda.

Coat of Arms and Badges.